# ALEX

# ALEX

## THE FATHERING OF A PREEMIE

JEFF STIMPSON

ACADEMY CHICAGO PUBLISHERS

Published in 2004 by
Academy Chicago Publishers
363 West Erie Street
Chicago, Illinois 60610

© 2004 Jeff Stimpson

Portions of this work have appeared in *Ithaca Child*, *The Village Family Magazine*, *Abilities Magazine* (Toronto), and *Laughing and Learning: Adventures in Parenting*, among others, as well as on the following Web sites: About.com, Cold Glass, Early Edition, Fatherville, Mensight, Premature Baby Premature Child, Sevenseasmagazine.com, Storknet, and Whim's Place, among others.

Printed in the U.S.A.

Library of Congress Cataloging-in-Publication Data
on file with the printer

ISBN 0-89733-528-7

*For Jill*

# CONTENTS

# JUNE TO OCTOBER, 1998

SOMEBODY YELLS "BOY!" Everything I used to want turns to mist when someone sails past with a baseball. Later I learn it's his head. I think it's gray. I peek on tiptoes as a clot of doctors dive onto the "Boy!," and beyond their gowns I glimpse hands and feet the size of a GI Joe's. "So small," I whisper. So small it kicks my chest. They slide him into a clear plastic box, and wheel him away.

Our road to parenthood had already been twisty. My wife Jill and I were living in Baltimore in early 1997, trying to conceive a baby. When that didn't work, we headed to doctors, who gave us appointments, exams, and odd things to do in cups until one evening in December we heard the nurse on the phone say, "Jill, your test is . . . positive!" So we quit our jobs at suburban Maryland newspapers and wheeled it back to New York City, where Jill is from. In the months since, we'd been pinballing from sonogram to sonogram to let doctors probe Jill as if hunting for a submarine. They said the baby was small, small, small.

They can tell a fair amount about a fetus just by looking at the sonogram: what it sort of looks like; how big it is; if it's moving the right way; if it's making the pre-breathing movements. Alex seemed okay for most of those things, but he was way behind in growth, which we discovered when Jill went in for a routine sonogram at around twenty weeks and was told that Alex was roughly a seventeen-week size.

Around this time, one of the doctors had begun to sigh a lot, and started to use the word "miracle" in a bad way, and not long after that four new letters landed in our lives: IUGR, or intrauterine growth retardation. Alex didn't just arrive prematurely: They chose to deliver him early, thinking that he would do better outside the womb than inside. Jill had also been given steroid shots to "develop" his lungs for this early delivery— though, in the time since, research has shown that steroids don't help in these cases.

The doctors were dating growth from before conception, which made no sense to me. But as our submarine dropped further down a percentile chart of fetal growth, the doctors began wondering when intensive care might be best. "Let's just hope you make it to twenty-eight weeks," the doctor sighed. Then "twenty-nine weeks." Then "thirty . . ." As the numbers climbed, the doctor's hands waved and waved in wider and wider circles, and she felt compelled to add that she'd be praying for us. They continued to monitor the fetus with, eventually, daily and detailed sonograms, measuring it and looking for specific signs of movement and particular behaviors, such as joints flexing, and pre-breathing movements—entering Alex in the first critical race of his life: develop, or come out.

Jill went on bed rest, sentenced to rented movies and my cooking. She rose only for sonogram appointments, which jumped from once a week to twice a week to once a day, which pretty much killed time until she was ordered into the hospital after a technician seemed at sea one day during a biophysical (the detailed sonogram), and the doctor didn't see the signs from the fetus she wanted to see immediately. In the years ahead, Jill would say that if she had it to do over again, she'd insist that the doctor wait half an hour, let her eat something, and try it all again. But a pregnant woman is rarely in a position to fight off panic and battle a doctor.

So we came to that Sunday, June 14, when Jill gave me the news and I said, "Okay." "I just hope the kid isn't too shocked," she added, looking out the window, her hand on her belly where the kicks continued.

Premature labor affects a fifth of pregnancies in the U.S., and annually some 400,000 premature infants—"preemies"—are born before the thirty-seventh week of pregnancy. The trickiness of predicting the outcomes for such fetuses has been documented. My family was looking at two and a half months early.

Tick tick tick went the heart monitor in the OR as I tied on my papery surgical mask and wondered how life was about to change. Wondered how I was going to screw up this kid. Wondered if I'd get the chance to screw him up. There was nothing to do but stroke Jill's head, listen to the surgeons' chatter and remember the comforting words of "The Neonatal Intensive Care Unit Parent Information Booklet," a hospital handout that begins with the observation, "We know this can be a very stressful time."

The Neonatal Intensive Care Unit, or NICU ("nick-YOU") looks like a baby hatchery: it has a clean, gluey smell and is crammed with carts and medical gear and clear plastic boxes called isolettes. Inside the isolettes, most of the arms and legs don't move; their owners seem pretty tired. Cries are muffled—one infant sounds like a crow—but red and green numbers on monitors constantly set off alarms, bleeps and bells that shatter any sense of a homey nursery. Jill has told me preemies can hear, and some parents fill a few cassettes with recordings of the NICU to play for their baby when it comes home.

In a premature infant, the lungs, digestive and circulatory systems are undeveloped. Preemies' most common health problems affect breathing, heart, brain, body heat and eyes—the latter problem may result in permanent blindness (Stevie Wonder was a preemie). Premature babies are at increased risk for apnea, in which breathing temporarily stops for twenty seconds or more. Maybe a lot more.

Someone has stuck a piece of white tape across the front of my son's isolette and written "Hi! I'm Alexander!" No other baby has a piece of tape. Tubes run into Alex's isolette. Blue tubes, green tubes, clear tubes, fat tubes, fine tubes. One carries in warm, humid air; another runs into his pinhole left nostril, and a wider clear tube goes down his throat. He opens his mouth wide, but no sound comes out because the clear tube is between his vocal cords. My kid is painstakingly crafted with miniature versions of my feet and with knuckles the size of these letters. My finger is monstrous in his hand. His eyes are closed, wrinkles rippling across his forehead just as they did on the forehead of my father, who also had thin hair. Alex has my nose. I open the porthole of the isolette and peer in. I look at his palm; his life-line is long.

"He is one tough little kid," his doctor tells me, then reiter-ates all that may yet go wrong. As recently as the 1980s, doc-tors were brutal with the parents of preemies, standing over isolettes and spewing predictions of everything from a quick death in infancy to a bad social life in grade school. Don't touch them, they'd say, don't bug them; their nervous systems aren't formed, and the case is kind of hopeless anyway. These days the medical profession has wised up a little—some nurses encour-age holding, for instance—but nobody will predict anything more than a day, sometimes an hour, ahead.

"Some babies fall apart within six weeks," the doctor says. "Some take right off. Your experience will probably be some-where in between."

I've never been a parent, but I already make a prediction of my own: a years' worth of worry, helplessness, highs, lows, daydreams and dread will be crammed into the next eight weeks until—at the soonest—Alex can come home.

"I'm optimistic," the doctor says.

Optimism floats us through the first week. Jill and I get plas-tic hospital ID bracelets, hers with "Mother" and mine with "Fa-ther" and both with the number "64092." My life becomes a pattern of days spent at work, then meeting Jill at the hospital over Alex's isolette. We cradle his head and touch his palms, watch him squint and learn to yawn. I write a letter to Alex, pregnant with feeling and significance. "You are part of that river of humanity that has had billions and billions of bright sparkles upon its surface. You're one of those sparkles now," I write to him.

Meanwhile Jill hooks herself to a pump to begin trying to lactate. But the stuff comes hard, and soon she hates opening the door of the pumping room fridge and seeing the full beakers of the other mothers; soon she speaks about full-term moms and their "bully" babies in the same tones she once used to describe other drivers on the Beltway.

Each night at nine o'clock that first week I leave Jill, who's still recovering in the hospital, and head home, arriving at about ten o'clock, and spend two hours juggling phone calls. Amazing how a 21-ounce person has started phones ringing from Tucson, Arizona, to Waterville, Maine. "Awful big name for such a little baby," my sister says. "Little guy, isn't he?" my brother says. The phone rings and rings until I get about four or five hours' sleep a night, and begin to feel like a parent.

Alex doesn't call, because he's busy. When the big ventilator gets to be too much, they attach a device that makes his chest flutter. They wiggle a tiny stocking cap on his head to preserve body heat. The dial controlling the percentage of pure oxygen in his air tube goes up to 70, down to 25, and gradually settles around 30 to get him used to breathing room air (which is about 21 percent oxygen). I look at Alex and I know that he doesn't know what he's doing here. He doesn't know what a "transfusion" is when he needs one on Tuesday night. He doesn't know what "jaundice" is when it sets in, when they haul out banks of purple lights and bake him while he lounges like a preemie movie star in a pair of tiny black eye shades. His right fist finds his mouth. We learn he may qualify for Social Security. Around that time, a grandma new to the NICU walks past Alex's isolette and looks at him as she would a car wreck. We tell Alex he's just met his first jerk.

This is how the first days go, before Alex turns one week old on Father's Day. To celebrate, Jill's mom sticks her head near the isolette port and breaks into "99 Bottles of Beer in the Wall." Jill and I squabble about who gets to change his diaper, which is about the size of a pack of playing cards; it's the smallest size they make, and it's too large on him. This is how the first days go, while our world goes up and down, mostly up: good heart, cloudy lungs; firm kick, yellow color. He pinks up, twitches in a way that lets me glimpse the baby that my child will become.

This is a very stressful time. Day to day I try not to stare at the babies and little boys on the street—hordes of them, a mob, a terrifying many because all, all are bigger than Alex. Time after time my stomach will not stop catching when I enter that bright room ("Hi! I'm Alexander!") and go once more into the bleeps, praying that no bell tolls for him. Praying, as I look down at my boy through the clear plastic and realize that I am the one who feels so small.

Alex turns a month old without ever leaving the hospital. I learn to call him a "preemie," a cute new word in my life that has let in menacing associates: "BPD" (bronchopulmonary dysplasia), "desat," "brady" (bradycardia, when the heart rate slows too much), and others that on every visit cause Jill and me to keep one eye on Alex and one on his loud, pitiless monitors.

An Irish nurse calls him "the wee man." But he's seven ounces bigger than when he was born, and so far this week he's gained about twenty grams a night. I think a penny weighs about twenty grams. Sometimes we take him out of the box and hold him for a half hour, hoping that ounces will never be this important to him again. Or to us.

Doctors tell us that parenting a preemie is a roller coaster. Jill says it's more like pinball played badly. Both similes hold up during a typical weekend with a preemie: Friday afternoon the head doctor greenlights our holding Alex skin-to-skin and gives his overall assessment of Alex as "pretty good." But when's the kid going to grow?

Not this Friday, which is a bad day. The doctors give Alex a spinal tap, then have to move his isolette once or twice. That evening the bells go off, as Alex starts "desatting," meaning the oxygen-saturation in his blood dips below 80 percent (not good—it should be very close to 100—but this happens to a lot of preemies). The numbers refuse to rise; the doctors wheel in an x-ray machine that must look to Alex about the size of a mobile home. "Don't touch him just yet," they tell us, "and come back in a few minutes." So we stand back like tourists watching a mugging while they turn the lights up and dive on him. Couldn't some of the reading be caused by his squirming? It's amazing what a baby's wires can get into. No, they tell us, no. The doctors never look at his face. Another doctor says Alex needs a diuretic to get fluid from his lungs. Later we're told we can hold him, but after the nurse finishes feeding another baby. Then a hideously young doctor flies by and bombs us with the word "pneumonia." Jill cries all the way home.

Everybody wants to know how he is. Why's he desatting? Why don't they feed him more? What kind of infection? Why don't you find out? Jill and I turn off the phone and open beers. We sit at the table and drink beer and talk about a time when others might actually understand something about our lives and when we'll understand how we can follow the nurses' advice and "take care of ourselves." "The hardest thing about this is telling other people," Jill says. "I wish there was a way to have a conversation with someone and have them just not ask."

On Saturday, Alex is fine. Jill holds him to her chest, and he stares up at her chin with eyes bluish and bright under a tiny wrinkled forehead, and goes to sleep. It's amazing what's possible again. As the poppa, I will announce that Alex has sucked his thumb twice that we know of, and is the only baby in the NICU who doesn't need a constant IV. Jill is filling more and more plastic containers with breast milk, while I watch and sometimes handle the timer. The doctors inject his milk with stuff that has initials.

Jill and I spend a week at her parents', which is close to the hospital, to save the time we spend on the subway hating the word "desat." We take the bus up each evening, and afterwards walk back south the eleven blocks, along the darkened park. We pass the same doormen and the same brooding museums. Ahead of us on the walk, never seeming to get any closer, is the brightly lit "1" of the Empire State Building. We sit on a low wall and weep or work out a strategy for the next time we walk in and alarms are going off.

Alex begins to grow. His eyes move around. A doctor tells us that yes he can see, but his brain can't process the information. The nurse takes him out of the box and I hold him, wishing that the people with the questions could feel his weight and could look down and see his head like a fuzzy ball on their chest. In his box we put a stuffed football rattle, a postage-stamp drawing of a sailing ship, a Tiny Toons Bugs, and a little teddy bear. On one wall of the isolette I tape a headline from the NY Post that reads, "Tough as Nails!"

Then it is another Sunday. "This will just take a few minutes," says the doctor as they turn up the lights and more and more doctors gather over him. He's moved a tube, so they say, and it has to be re-inserted. Jill and I flee into the empty breast-pumping room, then settle at the empty doctors' station and eat their jelly beans. Jill picks up a neonatal textbook—bad move—and reads that by six weeks many premature babies double their birth weight. Alex hasn't even gained a third of his. The few minutes drag to an hour. More doctors come in. We buttonhole two of them on their way out and learn they are anesthesiologists called in to supervise the insertion of a new tube. Alex lies squirming for almost ninety minutes while a plastic tube is shoved down his throat twice. Jill is ready to shatter when she asks if they can give him a sedative. "We don't do that to babies this size," the doctor says. There is always an answer. This time the answer is that Alex vomits during the tubing, and may have to go on days of antibiotics if he got any of the stuff in his lungs. "We'll know later tonight," a nurse says. The Tiny Toon Bugs has been flattened against the bottom of the box.

Jill cries halfway home. We sit on a bench near the park and she pulls back from the edge of a rant. I have no ranting in me. I just wish my new family felt better. I have a better handle than Jill on getting through this one step at a time, but part of me wishes I could rant. And to the right people. Once Jill and I had things to do this summer. But no plan feels as real as the hospital. When I see my son inside the box I know he doesn't give a dirty diaper for our plans. He's here, he's tough as nails, and somebody's going to pay attention for however long this takes.

People are still asking about Alex by the time he's seven weeks old and two pounds. He moves around and likes to take a bath in a plastic bowl. Recently he had his first tantrum, during which he resembled his mother. We're near tantrums of our own. Sometimes I understand other parents when I look through the plastic of the isolette and into his eyes, which are the color of the night sky when you're having a good evening. That face through the plastic makes everything else evaporate. At other times I hate clear plastic and I hate other parents and their fat children who grow. So does Jill.

"I'm not proud of that," she says. So? In two months Jill and I have had two days we'd call normal. The first was when a friend came in from Philadelphia and we spent Saturday in the park, and later had a real dinner in a real restaurant, with mussels and wine. Once I went to a model boat show. Jill has rediscovered thrift shops, and found a pair of shoes for $9. Another friend flew in from California and we went for a walk by the harbor. It was a sunny day, and there were many children. Then I went back to the hospital. Alex's room is a long, long way from sunny days near any harbor.

But mostly, I head to work in the mornings. Once or twice through the day Jill calls, telling me about her morning's projects and how she's late getting out the door. Then she travels by bus or subway or car an hour to the hospital, and from there in the afternoon she usually calls me to say that Alex is fine. I stay awake through the afternoon on more junk food than I ever ate in high school, and at five o'clock I take two trains and one bus to the hospital. There I flash my wristband to the guard and enter the second half of my day.

I take a deathly slow elevator up three flights. I walk down a corridor and into a room painted sky blue and peach, where the door of the one bathroom for thirty parents has needed oil on the hinges since Flag Day. In a room bright with bells and monitors, I find Alex in his box. I spend an hour speaking to Alex softly through the porthole, telling him how I know he can do it, and humming "Little Papoose" or something else intended as soothing.

I only know a few words to "Little Papoose":

*Lit-tle pap-oose*
*Lit-tle pap-oose*
*Rock-a-bye, rock-a-bye, little papoose*
*Lit-tle pap-oose . . .*

There are more words, which Jill knows, but after humming it to Alex for an hour even she describes the song with language that she, a new mother, should stop using soon. We leave the hospital and sit on a bench across the street. There, Jill says, she's come to know the dogs that are walked by, what kind of ice cream the vendor has, the block's lone speckled pigeon. Then Jill and I find a bus for home in Queens. Jill does the crossword on the way. I've never liked crosswords, but lately I lean over them with her. I hope one of the clues is never, "Last word of the full version of 'Little Papoose'."

We come home to a blinking answering machine. Just wanted to see how you're doing. Call sometime. Hope you're well. Just wanted an update from you guys. There really is just one message: Just wanted some answers. I leave an Alex update on the recording, hoping some callers will just listen to it and hang up.

We spend an hour watching "Larry Sanders" on tape and trying to log on to AOL. In cyberspace we find that our answering
machine did not field all the world's questions. So we broadcast
an update on his spirits; his movements and twitchings; his eye
color and finger length; his weight in grams, the all-important
grams, a goddamned unit of measurement that I guess I never
thought about before.

Some days are harder than others. Days when we get to
change his diapers are good days, because his middle soon grows
too plump for preemie Pampers. As a rule, though, Mondays
are the worst. Another week in the hospital, another week of
messages and e-mails and asking for a nurse's recommendation
before we pick up our kid. Jill and I sit in the living room by the
window. She cries often; I touch her leg. We call the hospital to
see how he's doing. "Hi," I say, "this is Jeff Stimpson. I'm calling about my son Alex Cornfield. I believe—" insert nurse's
name here "—is his nurse . . ." (For some reason we never dis-
cern, this hospital always refers to Alex by his mother's last
name.) Monday turns to Tuesday some time while we sleep.
And we never sleep enough.

One day Alex pulls out his breathing tube; a nurse later tells
us that when this happened, he looked around as if seeing the
world for the first time. He pants on his own for six hours, then
his brand-new chest muscles give out and the tube goes back in.
Two days later he pulls it out again. Back it goes. One night my
holding him just doesn't work; he fusses, he cries, the bells won't
stop. I put him back in his box. Jill suggests maybe we can just
visit him. "I—don't—want—to—be—here!" I hiss at her. The
intensity feels good, but she recoils as if smacked and over her
shoulder I see the nurse's head turn.

Some days are better than others. We plan the menu for his
kilo party—foot-long hot dogs, liters of Coke. Jill's sister Julie
suggests graham crackers. But night after night his weight bumps
slowly toward 1,000 grams. I try not to notice how many days
go by with Alex gaining only the weight of a nickel. "I'm sorry

it's all I can talk about," Jill has said in our living room, on street corners, on buses and in cabs. And to doctors. After a while, we wonder how much they're listening to us and our instincts about Alex, and how much they're listening to a pre-learned method of treatment. After a while, I get the feeling I'm talking to people who are treating their last patient, people so tired they feel free to say anything that comes into their heads.

Talking to the doctor one afternoon becomes one of those moments when Jill and I turn from sadness to anger. About mother's milk, for example: the doctor claims nature isn't perfect. Look at that tsunami in New Guinea.

Jill straightens in her chair, pulls in her chin and smiles with a calm tolerance that I haven't seen in a while. "Doctor, that is a specious analogy," she says. I see him silently mouth the word.

"And I used it right!" Jill says later in our study, over the open dictionary. That study will be Alex's room. Some day, if we can ever pick up these papers. The dining room table is also disappearing under bills, unopened mail, keys, bags, and everything else.

"It was a perfect word," I tell Jill.

"Really?" she says. "Really?"

We won't pick up papers tonight. Instead, before we go to bed, we sit again at the window, everything in our lives feeling heavy, trying to uncoil over a crossword puzzle, trying to remember that we got through another day without needing a little plastic box of our own.

Pretty soon Alex doesn't look like me anymore. "He's a little Jeff," Jill used to marvel. That was nice. "Who's Daddy's little guy?" I ask him. "*Who's* Daddy's little guy? Alex is!" We both know the answer, I guess, but several times his hand has found my nose. His hand is now bigger than some postage stamps.

Alex gained no weight for an endless while. In that time he seemed to take no notice of Mom and Dad's exhausted faces pressed against the plastic. He started out skinny, too, his arms and legs pinkish-gray straws. For a long time Alex had a thin plastic tube down his throat, and often an IV with a tongue-depressor-like white plastic board jabbed in his forearm or ankle.

Now he peeps when we give him a bath. He just started eating, and he'll clamp onto the nipple and suck and suck, his minuscule jaw working and his eyes bright over the bottle. He seems to be a focused person. He sleeps without stirring until it is time to stir. Then his head stretches back and his forehead wrinkles, his hands stretch forward and his legs kick once, and hard. If he has time he jerks his head and takes a whack at the nose tubes. Then he lies still.

He had just woken up one afternoon when I noticed his eyes had changed. The light into his isolette is dim, so I guess for a while I believed his eyes were simply still that special midnight. But that afternoon the light was better, and I looked at his face and he moved his head, and I saw a flash of chocolate.

He stared at me and blinked. "Brown is the dominant gene," explained the nurse, who had blue eyes. His cheeks began to balloon and his eyes to pinball around the room, wide and excited and mostly happy to be in the world.

"Isn't he cute?" says Jill. "Isn't he so cute and smart? And I'm not just saying that because I'm his mother."

Alex gains weight, and we gain hope. For weeks his chest was the size of a pack of cards, a pack of cards that heaved and heaved in the loop of no weight gain without better breathing and no breathing without more weight. We watched his chest heave as his weight staggered from three digits to four, from 900 to 1,000 to 1,100, to finally double his birth weight. Now, the Beanie Babies seem smaller. Now, perched atop Alex's 1,360 grams, I can see a day when I'll sling him through the subway, the day I'll drag him screaming from a toy department. A day I will look him in those brown eyes as I watch him drive away.

Tonight on my arm, Alex will feel like flesh and blood, instead of like porcelain. His eyes are Jill's color, but my shape. His feet have my arches, his face Jill's isosceles smile. When he sleeps he looks like Jill. When he yawns he looks like me. When he gums his feeding tube, he looks like my mother eating a nut. When he fusses and his eyebrows crash together, he looks like my brother when the Dallas Cowboys lose. When he sneezes he looks like a kitten. Somewhere in there, he began to look like somebody else. I'm not sure who.

These last few days have been by any stretch of the imagination, by any stretch of his parents' hearts, the worst. Today is Thursday. On Tuesday I held him, looking at the thin green feeding tube in his nose as Alex rode my chest and stared over my shoulder. He was looking out the window, spellbound by the brick wall across the alley from the NICU. That morning I sang him his song, to the tune of "Frere Jacques":

> *Al-ex-an-der, Al-ex-an-der,*
> *Is that you? Is that you?*
> *Yes I'm Alexander! Yes I'm Alexander!*
> *Ehn-ehn-ehn, ehn-ehn-ehn* (*ehn* being most of his vocabulary).

A mealtime variation of this song includes the lines,

> *Alexander's hun-gry! Alexander's hun-gry!*
> *Do not sing. Do not sing.*

He was relatively free of tubes. Alex had been free for a long time from a breathing tube down his throat. That's good because the tube ran between his vocal cords, jammed his lip to one side, and unless he was sedated his gag reflex would kick in and things would get nasty.

On Tuesday, I put him down, gave him his pacifier, and went to work. As I left, I glanced up at his numbers blinking red on the black box above his crib. The box, about the size of a cheap car radio, blares every time the oxygen-saturation in his blood dips below 80 percent. The box was quiet; his numbers looked a little low.

A quarter to midnight on Tuesday we call to see how he is. Dr. M. comes on. "I'm afraid," she says, "we're going to have to intubate him again."

Alex has caught a cold, which can kill premature babies with BPD. I had never heard the word "intubate" before last June. But on this chilly October night, it sends us to our car at about the hour we're normally finishing the crossword in bed. We try to speed into the city, but instead we crawl over a bridge that's packed bright red with tail lights. We don't speak.

"I can't believe we're going to lose him," I say at last.

Jill doesn't look up. "Please don't say that," she says.

We swerve up the dark streets of Manhattan. Then we park. Then we run. Then walk fast. Then run again.

We reach Alex's room, throw open the door and find the lights on bright, and a clot of people in ratty faded-yellow hospital gowns leaning over Alex. The black box is blaring. Alex is chomping on the pacifier, all five pounds of his power channeled through his jaws. He may be little, but he knows this many people are not supposed to be leaning over him this late at night.

"We'll give you a few minutes with him while we get ready," Dr. M. says. Six months ago, a vet said the same thing to us before giving the final shot to our cat. "Who's my little bunny?" Jill asks Alex. "Who's Daddy's little guy?" Chomp chomp chomp.

It hits me then that when the tube goes in, Alex will be silenced. Alex will no longer be the guy going *ehn-ehn-ehn-ehn* on my chest, no longer the guy with wide eyes looking across the alley. He'll be what he was four months ago, when he was born: My son, but not a person in the same way, with a gaze and chomping jaws and *ehns* of horror at preemie massage.

One of the doctors says that sometimes, with kids, instead of a tube you can do an oxygen tent.

"Well, can we do that *here*?" Jill asks.

Calls are made. While Jill and I sing him the theme from "The Flintstones," a technician arrives with a plastic box that won't fit snugly down on Alex's neck. Then the tech returns with a plastic tent so big Alex could use it as a life raft.

Jill puts Alex to her chest. Chomp chomp chomp. The red numbers rise, stop, rise. "That's the best he's been all night," Dr. M. says.

The numbers hold as they rig the oxygen tent. By now it's almost two a.m. Jill and I take turns singing "Meet the Flintstones" and "Al—ex—an—der." Then we slip him inside the tent and his face goes fuzzy behind the plastic. Through the top of the tent the tech threads a tube for warm oxygen, but for several minutes only cold air comes out. The red numbers sink as eight adults stand there in the middle of the night and watch one baby work a pacifier.

"I'm glad we came," I whisper to Jill. "I'm still glad we came."

Dr. M. appears and says, "You two will have to step out."

Jill and I go to the waiting room. It is empty; the TV is dark. We collapse on the fat blue cushions. On the table nearby someone has left a soda can and half a cup of coffee. I think how people more suited to be parents would either be home sleeping or would have dragged some family member out of bed, too. Jill and I talk in circles about how well he was doing. I think about giving him baths with his little rubber ducks and about watching him watch the building across the alley.

I swat the coffee cup. It makes a satisfying brown spray across the sick-yellow wall, under that goddamned framed quilt.

About fifty years go by. No one comes out to talk to us. Then Jill has had it and heads back in. "They could send someone out here!" she says. I don't know what to say. Part of me wants to demand answers. Part of me wants to be patient. I watch my wife hurl herself against the door of my son's room.

There is the crowd, there are the robes. There are the faces, all awfully set. Somewhere in there is Alex. "Can you tell us what's happening!" Jill says.

"I need you out of here now!" Dr. M. says.

"Well, send somebody out!" I say.

"We will."

Back to the waiting room. I smash a trash can. Jill just cries. By four o'clock, it's okay to go in.

There lies Alex, transformed, with a clear plastic tube jutting from the right side of his mouth. His eyes are closed. Beside him the vent wheezes and wheezes, a sound I thought my family had left behind weeks ago. "I'm sorry," Dr. M. says, "but when you came in I was right in the middle of putting the tube between his vocal cords."

Jill and I leave, because there's nothing else to see and certainly nothing else to hear. We walk back to the car on the corner, and start down Manhattan towards the Queensboro Bridge. We make every light; we dash across the bridge. We get a good parking spot. Sometimes it goes that way when Alex has had a rotten time.

I fall asleep around five. What if the vent doesn't work? What if I never hear my son again?

The next day starts at ten. Jill and I get to the hospital, where we meet her mother coming out from knee surgery and from visiting Alex. She says he looked pink. "We were here until four," I tell her.

Alex is how I left him. His eyes move, his hands find the tube. At least he doesn't have that red-rimmed, run-down-by-a-truck look. Three or four days, they say, and they'll wean him from the tube and the sedative. Another holiday weekend I'll spend telling Alex what I've told him all summer: "Daddy knows you can do it, Alexander. Daddy knows you can do it. *Al-ex-an-der, Al-ex-an-der, is that you?*"

Yet another doctor tells us, "Some babies with BPD get this and get over it. Some babies with BPD get this and don't get over it." When that doctor has left, Dr. M. grips Jill's arm and says, "Alex is *going* to get better!" Okay. I stare down at the gauze over his eyes and the IVs in his scalp. People have asked me if I think I'm being tested. No, I don't. A test is something you take only to see if you could go through the real thing.

No bath, of course. We don't pick him up. Jill strokes his head. Three or four days.

The first of those days is Thursday. At 3:20 Thursday afternoon the phone rings in my office. "Hi, it's me," Jill says. "Alex had an episode."

The doctor had examined him and left; Jill visited him and was about to leave; then the nurse was on him. Then she called for an emergency team. "She said it wasn't really an emergency, that she just said that to make them come faster," Jill tells me.

A lie. For thirty minutes my boy lay in his crib, a tube down his throat and about a quarter million dollars of medical expertise wapping his chest and trying to pry him from the depths of a bronchial spasm.

Later, on the other end of my phone, I have the attending doctor who pulled him back. "Is my son dying?" I ask.

"There was a moment there," she admits.

Then back on my phone is the nurse, speaking in hushed tones. My knees tingle. "Mr. Stimpson," she says, "your wife was about to leave and I don't think she should."

On the subway ride to the hospital I think how I'd cut the throat of everyone in the car to save Alex. I think how Wednesday morning was bush league. I think how Tuesday morning must have been eons ago.

How I found Alex that afternoon is how he remains. Motionless, except for the rise and fall of the vent working his lungs. IVs stick from his feet and hands, feeding him a confluence of drugs—mostly sedatives and a paralytic called Pavulon, because when he moves his oxygen saturation plummets, and the black box is always up there waiting. He lies pale and still, his eyes open. The nurse gently tapes a strip of gauze over them. "Thank you," I say.

The attending physician spends half an hour with us on the blue cushions in the waiting room, where someone has washed the walls and righted the trash can. The doctor is positive she does not know what happened. I venture that it was panic fueled by too little sedative, followed by an asthma attack. Maybe, maybe, she nods. Jill and I talk to her until our words run out.

The next day is Friday. At work I take Alex's pictures off my desk and place them in a drawer. They are of him on cannula and in a red knit hat; in them he is plump and sassy. *Yes I'm Alexander, Yes I'm Alexander* . . . Now and for God knows how long, his progress will be measured in milligrams of sedative and minutes free from Pavulon. No more baths, no more looking out the window, where brown leaves flutter past the glass. No more crying in this room right now. At least no crying from a baby.

Then I pull Alex's pictures from my drawer and put them back on my desk, kissing the cool glass of each frame and apologizing to my son. All that day, and every day since, I try to not move my lips as I walk the streets muttering, "Daddy knows you can do it, Alexander. Daddy knows you can do it."

# NOVEMBER AND DECEMBER, 1998

I GOT UP AT 4:30 this morning, and now it's almost eight p.m. My eyes are raw, my head is light, my legs ache, and I think, "I've been a *lot* more tired than this lately."

It has been five months, and Alex is okay except for breathing. He spends his time on a vent of one kind or another, the oxygen pumped into him slowly scarring his lungs, making it tougher for oxygen to be taken into his blood. But he's getting there, I guess. He's been getting there ever since Jill and I stood outside the hospital and said things like, "At least it isn't turning into a hot summer." Now we're still standing outside the hospital, hugging our coats closed while the leaves swirl around our ankles and Alex climbs out of October. He's feeding from a bottle again, looking at the ceiling, gaining weight. And yet, "You have to be the best person you can be for when he comes home," they're telling us again. They love to tell us things, as our lives are still laid bare under hospital neon. I've lost whole nights of sleep since June.

Other nights have just evaporated. And he isn't even home yet. Parents of healthy full-termers say, "You'll be happy to get six hours when he comes home!" Okay. Just remember there's a world of difference between getting up at two a.m. to rock a baby to sleep, and getting up at two a.m. to speed him to the ER before his lungs give out. These days, the morning coffee slides uselessly over my tongue. By 9:30 my bones feel like balsa wood. By noon I need aspirin. By afternoon, my head grows heavy and my sight grows weak.

Most nights I leave work at five p.m., and catch the subway uptown. Sometimes at the hospital door the security guard still asks to see the plastic ID band, rotted off weeks ago, that was fastened onto my wrist when Alex was born. Alex still has a tube up his nose, but the weight is returning to his face and he's taken to bopping his arms to cassettes of Pete Seeger and Chet Baker. He chomps on his pacifier, bouncing his eyes across the ceiling and across Jill's face as she reads him a baby book: "How cute is baby? *So* cute! How smart is baby? *So* smart! How sleepy is baby? . . ."

When I rest him on my chest, I close my eyes. I feel his five pounds seven ounces and think, "There is a future here." Who's Daddy's little guy? Alex is. To watch him sleep is torture as my head lolls forward. Then I open my eyes and he opens his and seems to ask, "How much longer?" What a cute, smart question! For about 130 nights we've called to check on Alex's condition before we went to bed. We've asked for the nurse. She— they're all women—has said "Hi." We've said how are you? She's said fine. There the conversation has often settled until we asked how in hell Alex was doing. I would like to care how the nurse is feeling. But I don't.

Recently within me, something has worn dangerously smooth. Like that Saturday in September when Jill and I drove in and we got stuck on a narrow Manhattan street behind a garbage truck, and I almost ran down a garbage man.

We stopped right after that, and the guy appeared huge in my windshield and said, "Did you see me? Did you *see* me?"

I saw you, I saw you, I tell him.

"Good. Next time I'm gonna lay on the floor!" I still don't know what he meant.

To release steam, Jill and I make fun of the staff. Some doctors and nurses are nice, like some garbage men. Others aren't. We call one resident "The Easter Bunny" because she always shows up with a pink expression and she lacks only floppy ears and green plastic grass. One nurse told Jill not to swear. One

doctor says Jill "questions authority." When asked Alex's ca-
loric intake, another nurse asked Jill to multiply two three-digit
numbers in her head; we call this nurse "The Mathematician."
Most of the hospital staff are like cops: courteous, chilly, hurried, and informative until you run into their invisible wall.

Jill has come up with a Flintstones NICU, which would use
loincloth diapers, a breathing vent powered by the weight of
rocks tied with vines, and a respiratory alarm that's just a bird
squawking "Baby's Awake! Baby's Awake!" I've come up with
a NICU based on that "Twilight Zone" where Dennis Weaver
is a convicted murderer set to be electrocuted at midnight. Except he doesn't fry, but just relives his last day over and over
with the same faces in different roles. One day the guy who's
the warden will be the guy in another cell, and the day after
that he'll be the district attorney.

I have to leave soon, as the headache drills upward from the
back of my neck. Off to visit Alex yet again in the place where his
air comes out of the walls and all containers are labeled with
masking tape: "Linen," "Respiratory," "Hi, I'm Alexander!" The
nurse will ask me if I want to hold him, and I'll say hi to the
doctors. Yet I know that someday soon when I go in, the faces of
the nurses will be switched around. A few of them may be the
moms, a few will be faces on the subway, the hospital security
guard will be one of the dads, and one of the doctors will be
sweeping the floor. Alex will be more or less the same.

Alex has hernia surgery this morning, and I can't find the
coffee cup I use on the subway. It's Monday. I want the cup. Jill
says she doesn't know where it is. Most kids walk out of the
hospital afterwards, and even walk home if they live close
enough. Alex doesn't have the lungs to do that.

At 8:20 a. m., at the counter of the Queens Boulevard
Dunkin' Donuts, I am not waited on before a Chinese woman
who came in after me. It's an honest mistake, I guess, and soon
I order a small with milk and one sugar, and climb the station

steps to the 7 train. I get off at Times Square at 8:45, and head down Broadway because I simply cannot face the mobs of Long Islanders on 7th Avenue.

9:10: The label of my scarf catches on the handle of my office door. I see my coffee cup on my desk. Five minutes later Jill calls, and says she got a phone call saying they're taking Alex early and need our verbal consent. They're also going to biopsy a piece of him for a bone condition. The odds of his having this condition are 15,000 to one, but they've found bone fractures of what they choose to believe is mysterious origin. Jill says that the doctor who phoned didn't know Jill's first name. Jill adds that she's going to bring her knitting for the wait.

At work, I send one e-mail and forward a wrong number before I leave my office at ten, and within minutes I am befuddled by the redesigned East 32nd Street subway station. Is my six-pound son under the knife? Will I find Jill crying and her mother holding her with that "I didn't think being a grandmother was going to be like this" look? I recall what the nurse said yesterday: "You'll be in for a tough day tomorrow."

On the train, two MTA workers are talking loudly about repairs in Queens. One has a cool baseball hat: tan, with the logos of several subway lines. Down the car, two other guys in leather jackets are transporting cartons of oversized baby books. I read *Horatio Hornblower*, and make good connections all the way. By 10:45 I'm at the hospital. In the NICU, Alex's room is deserted. His Beanie Babies are heaped in one corner of the crib, Rainbow the Iguana staring from the top of the pile. The monitors are dark, and his blankets are flat and cool. He's gone.

Jill isn't there, either. Turns out Alex hasn't been wheeled upstairs to the seventh floor, as we'd been told, but to the fifth floor of a different building. We're also told there's no waiting room near that OR. I call Carmel, Jill's mom. She says they phoned her by mistake earlier in the morning. She sounds disoriented, and thinks it's ten minutes to ten. But she says she'll come.

I head to the lobby, thinking, Hornblower-like, that this is the best point at which to intercept Jill no matter what direction she comes from. I will wait until 11:10, then proceed to the 7th floor, then back to Alex's room and then, if necessary, to that different building and ascertain for myself that there's no waiting room. I wait and I read, at my strategic point. By the ice cream machine, a mother is rigging a baby into a backpack. On the phone near the security desk a woman asks, "Can you tell me if she had a baby yet? And as far as you know everything is all right?" Everything is all right. She screams at the other mom and the rigged baby: "Guys! It's done!"

At 11:10 I find Jill on the plump blue cushions of the waiting room outside the NICU, untangling yarn. The TV is on. The doctors have told Jill nothing. She wonders where I've been. Turns out she walked right by me. "I yelled at his nurse," she reports. "She kept saying, 'There's no waiting room at that OR'. I said, 'I know! You've said that five times!'" John, an orderly we both love, comes by to give her a hard time. But he sees it's the wrong moment: His jokes fade to mumbles and an assurance. He goes away. We see him a few more times that morning, and he looks at us but doesn't speak.

At 11:15, I suggest that it would be smart to eat something during this lull. "I want a hot roast beef on rye toast, with mustard on the side, and salt and pepper," Jill says. "If they don't have that, bacon and egg on a roll."

I return half an hour later. I got myself hot roast beef on wheat; it chews like cloth. Jill can't believe I forgot the salt and pepper and didn't get a plastic knife for the mustard. She snaps on her jacket and is heading toward the elevator when I'm hit with the masterstroke that in the nearby NICU administrative offices are NICU administrators, sitting at desks. Top drawers of work desks always contain salt packets. One of the administrators uncovers two.

Over lunch Jill and I bet on when we'll hear something. Jill says 12:10. I say 12:25. The TV drones and drones. Sticking out from the wall near the waiting area is a round two-sided clock. One side tells us it's just before noon. The other side, which we cannot see but know has been broken for weeks, says 3:30. Someone named Nan, who apparently has been detailed to act as liaison between the OR and us, stops by. Everything has been set up well for the surgery, she reports.

The TV-mooner leaves the waiting room. I reach up and unplug the TV. "Stick the cord behind so they won't see it's unplugged," Jill suggests. There's a scene in Hornblower where he's blowing up an enemy fort and hides a burning fuse under a dead guard.

Carmel shows up at noon with ham and cheese sandwiches, and olives for Jill. Jill knits while I attack the ham and cheese. Carmel shows us the sailor suit she has bought for Alex. At 12:10 Nan swings by and tells us that things are going well— she seems to have a CNN-like connection to the surgeons—and that we should know a lot more in a half hour.

Carmel, Jill and I chat about English novels, Carmel's childhood in El Paso and what the Mexican maid thought of her brother, then about Carmel using college German to negotiate an inflated hotel bill in Europe. The TV is still off. We all do the *Times* crossword, passing it around after doing about three answers each. In between her turns, Jill knits. Then she says she screwed up the stitch. I lose my pen.

12:30: the elevator opens and they wheel out a baby in an isolette. "Who's that?" I ask. "I don't know," says Jill. "Is that Alex Cornfield?" Jill asks. "No," says the nurse, "it isn't." I see a little fist, then a little face that isn't his, and feel proud that I could probably pick my son out in a gymnasium full of isolettes.

Nan reappears, and we ask what's going on. She gestures to the elevators. "You should see them come right back here," she says.

Five minutes later we see them come right back here: Three adults escorting one six pound baby, one on each end of his isolette and the assisting surgeon wheeling his vent. I glimpse a red number "100." One hundred is good. They pilot Alex back into his room and four people in yellow robes and masks descend on him to re-hook plastic tubes and try to get the rest of the numbers to look as good as the 100.

"It went fine, really fine," says the assistant surgeon.

"You might want to stay out a minute," a nurse tells us.

Alex has a peaceful look, his eyes shuttered in sleep, his complexion grayish-tan with a deepening pink in the cheeks. And as they lift Alex naked—except for his breathing tube—I see he's a different man. That's all I can see as Jill and I hustle to stay out of the way. Jill notices they've put an IV into the same wrist that was fractured; the bandage around the IV is tied in a bow. The head surgeon appears and tells us Alex was "vigorous." "Oh, very vigorous," the doctor says.

Jill has to leave soon for a 1:30 lunch with a friend; I go to the waiting room to send in Carmel, and to gather the yarn, the newspapers, the coats, the bags and the other crap. When I get back, Alex is still asleep. Jill sings to him a while. At quarter to two, his arms are moving up and down and his lips are pressing together, then parting with little squeaks. They shoot him with a clear pencil of morphine.

The pink gets pinker. "He'll sleep now," the nurse says. There isn't much to do, so I sing to him a minute and head to the subway and back to work.

On the train platform, I feel the ham and cheese in the bottom of my stomach. All the other people getting on the train look awake. I don't think I do. The doors of the train rumble shut, and it starts to hit me that this morning went pretty well.

Twenty-four hours before Jill and I begin to "nest," or volunteer to join our son Alex as unwitting patients, I'm walking home in Queens and I pass a mechanical Santa. He's in the window of a ground-floor apartment, about two feet tall, washed in red and green light. His arm goes up and down, up and down, up and down. He's bigger than Alex, but he does raise his arm in a similar way.

They say that in a few days, Alex can come home. But before this struggle ends, Jill and I seem to be required to "nest" overnight in the hospital.

The night before, the nurse shows me the nesting room. "This is where Alex will be," says the nurse, indicating a clear plastic bin, cushioned with one pink and turquoise blanket atop a table of fake hospital wood. Beside it, the monitors are dark and the bells asleep. This is a back room, off the NICU. It has two windows with venetian blinds, sky-blue wallpaper, a TV, a dresser, a table, and a night stand sporting a lamp on which a wooden clown with a wooden dog sells obese plastic balloons. The lamp is bolted to the dresser. The room also has one wastebasket, in the bathroom. Dust blankets the air vent. One thin pillow sits at the head of each bed.

I go home. I get to bed at the usual time, about 11:30. After I brush my teeth: I wipe off the faucet, pick up Alex's picture beside the sink, kiss the cool glass of the frame, and tell him, "Daddy knows *you* can do it, Alex." In the bedroom, I reach over the bassinet and hang my clothes. I often bump the bassinet. It will rock and sway, rock and sway, squeaking as if from far away, even after I reach up and turn out the light.

Five hours later, I'm awake. I realize what today is. "Get plenty of sleep before nesting" was the on-line advice of preemie parents who've graduated. Many of these parents e-mail us. "Your words bring back memories and feelings that you think you have stuffed away forever," said one mom. "Lifted my spirits," said another. And, from a NICU nurse and mother of a preemie, "You've made a difference, not only for your own family but for many others."

Thoughts of such words wake me up, so finally as the minute hand drags toward the twelve, I get out of bed into the dark bedroom, figuring getting up this early will be neat to remember and figuring that, if you have to lose sleep, better to do so excited about seeing your son than worrying over whether he's still breathing.

I've got mail, so I spend the pre-dawn hours pushing the mouse and tapping the keys. Correspondence done by six, I lapse into two hours of Duke Nukem. The day's work begins with exhausting my jet-pack and picking off drones with the rocket launcher. I toy with the idea of going out for breakfast, but instead try to fetch Duke's shotgun with no air left in my scuba gear. Jill gets up at eight and drinks the coffee I brewed after draining the pot before dawn.

I arrive at work having been up five hours, feeling like a farmer. Tonight I'm going to become the real daddy of a six-month-old boy! By mid-morning I'm low on fuel, and blow $2 on bacon-and-egg on a roll. The sandwich sits on my tongue. Haze blankets my eyes, but I tingle at the thought of doing the crossword and spending all night with him. For five months, almost every day, there's been an Alex-related answer in the *Times* crossword puzzle. "Gram." "EKG." "Vent." "Alex." In the past week, though, Alex clues have dried up.

The haze deepens as I have three tangelos and two bananas for lunch. What am I going to do twelve hours from now when he's hungry? Jill calls to say meet her at Broadway and 72nd Street at 5:45. I hit the vending machine downstairs, blow $1 on cheese n' bacon-flavored Tato Skins and white cheddar-flavored popcorn. I get a drink at the water fountain down the hall, and the bubble rising in the tank echoes in my head. Computer crashes nag me all the way to 4:30, when the sun finally deserts an unseasonable 65-degree day.

I meet Jill and we walk, killing time in Barnes & Noble until we meet her parents for dinner in a Vietnamese restaurant. Jill has the steak cubes; I have the noodles. After that, we head to her parents' house and I take a shower.

"My mother told me, 'Keep him up late! Keep him up late!'" Jill says as we sit on the bench on the street at 8:40 p.m. Theory being, I guess, he'll then sleep through the night. We hold each other's hand.

We go in and find the nurse feeding him. He's smiling and grinning, chomping on a pacifier and about to get a dose of hydrochlorothiazide, a diuretic to help get tiny amounts of fluid out of his lungs. "It's refined, so you have to shake it," the nurse warns. "When they see you," Jill says to Alex, "people are going to want to take you home."

The sky-blue wallpaper is still there. So are the clown lamp and the velvety lint on the air duct. No wastebasket has been added, and though there are two light switches, only one seems connected. It floods the room with white neon. "Like a crummy hotel room," says Jill, dropping the blinds.

There are things we have to know now. The nurses and doctors try to convince us of this as, six months ago, they tried to convince us that there were things we were better off not knowing. Alex's night nurse asks us if we know syringes. Oh yeah, I say, we had a diabetic cat and we used to give him insulin.

Alex is eating now. But they started him back on corn oil a few days ago, and he has a touch of thrush coming on. After about 50 ccs, spit-up bursts out of his lips in a quick yellow stream. We clean him up and the nurse trundles him back— unattached to the oxygen that he still needs. He lives on a monitor that has red numbers and a monitor that has green numbers. The red-numbered one blares incessantly, it seems, because the newborn-sized sensor no longer adheres to his foot. Alex has my arches, and his big toe curls up in a kind of sneer, just like mine. The red-numbered monitor is a pulse oximeter, or pulse ox, and it measures the oxygen saturation in his blood. Its alarms shatter the air in the crummy hotel room.

Jill washes his foot. "I just want to fix this pulse ox because I'm about to kill myself," she says.

We're settled by about 11:20—I'm coming up on 19 straight hours awake—and though Alex is concerned at first with his new surroundings, he settles quickly. His eyes bounce around the place and his head moves, but when I put him on me and lie on the bed, he goes to sleep.

So of course the nurse must come in. She is from Boston. We talk about New England winters and Fenway Park. To help his breathing before he eats, Alex must inhale misty medicine through a rubber mask. The nurse watches me hold the mask to Alex's face and tap his chest to loosen mucus. She chats about the Patriots moving to Hartford, then warns us about all the procedures we'll have to do for Alex when he comes home. Jill replies, yes, but we won't have to do this stuff forever. The nurse then says, "I just don't want you to think you're ever going to have a normal baby."

In six months Jill and I have learned you can confront the nurse, which results in a few moments of strained silence and, after you go home, nightmares of what she can do to your baby after you leave. You can punch her and be barred from the NICU. You can have her fired from your case. But we're in this nursing room because we're close to the end, and we just stand there.

She leaves. Alex chomps his pacifier. We feed him. Inside the two-ounce bottle, the bubbles climb in the yellow formula. In half an hour he's done, more or less. He burps like a tiny sailor and we lie him down. His eyes are bright. The pulse ox erupts for no reason. We pat Alex. "Wouldn't it be a good idea to let Mommy go to sleep for a while now, buddy?" Jill asks him. She turns to me; our faces are white in the neon. "I don't feel I can take my clothes off here," she says. "I don't feel I can brush my teeth."

Twenty hours now I haven't slept, and my own eyes burn. Pat pat pat pat pat pat. It's 1:30 by the time I've brushed my teeth by the push-pedal sink and put my head down on the thin pillow. The room is dark and quiet, and my head sinks into the extra pillow Jill swiped from the breast-pumping room. I go to sleep quickly.

At four a.m., Nurse Normal flicks on the neons and says she needs to wake Alex to feed him. It's as if Jill and I have decided to stay up forever. Jill is already up, but wonders about the sense of trying to force-feed a dozing six-month-old. Alex is undersized, the nurse says, and we need to keep up the feeding schedule so he'll maybe one day come close to normal.

Back to sleep for me. I dream about Alex and a seaside resort, and intruders trying to break into our cabin. I awake to find breakfast on a hospital tray. Cheerios and a roll. A differ-

ent nurse brings in vitamins for Alex. Jill is sleeping by now and
I'm not. The vitamins have to be mixed. The nurse tries to wake
Jill, who fell asleep about an hour ago.

The nurse is a fresh reinforcement, and chides Jill. "You have
to learn how to do this," the nurse says, putting the vitamin bottles
down beside Alex's bed. "You have to learn how to do this."

"I just got to sleep," Jill says. I'm staring at Alex. "My hus-
band just told you he'd learn how and teach me later . . ."

"Well yes, but you really have to do this too . . ."

*"MADAM!" I bark. "You will leave my wife alone! She
was awake and caring for this baby while you and I were both
fast asleep last night. You will not bother her, but instead you
will instruct me!"*

I don't bark any such thing. I stare silently at Alex. I wish
that they would leave Jill alone before I take one of their heads
and bang it over and over on the fake wood tabletop until,
eventually, Jill gets up to stop me. "There should be another
wastebasket in here," the nurse says.

I mix the vitamins. Jill goes back to sleep, and I shut off the
pulse ox and am immediately sorry. I worry about cardiac arrest and death. No more fitting place for a baby to die than in a
hospital. My family sleeps. I read *Hornblower* and this extra-
long day in the day in the NICU continues into early afternoon.
Alex suffers neither cardiac arrest nor death—but he does spit
up twice, turning the floor sticky.

It is suddenly 1:50 p.m., and out the window I see it has become another day for normal people. Jill and I sip take-out coffee
and give him a bath in a bowl. We plot our escape, not from our
baby, but from our baby in the hospital. We tell the nurses that,
sure, we will nest again next week. But I doubt we will.

I'm starting to think that in the years ahead I'll remember
all of Alex's nurses as one big Nurse.

He has a harem, in faded yellow gowns stenciled "Property
of Medical Center." Some of the members of the harem are

Kris, Dee, another Dee, Jacky, Lynn, Ellen, Frieda, Ricki, Phyl, Sylvia, Penny and Emma. Kris used to work in a modeling agency. She wants a baby boy of her own, but would prefer to meet a nice guy first; her dentist is "gorgeous." Dee 2 is Swiss and came here as a child, but never lost her accent. She's from near Zurich, and her son's in California trying to be an actor. Her daughter has kids now, but used to act on a soap. Dee #1 likes to ski. We fired a different Debbie, and I don't really want Delores again because she called Alex "a little white boy." Jacky is Irish. Lynn is Scottish, and hates London. Kelly is from New Zealand. Phyl is the only nurse who talks baby talk to Alex. Ricki once made Alex stop crying by demanding to know, "What's going *on* here?!"

In the past six months, Sylvia's knee went bad, Ricky's son finished baseball camp, and Kris went to Norway and had a long weekend in North Carolina for a wedding. Other stuff has happened to them, but to tell you the truth after these months, they have formed into one gigantic ball, like the rock that almost gets Indiana Jones. None of them is my buddy, and there's always a fresh reinforcement when one of them gets tired and leaves.

The huge ball is rolling closer to me and Jill, a snowball big as a hospital, loud as a hive, one big nurse with pet sayings:

Every baby's different.

These babies take time.

You're going to have to be ready when he comes home.

Six months. I refuse to say "half a year." This is the kind of stuff you refuse to say when you've been visiting your baby in the hospital for a period of time no longer most efficiently measured in weeks. Six months is not as long as it could be: I was recently telling an outside doctor about Alex's birth and the doctor asked, "June of what year?"

Alex stares at your face as you feed him—Kris thinks he has a crush on her—though according to the doctors he still has the blurry vision of a newborn. With inch-long fingers and finely

creased knuckles he reaches for the bottle of formula. Between
his lips appears his tongue, pink and hungry and the size of a
grown-up's fingernail. A few days ago I got a whole bottle of
formula past that tongue. I was proud, though it was only about
as much liquid as an adult might spill on his desk and wipe dry
before even needing to swear.

"Good job, Dad," the nurse said.

Alex also uses those tiny hands to shove away medications.
Sometimes his least favorite is Albuterol, a mist given through a
plastic green mask that fits over his eyes and mouth until he looks
like a little jet pilot. Sometimes he sleeps through this, as the
vapors seep into his lungs and widen the airways. Sometimes he
squirms. Lately he squirms with purpose, arms and legs beginning to buck with what looks like a toddler's coordination.

There are things you're going to have to do, the Big Nurse
tells us. Looking at Alex's future bedroom, I presume one of
those things is "sweep." But at least the air conditioner is off
the floor and we're almost ready to move the couch out. We
have to do something with the crap that was on the bookshelf.
We'll have to move the dresser back, and, as Alex has breathing
problems, we'll have to get rid of the big living room rug. We've
moved his bassinet to our bedroom and piled it high with plush
animals and other stuff.

That stuff has been there a while. Alex is back on CPAP, a
thick nasal tube that does the breathing for him, because last
weekend his hernia kicked up and, again, something collapsed
in his lungs. This has happened before, as we know. On one
bad, bad day, Dee patted him and put drops in his eyes because
Alex had to be artificially paralyzed and couldn't blink by himself. Dee's face still wilts when she remembers. She still drops
by Alex's room on her day off, and once when she had Alex for
the day Jill and I came back from lunch and found him on her
lap in the rocker. She was touching his cheeks with her fingertips, and they were smiling at each other. She handed him back

to us without a word and went out to the nurses' station. I wish she had stayed.

The next day, Kris was back. She leaned over the crib in her faded yellow robe, telling us what medical science can do for a baby with bad lungs. Alex looked up at her and she looked down at him, and all the time she spoke of him she kept his hand cupped inside her simply gigantic palm.

Here are some scenes from the week Alex was home:

—Our study transformed by powder-scented blankets, Rainbow the Iguana and the other Beanie Babies, a bassinet and a towering dark-green oxygen tank. In the bassinet he slumbers like a baby painting on a grandmother's wall: lips apart, eyes in soft slits, skin pink and smooth.

—On the first night, he sits with us in the living room for our dinner of pizza and Hershey's Kisses, and waves his arms and sucks on his pacifier. "We're Mom and Dad," I tell him, "and this is the halogen lamp." Soon, when I hear him cry, my first thought isn't that it's some kid outside. "What's the matter?" I ask him. "What's the matter? Oh I'm sorry, Alex. They don't make baby food anymore . . ."

—I shower on the first night; I finish with five minutes to spare before the overnight nurse arrives. "What's the matter?" my wife Jill asks in bed on Monday night. "Well it's just weird," I say. "Two people are here tonight who weren't here last night."

—Beside him, the lullaby plays on the Walkman: "Stars shining, number number one, number two, number three good Lord, bye 'n' bye . . ." We're together, after half a year, under one roof. Under that roof, the pulse ox tells us nothing. Saturation levels of 99, then 35, then 85, then 60. A Martian wouldn't sat like that. The company sends out a technician in a leather jacket and coconut cologne who straps the sensor on his own finger and announces that the machine is, in fact, accurate. We call the emergency line. "You've seen him at 55 on the pulse ox in

real life," says Dr. T. over the phone. "You know that isn't right."
Indeed: 55 is well on the way to dead.

—On the second night, I finish the shower with twenty minutes to spare. The days shatter into feeding times and prepara-
tion times for feeding, into screwing together his nebulizer and
untangling his oxygen cord. By the third day, a rhythm surfaces. Feedings we cut to 30 ccs, given twice as often. I make a
big chart of all the stuff we do and at what time. Unused diapers blossom around our apartment.

—The smell of chili wafts in from the kitchen, where Jill
works with beans and onions to bring life back to normal.
"Where are the notes you're keeping on this?" Jill asks. "It's
quarter to eight and we're eating dinner. I just want to say that's
a lot earlier than normal." She turns to Alex with a bottle. "Take
this, baby, so Mommy can have a life."

—On Thursday we spend four hours getting to and from
his eye doctor. I trundle Alex out of the car, trying not to bang
the portable oxygen tank that weighs a ton, watching his eyes
narrow in the cold misty rain on the roof of the hospital garage,
wanting him to never feel the cold rain. Jill and I struggle to the
hospital, and suddenly glimpse the end of his oxygen tube dan-
gling in front of us on the sidewalk. In the waiting room, another mother calls his face handsome and mature.

—We get him home. I play Michael Feinstein in his crib. I
print out a ream of congratulatory e-mails. I spend five hours
trying to write a check for the electric bill. I think about all the
other stuff I liked to do—computer shoot'em-ups, e-mail—then
I twist the bottle to get those final yellow ccs down Alex's throat.

Then the week ended, and a lot of other things with it.

# DECEMBER, 1998, AND JANUARY, 1999

WE TOOK ALEX TO three appointments that week he was home. The last began at eleven a.m. on Friday. They checked his oxygen and twisted at his hips, and then they quizzed Jill and me separately about how the feeding's going at home.

At 1:30 we were nearing the end; the nurse had only to re-tape Alex's cannula to his cheeks. It was a pretty warm day. We brought sandwiches of ham and cheese, and tangelos, and his bottle, which he sucked. Jill had also brought an Agatha Christie novel, and it jutted from a pocket of her purse on the floor. I could see the title: *Is There a Doctor in the House?* Later Jill wondered why she couldn't have brought a book entitled, *Life Is Beautiful. Go Home.*

The taping turned ugly. Alex squirmed. He cried, and cried and cried. Strong for seven and a half pounds of kid. He cried and cried, and Jill picked him up from the nurse and his lips turned the color of grape gum, and then he stopped crying in Jill's arms. The resulting moment of silence lasted about ten years until the nurse yelled, "Get Susan!"

I'll never know who Susan was. The nurse carried him, her face frozen as she yelled. Alex was limp as the dead. I ran down the hall. "I need a doctor!" I shouted at a guy on a phone. I picked him because he had glasses and gray hair and a nice tie.

He hung up and followed me into the exam room, where he flipped Alex over and turned to Jill and said, "Tell me what's been happening."

Jill shoved me into another exam room nearby. She seemed on the verge of laughing. From the doorway I saw our exam room fill with a mob, the backs of dozens and dozens of heads, haircuts neat and scraggy. They bobbed as if trying to glimpse the world's tiniest Michael Feinstein fan.

"Sir, clear the doorway," a guard said to me.

"I'm the father," I told him.

*Oh well then, glad I'm not you.*

Alex had suffered some sort of blockage, the doctors said. He had choked, and was actually breathing on his own when they rammed a plastic vent down his throat for transport to the Pediatric Intensive Care Unit. "So I'm not going home with my baby," Jill said to a nurse.

"Maybe you should just sit down, you know?" the nurse said.

"I think he'll be all right," the doctor said.

Then Alex was gone, replaced on the examining bed by spaghetti of tubes and wires, torn white paper, a wide and ragged pink stain. On the radiator, I found the cannula we'd been trying to change. His little gray long-johns lay on the floor beside the bed. Jill zeroed in on a blue sock. "I found the other sock near a retractor," she said, eating my ham sandwich.

In the PICU we marveled at the ice machine and the microwave—Neonatal Intensive Care had nothing like that for parents—and spent a couple hours watching them sedate him; then we went home, numbed into what Jill called "auto-pilot" by knowing that we were back to the routine. Before leaving the hospital, we found a bulletin board where parents had written messages in crayon. In blue I wrote, "Daddy knows you can do it, Alex."

Now Alex lies unmoving. The tube is down his throat, he has IVs in his head, right hand and feet. He has sprouted tubes in all the old directions. "Remember who was in the bed with us yesterday morning?" Jill asks. It was him. I remember that as a dream, and the new week begins:

—A PICU resident explains that rotating the hips is a common examination of babies, and that they all hate it. "You have to be careful not to pull them out of the sockets," she says, "or then you have to treat that." Dr. H. tells us she shares our frustration. But we've been six months in this mess. "You can't share it completely, doctor," I tell her.

—On Sunday afternoon they try to pull out the tube. I suggest an oxygen mask. It doesn't work; Alex's numbers fall. 79. 78. 77. 76. 75. 74. 73. 72. 71. Beep. We play him the lullabies. "Stars shin-ing, number number one, number two, number three good Lord . . ."

—Says Jill's mom, "Tell Jill I'll be over next week. I will rearrange appointments for the next several weeks and come hell or high water I'll be there, and I'll bring bread and cheese, and a piece of fruit." I ask Jill's mom to call her dentist to cancel an appointment for me on Monday; to remind herself, she writes his name on the palm of her hand.

—"Look at our Friday afternoon. Look at our Sunday evening," I tell one doctor. "You can see why we're not impressed."

—Jill cries, her shoulders shaking, on a park bench. I stare at the new hospital entrance we use, for the new wing he's in. The entrance is one door north of the entrance we used for six months. "This is like a job you hate," Jill says, "a job where you hate all your co-workers, except one."

—The nurse says to bring him his frog Beanie Baby. Our former neonatologist tells me that the "aggressive questioning" Jill and I did since June affected the course of Alex's medical treatment "to his detriment." His current doctor tells me this morning that unless Alex gains weight, he will die. I don't know how much more I'll talk to doctors.

I survive right now by thinking of Alex as gone. And the baby I knew that first and only week home is gone. How he stretched and yawned, how he looked around in bed with me and Jill, how his mouth curled when he didn't want to eat. But

I am glad that the study still smells like powder. As I type this the scent hangs in the back of my nose, like a memory of some candy that they just don't make anymore.

It's one in the morning on the day after Christmas, and I'm playing poker on the computer. I've felt lousy on a lot of Christmas nights before this one. But I've felt better on a lot of them, too, and that's what I'm remembering as I draw to a straight. I remember petting a tiger cat in the reddish glow of the tree in our living room about twenty-five years ago. My mother was in the kitchen, my dad was probably watching TV. This was in Bangor, Maine, in a ramshackle old three-story house where the roof always leaked. I was in pajamas. It was Christmas night at about 8:30, and the base of the tree was naked save for a sprinkle of pine needles. I think I got a little pool table that year.

The next Christmases I remembered were from the mid-1980s, when I went home for a few weeks. I remembered deep snow and hollow-cold nights walking to the car in the mall parking lot. I should have been Christmas shopping in the mall, but spent most of those nights playing pinball. Come Christmas Day my older brother and my mother and I would rip the packages apart. One of us would unwrap while another would dig under the tree and another would thank whoever gave us something. In the afternoon, my brother and I would go play pinball after my mother had given each of us a roll of quarters. I was in my twenties and he was in his thirties and we both should have had better things to do, I guess, but I still loved those Christmases.

This last Christmas capped a tough year. This was the Christmas I came home from seeing Alex and on the way home ran across a woman in a deli. She was arguing about having bought a dead battery. *"See?"* she demanded of the guy behind the counter. "I'm pressing it and it isn't going up to 'Good.' It's staying at 'Replace.' It's been on your shelf too long."

The guy said something to her as I stood behind Jill. We were buying tomatoes and thinking about Alex.

"I bought it for a Christmas present and I want to *make sure* it works," the woman said. She was having a rough Christmas.

Maybe the battery died in the cold. This Christmas felt like Christmas in Maine: below-freezing temperatures, with a wind. Snow squeaked under your boots, and God forbid your wife left your earmuffs in your mother-in-law's hospital room. This Christmas I have three days off from my job at an accounting magazine. I spent some of that time picking Alex's nipples and bottles out of the drain rack and putting them in the cupboard, tossing them behind the baby food he may never eat. A lot of things besides batteries weren't working this Christmas.

They keep Alex paralyzed with a drug, which is good, because if they didn't he'd rip out his breathing tube and vent. Because he's paralyzed, they have to put drops in his eyes, and suction away his spittle whenever it bubbles out around the tube. They feed him through a yellow tube. He doesn't move. I've blotted out the image from my mind of what he looked like when he looked alive.

"I keep thinking of bathing him at home," Jill says, "and telling him, 'Now you're a boy in a bathtub. Now you're a boy in a towel . . .'"

I figured Alex would return to the hospital. But I figured he'd have a few weeks home, then four days in the hospital, not four days home then a few weeks—or more—in the hospital. I hate the word "hospital."

Jill is asleep right now in the other room. I'm in the study, which is supposed to be Alex's room. Behind me is a bassinet, blankets, his Beanie Baby Bat, a rattle, wipies, and on his dresser a changing pad and a wooden tray of diapers and the medicines he needed. We don't know if we should put this stuff somewhere. At least the home-oxygen guys came and got the tanks.

One of his former night nurses calls. "Merry Christmas," she says. "Yes," I reply.

They're saying Alex may need a tracheotomy. A trach is another tube, stuck in a hole in his throat to help him breathe. On it, he can barely speak, and he will cry soundlessly. The doctors consider this tube the best step. "I've given you my best medical opinion," one doctor said today. Yesterday she told us Alex's outlook "isn't dismal." There are doctors all over the place this Christmas. Yesterday, Christmas Eve at about 4:30 p.m., a psychiatrist told me there wasn't much I could give Alex right now.

She was the first psychiatrist I've ever talked to as a patient. She was also the first person to call the stress on me and Jill "inhuman." I watched the lights twinkle in the windows of the housing project across the street from her office.

But for this Christmas I can at least give my son alternatives to a trach. Jill and I visit her mom in one hospital on Christmas Day before heading up to another hospital to see Alex. While Jill visits her mother, I duck into the Pediatric Intensive Care Unit of that hospital in hopes of leaving my phone number. Instead I dig up two doctors who listen to the outline of Alex's case. One says that in his opinion our hospital is doing the right thing.

Also on this Christmas I'm trying to recover from a doctor telling me that asking so many questions altered Alex's course of treatment during his first half year "to his detriment." When he heard the comment, my brother asked, "Is that legal?" Probably. Everything this year has been legal. Thus proving to me the difference between "legal" and "right."

For Christmas dinner Jill and I have roasted peppers, with nice bread with feta cheese. We rent *Sour Grapes*, a movie about cousins who get into a fight over slot machine winnings. One of the cousins castigates a TV star and the other almost murders his mother. Midway through we phone the PICU. The nurse says Alex can take being handled better tonight. Later Jill and I stay up until one a.m., searching the Web for the word "trach." Beside us slowly twirl the Mylar balloons I bought at Rite Aid that week he was home. One says "Congratulations!" and the other says "It's a boy!" They're gradually sinking closer to the floor.

The Sunday after Christmas we get up at eleven a.m. I sip my morning coffee at ten past noon. We call the PICU, which is in the same hospital and just one door north of our old NICU entrance. The nurse tells us that his oxygen needs are higher and he needs mucus suctioned out every hour, but that his x ray looks better than yesterday. By afternoon, I haven't even dressed. I watch the Jets beat the Patriots. I wish my boy were here to watch it with me.

There are four days left in this year. I don't want to think about New Year's Eve. Jill and I will probably be at a party directly across town from Alex's hospital. It's a nice apartment, with a big window in the living room. On New Year's Eve that window will be black and shiny. I'll look past the reflection of my face, past the treetops of the park, and I will be able to see the building where Alex will be for yet another day without an orange cat.

In the frigid air on the way to the bus stop after I've seen Alex, I pass a man and woman waiting for a bus. For some reason, they're standing half a block from the stop. I don't tell them. The bus pulls up, the door opens and I get in, and the door shuts. The man and woman come running, but too late. They bang bang bang on the door, but the driver just pulls away. I hear the man and woman swear.

"He wants the bus and he bangs like an animal," the driver says to me in the rear-view mirror. I smile under my scarf and think, What if that guy takes a faster bus? What if he meets us up ahead, and as I'm getting off he pulls a semi-automatic and peppers the doorway with bullets, almost hitting me twice in the chest? *Try it, you son of a bitch,* I think into my scarf.

It's just that this bus thing occurs on the evening following the afternoon when Dr. F. pronounces Alex "seriously ill."

"So next down is 'critical'?" I ask.

"I don't make those distinctions," he says.

We're talking about what might happen now that some of my son's upper right lung has collapsed again. We want them to give Alex a short course of steroids for his lungs, thus paving the way for an eventual move onto a gentler vent. But Alex has developed some kind of infection in the hospital, and steroids would now be dangerous. "Alex is very sick," Dr. F. says, adding that we're always going to be walking a fine line when treating Alex.

He seems as stable as a baby can be when he has a tube of plastic down his throat. Alex has a TV over his crib where he lies with Rainbow the Iguana; behind them both is a pile of tubes and wires, yellow and clear and black, that connect Alex to machines. He usually has a hat on and doesn't move because they have to keep him paralyzed and sedated. If he moves too much, the little air sacs in his lungs deflate. They're doing everything to keep him alive, if not moving forward. Jill and I tape up a picture of Alex when he was better.

"This is really him," we say. "He has a lot of character."

"I'll bet," the nurses say.

"These preemies have nine lives," says the doctor who revived Alex most recently.

Parents of preemies do not. Nobody will nail down what's wrong. They mention bad-lung "spells," which sounds one step above "evil humours." Dr. F., who doesn't draw those distinctions, draws Jill and me a picture. The drawing starts nice enough, with what looks like a huge lab beaker sitting on top of a culvert pipe. Then Dr. F. adds arrows showing how the air is supposed to move in and out of Alex; then he adds circles to show the air sacs, and then a deep, deep, deep line to depict scars in my kid's lungs. Dr. F. bores into the paper with his Bic, scratching that line over the same few inches, back and forth, back and forth, until we all know what a "spell" is.

We need luck. Jill isn't very religious—at least she wasn't before last June—but she knits Alex a "bendl," a bracelet of red yarn. The night before she slips it over Alex's paralyzed hand, she sleeps with it under her pillow. "I woke up the day after I gave it to him and felt under my pillow and I felt so sad I have nothing to give him," Jill says. "I couldn't find anything of yours. A tie tack didn't seem right . . ." Jill also thinks this is like having a dying baby.

"Except that ends, and you pick up the pieces," she says. "But here, we just have the pieces."

Alex moves a bit on Saturday. When I come in he's staring into space, but when he sees me he wiggles and the corner of his mouth that is free of tube and tape makes a little sideways spike. I think he sees me. This is playoff weekend, and before the game comes on, I open the present a hospital volunteer brought him for Christmas: a foot-long plastic bar threaded with a spinning mirror, a panda head that plays music when you push the nose, a dangly black plastic triangle, and a clear ball filled with red, white and black plastic balls. "Encourages the development of baby's senses of sight, sound, and touch. Help your baby learn and develop one fun step at a time!" the box reads. I look out at the daylight turning to gray, black branches cutting the clouds like power lines, and think, "This could be an okay night." I step to the kitchenette to make a cup of Sanka.

When I come back I find Alex sitting upright, his back against the nurse's hand. Beside him on the sheets is a peach-colored pool of spit-up. Lots of mucus, says the nurse who holds him, and the other says, "Want the Vec?" Vec is the drug that paralyzes Alex. The nurse nods. Soon Alex stops moving, his eyes droop into slits, and I help the nurse close them the rest of the way. I watch the game with the sound off, but the hearing-impaired captions are on. When the Cowboys are down by twenty, they intercept a Cardinal pass. "Arizona just put Dallas on a respirator," the announcer says.

Sunday night we get a different nurse, who must cover two patients, and in the other bed a baby screams like a navy jet. Alex is quiet, but his bells erupt when the nurse has to suction him. She calls over a doctor to help. The doctor's busy, and eventually, I just suction Alex with the fine clear tube and the tiny vacuum device to suck the mucus out of his throat.

Next day Jill and I hold Alex, and he does so well the doctors even consider lowering the vent settings. Then, as we're about to leave, a doctor we call "The Iron Lung" tells us that "we" had decided to put off lowering the vent settings for a few days.

The announcement crushes us. "I know you want to trach this boy!" Jill fires at him.

"No, I do not want to trach this boy," Iron Lung replies.

Later that evening, Jill makes up a title for a book Iron Lung might write: *I Love to Trach Little Babies and Make Their Mothers Cry.* Wherever paperbacks are sold.

And one night not long afterward, Dr. H. heads toward us to talk about "long-term prospects." "Just a minute," she says, "I have to get a chair . . ."

"Oh God, she has to get a chair!" Jill whispers.

Dr. H. listens to what we want to do. Then she tells us what she wants to do, and suggests we do what Jill and I want, only wait a while. "Deal?" Dr. H. asks.

No deal is without price. My price is that a year ago I would have sided with the man and the woman who were banging on the bus. A year ago I would have boarded the bus more slowly, and advised the driver that other people were coming. But I've banged my share of bus doors since the summer sun burned hot, and I've stood in the hospital and watched the numbers on my baby's monitors add up to July Fourth, Labor Day, Halloween, Thanksgiving, and Christmas. Even as Jill begins to hold him again, we hope Alex can have his first birthday somewhere far away from here, only one door north of where he started.

"Doctor, we'd like to transfer Alex."

Alex sleeps, drugged and paralyzed, between us. Dr. T. leans forward, leading with his right ear. "Excuse me?"

"We would like to transfer Alex," I say. Jill and I agreed I'd be the one to ask. "Very good," Dr. T. replies. "I'll tell the attending tomorrow."

Yesterday, the day before I made the request, we had visited the hospital we wanted to transfer to. The place had two pay phones—our hospital has one—and two clean bathrooms. There were three waiting rooms, with tables and soft chairs and a spotless carpet of orange and green and gray. In one waiting room was unvandalized origami under glass. There was a picture of a boy in a space suit planting the "Pediatric ICU" flag on the moon. Inside that PICU, every kid has a private room named after a planet. The monitors showed the vital signs in different colors; none of the equipment seemed scratched. In our PICU, one of the things they use to measure Alex's blood gas has been broken for days. Jill said the difference between this place and our current hospital was the difference between the New York City subway and the starship *Enterprise*.

In the *Enterprise* PICU, we asked to speak to the attending doctor. Turns out he's Dr. K., with whom I had discussed a transfer back in November. He was about forty, Greek, hair still dark, though he no longer had the mustache of his ID photo. On the lapel of his white coat, a button read, "Not always right. Never in doubt." We showed him Alex's snapshot, taken in better days; bringing it was Jill's mom's suggestion. Dr. K. had a seventeen-month-old girl, and his face ignited over Alex's picture. "We're not born with holes in our throats," he noted, and called bronchopulmonary dysplasia, which Alex has, an "abstract concept."

Dr. K. agreed that Jill and I have "a responsibility, an obligation" to do what we think best for Alex. I liked the *Enterprise*. By the time we visited Alex that afternoon back in our subway hospital, Jill and I had made up our minds without a word, much like the way we decide on spaghetti for dinner. Jill called her stepdad, who wondered if a weekend was the best time for a transfer. I agreed—my idea about hospitals' round-the-clock operations has changed since last summer, like most of my ideas about hospitals.

Just hours after we announce our intention to break up with our current hospital, a nurse is lifting Alex into my lap so I can hold him. "He'll be happy now. He's been waiting all day for this," says another nurse. But something happens to the tube in his throat.

Alex's face turns the color of fruit punch, and when the nurse whisks him back to bed and cries for assistance, his head lolls. Dead again, I think. They put the ceiling neons up bright, and The Cluster of Doctors engulfs Alex. He takes a ton of sedative, but they finally get the tube back in. His numbers pop up.

The cluster scatters. "You guys okay?" the nurse asks us.

Jill's face is a pan of milk. "Bush league," she says.

Later we stop at the bathroom before leaving. I'm waiting to go in after Jill when a woman breezes up to the desk nearby, says she's a doctor there for a conference and where is the ladies' room? Right there, the woman at the desk tells her, and walks away. Jill comes out and the woman starts in. "Do you mind if I go in first?" I ask. "Actually I do," she says, and moves inside the door.

I should have made clear I was next. I should have made it clear my baby has been in the hospital for eight months, and that I'm tired. I should have killed her.

"Nothing good is going to happen in this hospital," Jill says.

On Monday Alex has a good afternoon, bouncing on mom's leg to the tune of "William Tell." Then Jill says that there's a "wrinkle" in the insurance: They want a letter confirming that Alex's transfer is a "medical necessity." "I don't suppose you want to go to the desk and see if the doctor wrote the letter?" Jill says to me. Again I have a chance to feel manly.

Dr. H. didn't write the letter, but she did spend three long chunks of time on hold with the *Enterprise*. "First you have to find out their phone number, which is, like, the world's greatest secret," Dr. H. says. "But that's good . . ."

We like this doctor. But anyway, the letter?

"I've written these letters before," she says. "I once talked to one insurance company doctor—that must be an awful job— who just couldn't believe that we'd had a baby on a vent for four months. He said that was just an impossibility!" Later it struck me why she might have been having this conversation: another set of parents had been working on a transfer.

"We all have the same tools," Dr. K. said to me once, referring to different hospitals. "We just use them differently." Indeed. This hospital believes in venting and trachs—it is a revelation to me that hospitals and their physicians "believe" in things, that complex medicine seems as much art as science—and the hospital where we want to transfer Alex seems to do thing differently, and has a growing reputation for pioneering respiratory procedures in preemies. We're betting, in short, that the *Enterprise* can get the vent out of his throat faster.

Eventually Dr. H. faxes the letter. I call insurance the day after and they promptly and crisply assure me they never got it. The caseworker gives me the fax number, and says that when she does get the letter she'll forward it to their medical review board. "But I think he's in a meeting this morning," she adds.

She then sort of asks me for the parental run-down of why this transfer is a medical necessity. Sure in my heart that the transfer is needed, yet unsure of my adjectives, I tell her how BPD is a new condition that may need one of many, varied treatments. It's not like we're asking for a transfer to Bubba's House of Lungs and Lubes, I think.

The caseworker doesn't foresee a problem. But they may not pay for the ambulance.

Over the next few days, I get ensnared in waiting for calls, waiting for people to make calls to other people, then dialing the damned phone myself to see if people are making the calls. It becomes a cloverleaf ramp with no exits, and in between dialing and rubbing my mashed phone ear, I plan what will happen depending on approval or disapproval. One means appeal, delay, working with those we wanted to ditch, and tight chests for Mom and Dad. The other means waiting for a bed, discharge forms on one letterhead and admittance forms on another, and tight chests for Mom and Dad.

Many of the afternoons come to resemble each other. During one afternoon, it becomes three hours since I was last told

I'd have a callback—from whom I can't recall—and I'm trying to gauge the best moment to call the insurance company.

My insurer needs a name of an admitting, in-network doctor in the *Enterprise* PICU that is in the network. I call Jill, and she wants me to run this past her stepfather. I say no. He's a renowned corporate lawyer, and I think of him as the last reserve if it appears storming Fort Insurance will fail. Besides, nothing is clear yet. I tell Jill to take a nap and I call our current PICU. They say we're all set. Uh-huh. I seem to straighten all this out by four o'clock. Everybody says they're happy.

Then Dr. H. tells me that the *Enterprise* PICU at the second hospital is overflowing, and they're sending patients to my *current* hospital! Maybe the transfer will happen Friday.

On Thursday, promise evaporates when the insurance company needs a call from either the discharging or the admitting doctor, confirming that Alex has in fact transferred and didn't stroll to the second hospital on his own. "I need to hear from, you know, a medical doctor. Just somebody besides you," my caseworker says. I phone one doctor, fax another. Yet ninety minutes later I'm still not sure I've uncorked any money. I try my caseworker, to see if she's heard from either doctor. "You just keep *calling*!" she says.

An hour later, Dr. K. phones me back and says this is the first he's heard that we want him to be Alex's doctor. But he agrees; I say we're delighted. He might be delighted that we're delighted, but he still needs documents and history on Alex before his decision can be final. My heads starts to pound, and I try to make clear who must talk to whom before I can succeed in having my son budged.

The calls peter out, as does the day.

On Friday Jill takes over, sending documents to the admitting doctor after first calling to make sure someone is there to catch them as they flutter from the fax machine. Later Jill tells me that the admitting doctor is "working on it." By 3:30 p.m., Jill has heard back from the admitting doctor and I've talked to the discharging doctor. They've talked to each other and are shooting for Sunday or Monday. Jill wants to call the insurance company. I think that's a bad idea—but if we don't, and soon, we may get jammed into paying out of pocket (out of bank, more like) for a few nights in a hospital.

Jill adds that she won't come in today. "Tell Alex Mommy isn't feeling well," Jill says. "Tell Alex that Mommy loves him and misses him and thinks of him all the time."

We hang up. I call her back in a minute and tell her I'm sorry I made her feel guilty about not coming in. She says her stepdad says transfer Alex: The insurance company gave us tasks, we performed them, and that's that. Dr. H. tells me they'll spring for the ambulance. "We usually do it as a courtesy," she says.

Saturday afternoon at our soon-to-be-former hospital feels like a last date. Dr. T. approaches us and starts talking about their plans for Alex—diet, vent settings, IVs—but the list comes out in a monotone, like upcoming holidays you know you won't be spending with your current love. Jill and I announce that we will try to transfer Alex tomorrow. "They'll call us if they have a bed," Dr. H. says.

"They told us you have to call them," Jill says. "I'm making the request you call."

Next morning, Super Bowl Sunday, my eyes come open to see Jill's thumb, which is pointing straight up. She clutches the phone to her head; she's smiling. A bed has opened at the *Enterprise*. I'm halfway through my coffee when the admitting hospital calls us for insurance information. It all begins to sound real.

"I think it's going to be a long day," Jill says. We slice salami, wrap it in plastic and stuff it in my bag. On the way Jill buys two bacon and egg sandwiches, and also for me an apple-crumb donut.

We get to the hospital and a resident is trying to contact the *Enterprise*. Jill predicts something will happen by two p.m. At five to noon we both call the *Enterprise*. "I'm sick of making all these calls alone," Jill says to me. She nonetheless does all the talking.

We have eaten the sandwiches by 1:30. I then have a few forkfuls of hospital chili, and Jill eats the cornbread. There's an apple turnover for me to top off the donut. The Super Bowl pre-game starts, and there's a good Yahoo! commercial about a Russian peasant whose monkey keeps throwing stuff in his girlfriend's soup. At three p.m., Jill and I step out, hoping that a hospital transfer is like a watched pot.

But I believe the window is closing. We come back. Alex thrashes and we ask for a sedative. Half an hour later, Alex's nurse is on the phone with somebody, and another nurse comes up to Alex's bedside and walks off with his book. I hear a respiratory therapist say something to our nurse about "five." A transport harness sits nearby, aluminum braces swaying like a swing set in the breeze. At a quarter to four, Alex's nurse rounds the front desk and bears down on us.

"We're rolling!" she says.

Jill scrapes up Rainbow and the Beanie Babies and the tape player while I break down the bouncy chair, and we both pull down the inspirational headlines and photos that we've taped up since Christmas ("Alexander Says He'll Take Step Forward in 2000"). I phone Jill's stepdad, who is having a Super Bowl party, and say we'll be there by the second half.

The ambulance crew wheels in a stretcher that is about six times longer than Alex. Jill chats with them while I stand out of the way by the $O_2$ tanks, my earmuffs on. "So four can sit in the back," someone asks. The nurse says no, she'd rather have room to move around. Jill will sit in front. No, I tell her, she'll in fact come with me in the goddamned taxi, her and the four shopping bags that are stuffed to splitting.

We take a cab, pay the $12 fare and then sit for a minute on a bench in the middle of Upper Broadway. Jill scans the streets for coffee shops while we talk about Alex's strengths and catch our breath. I have no idea what time it is.

Then we go inside and find Alex's new room and new nurse. The nurse shows us in and we start emptying the bags and put-

ting the stuff into exotic new cubbyholes. Alex has some apartment here: furnished, hardwood floors, sunny view, newly reno-
vated, cable-ready w/VCR, semi-private entrance, 24-hr. security. The room is called "Halley," and it has stars and planets and
a silver-gray space shuttle painted on the dark-blue wall. One of
the cushioned chairs folds out into a bed. I note that the room is
bigger than my first two New York apartments combined.

They wheel him in at about 5:30. He slept the whole way.
They hoist him into a new bed and begin plugging him in. The
new respiratory therapist is a tall man who looks happy.
"Daddy," he says, leaning over Alex, "tell him to stop."

Is he doing something wrong?

"Nah. He's being normal. He's moving his head and I don't
want him to move his head . . ." Alex's new nurse jiggles his
bed. He loves that.

We head to Jill's parents' at about six o'clock, after Alex
has fallen asleep again. Will insurance approve? I ask myself as
the Broncos beat the Falcons. Alex has a phone in his room,
and we call the strange new number; the nurse says he smiled a
few times in his new home. Later, the night nurse asks what he
likes. "Touch his head. Sing to him," Jill advises. "Tell him about
your boyfriend problems." We left him sleeping amid new colors and new curtains. The sun was painting the tops of new
buildings outside. Actually, aside from those of the hospital,
most of those buildings are abandoned and others drug-invested.
But they look new to me, and his room looks new to me.

A few days go by, and nothing bad happens in Halley. Jill
and I feel pretty good. Maybe moments are ahead when the
lights will go up bright and Alex will vanish inside yet another
cluster of doctors. But now, for the first time since July, I actually find it hard to stay depressed. For that reason, I stamp this
move "Approved."

# FEBRUARY TO MAY, 1999

I DIDN'T SEE ALEX for two days—worked late—but on the third day Jill phones to say that he's smiling a lot in his new home, and to confirm that his favorite thing in the world is a foot-long version of the purple Teletubby Tinky Winky. Over the phone I hear Jill making it talk to him: "Eh-oh, Awecks! Eh-oh!" She has the high tones down pat; I can't do it as well. "Eh-oh, Awecks! Eh-oh! Again! Again!" In the background I hear him gurgle.

I still can't get over that he makes noise. Jill asks if I want to talk to him. There's a moment of silence before I hear a sound like the sound of other people's babies: "Glug-*gaa*." I picture how his face splits when he smiles, the corners of the lips dimpling. When he gets really excited and smiles until he can't smile any wider; he just hisses. Jill says he's also kicking his legs.

The only bump: this was another day of "CPAP belly," where the machine that helps him breathe pumps so much air into him that his stomach distends. The doctors are on it. One of the first things they do is give him a mix of helium and oxygen, "heliox," which they say is easier for Alex to breathe in his current state. They're also aggressively turning down the vent settings, getting him to breathe more and more on his own.

"Glug-gaa."

"Who's Daddy's big guy?"

"Gaa."

Monday and Tuesday sort of meld into one day. At a quarter to six on Tuesday I'm still in the office, working late as the sun surrenders in orange over New Jersey. The office is silent. I'm going home soon. Since last June, one talking hospital robe after another has told me to take care of myself. So I got myself home early on Monday. Then on Tuesday a meeting blossoms at five o'clock, and I decide to take the unprecedented step of not seeing Alex for two days in a row.

I work on other things. I phone my caseworker at my insurance company and hear her say that my policy pays for almost all hospitalization for my family. Sometimes I've found it hard to concentrate on this job, but this insurance news propels me into the office of Howard, my boss, and makes me fling ideas at him. "Earn it," something whispers in my head as I talk, "earn it earn it earn it."

After work I don't immediately board the Queens-bound bus, but linger in Macys picking out baby onesies: blue checkered, blue with a puppy, soft brown and amber with a kitten. What will the nurses think is cute? The onesies I pick are in sizes for age six months and a weight of fourteen pounds. Alex weighs eleven pounds. "Keep the receipt," Jill had warned, concerned not so much about Alex's weight as Daddy's taste.

On Tuesday, Jill picks up recent pictures from the one-hour shop. In one photo, she is talking while Alex stares at her as if thinking, "That's so cute. She's making grown-up sounds." That was a week ago. Jill reports he's drooling a lot and may be cutting a first tooth. "And oh," Jill reported, "hands to the mouth big time." He didn't do that on Sunday. That I can remember.

Later on Tuesday night, the amber kitten onesie passes inspection, and the blue checkered earns a nod. The onesie with the blue puppy, however, prompts Jill to ask, "Did you keep the receipt?"

Then it is Wednesday. No meetings or deadlines this afternoon. I promise to bring in some of the pictures for my coworker Mike, whose wife is a speech pathologist who's given me a lot of advice. Mike and his wife have a nine-year-old son, and for Mike the boy's babyhood seems like yesterday. "They change every day," Mike has said. "You come home at the end of the day and you can't believe it."

I stick my head into Howard's office at 4:30. "If it's okay, I'd like to duck out a couple minutes early," I say, "and head to the hospital." Howard has a grown son who is in the navy, near Iraq.

"Have fun," Howard says. "Tell Alex I said hello."

On the subway to the hospital, I feel that first-date tingle, when every minute brings you closer to feeling something that you feel nowhere else and with no one else. At the desk of the hospital lobby I announce myself to the guard: "I'm here to see my son Alex." A crowd funnels into the one elevator and the doors rattle closed, and the thing stops at every floor on the rise to eleven, his floor.

In his room a woman on the cleaning crew is sweeping; she smiles at me. Daddy's here, she thinks. It's beginning to dawn on me what women think of a guy who spends eight months tying on a hospital gown and leaning over a metal crib to say, "Who's Daddy's big guy?"

There's the crib—no doctors, thank God—and the lights are off. Someone has tipped Tinky Winky onto his side, and the doll's legs hold up the heavy plastic air tubes behind my son's head. Alex is asleep, dressed in gray with little white animals, his legs making a fine diamond that meets at the toes of his blue Old Navy socks. Does Alex know who's here? The man who would be Dad, the endlessly older man to be worshipped until about the year 2010? A hero who will gradually degenerate into an unreasonable pain-in-the-ass who lords over access to the Internet and, later, the car keys? I don't know. I know that I'm here, Alex is here, and there's one thing to say. "Eh-oh, Awecks. Eh-ho!"

Dr. K. tells me that some BPD babies are prone to fever. No one told me that before. They hit us with more new details about BPD. The nurses and I quiz each other about the periodic table of elements. Jill names all the metals. We ask about the level of $CO_2$ Alex might be retaining because his lungs are weak. "I don't think he's retaining much," the doctor says, "because he's satting well." Then an alarm goes off. We ask if the doctor knows what it means.

"Yes," he says. "It means I have to call the nurse."

The nurses like watching Alex. When he's resting and a doctor comes in, these nurses say things to the doctors like, "Wake him up and I'll kill you." At one point Alex turns his head back and forth, shaking the tube in his mouth; his face goes strawberry and he coughs. The nurse isn't alarmed. "You're very talented to be able to do that," the nurse tells him. Another nurse says that when she's getting to know a baby, she tries to listen to parents. This staff has had five days to say something abusive to us, and has failed.

They say they'll do nothing and they're sorry they want to go so slow. But they work Alex toward extubation like an arrow moving across a map on the History Channel. His vent settings—the number of breaths the machine takes for Alex—drop to 20, 16, 14, 12. Jill notes that these guys aren't afraid to turn a vent knob to the right. "We don't like to intubate," everyone says in the same way they'd say, "We don't like to walk into oncoming traffic."

"It's like making a recipe," says one nurse, an eighteen-year NICU veteran who explains the myriad treatments for preemies. "We try to leave them alone and let them do it on their own." She adds that she's seen BPD babies much worse than Alex do fine. She says her son in high school has a friend on the soccer team who was a preemie. "Six-foot-two, 190 pounds," she says. We tell her that when Alex was intubated, doctors elsewhere worried about his carbon-dioxide retention. "You try breathing through a straw," she tells us. "Maybe you could do it for fifteen minutes. But after a day or two, your $CO_2$ would go up too."

Jill and I go home each night feeling lighter than we have in months. Once on the subway, Jill can't find her keys. I remind her that she took them out to rattle at Alex. "You wouldn't have put them in your coat pocket after that," I say. "You weren't wearing your coat in Alex's room. Maybe your purse?"

She finds bread and cookies, but no keys.

"Jeans, maybe?" I say.

She finds the keys. "Oh, you just know everything, don't you?" she says.

We sit in silence for a few stops. I hope that back in the hospital they have his music on.

Though the new hospital is about two miles north of our first hospital, the commute from my job is quicker: twenty-five minutes, and five stops on the A train (which, coincidentally, is my brother's nickname for Alex). I get to the hospital early and hold Alex on one of the first nights when he seems to be coming back. His head's on my forearm, brown eyes calm, minuscule nails scraping my wrist. I run my finger down his neck and ignite the first smile in days.

But at 7:30 p.m. I have to head home. I put him back in the crib and straighten the tubes and wires. But there's a crease between his eyes. He kicks off the monitors. Not happy, I tell the nurse. "He's wondering why he can't go home, too," I say.

"'Where's the fair in that, Dad?'" the nurse says. I look at the crease. Alex looks back at me.

"Good question," I say.

A few days later, Alex is moved to a smaller space in the hospital. The room has three beds; there is another baby and a little boy whose legs and arms are crimped with what I think is cerebral palsy. Alex is last in line. The space between his crib and the wall is twice the width of a rocking chair. The boy with the crimped legs is on Alex's other side. "His m-o-m hasn't called today," we overhear that boy's nurse say. She holds him as his head lolls. He watches "Bingo" and "Barney" on video and kicks at the pads lining the rails. He has nice hair. I hear he has a good time with the Pets on Wheels puppies, and I hope Alex has that kind of fun some day. Later I see the boy laughing and following the nurse with his eyes. I hear that he's almost six.

The nurses rig a baby seat for Alex and cushion it with towels and sheets. We sit him up and prop the pacifier in with Rainbow and other Beanie Babies. He gives a pink smile, all gums, angles dimpling the corners of his mouth. My chest lifts as if filling with helium. Looking around the new digs, I think of what the neonatologist said in the other hospital. "You just have to trust your doctors," he said.

Trust is a hard thing to come by a few nights later, however, when just before we go to sleep, Jill looks at me and says, "I think Alex has brain damage."

Alex is beginning to reach and grab, accomplishments that usually begin with him raising his arm, studying the target, and swatting. Swatting is right on course, according to the handout that the physical therapist left. The handout is written from the baby's perspective: "When I miss, kiss and nibble the fingers of my hand and say encouraging things." I kiss his hand, nibble his fingers and say encouraging things.

Brain damage.

Tomorrow Alex has CAT scans of his head and chest. They believe he has dilated ventricles in his head. Once upon a time I didn't know how to spell "ventricle," and I'm still unsure what a CAT scan is. It's supposed to be a little like an MRI, which I had last year. They slid me into a tube for forty-five minutes. About an inch in front of my nose was the cream-colored plastic roof of the tube, where for some reason I expected to find graffiti. Occasionally the tube would bang and bang, something to do with the magnetic field pulling on my herniated disks. People told me it would be terrifying. But I had my ears plugged and almost fell asleep. Alex also has a urinary tract infection, his fourth. This is unusual, they admit. So Jill went online and found out that such infections may point to cerebral palsy. "But 'cerebral palsy' can mean a wide range of things," she stipulates, sitting in the living room chair for about the billionth time since Alex was born. The corners of her mouth turn down and her eyebrows crash together.

She is tired. So am I. Alex's skull seems like the perfect nest for trouble. Trouble holds out its hand. A son alive but not with us, a baby who's a patient, and whose parents need a pass to see him. This is what we are when we sit in the chairs in the living room and I look at Jill against the blank wall and she says, "Brain damage."

On the morning of the test we get to the hospital and head for the CAT scan area. There, in the waiting room, a bald boy tugs at his mother and shrieks in one unending syllable. We find a technician. "Look at my schedule," he says, tipping the clip-board so I can see a sheet of white paper covered with squares. Almost every square has writing in it. "Today for sure," he says. "I just can't tell you when right now."

We head upstairs to Alex's room. He's sleeping and we settle ourselves, sharing a cup of coffee. By late morning we've sat Alex up and changed him into the T-shirt on which Jill drew an elaborate chicken. Alex looks us over as Jill squeaks a yellow plastic duck. She points out that the scan will tell us nothing about Alex that wasn't there yesterday, that isn't there today, and that won't be there tomorrow.

"Somebody's pretty perky," Jill says, looking at Alex and squeaking the duck. "But is he going to wind up bald and shriek-ing at me in a waiting room?"

J., the six-year-old in the next crib who came to the hospital for three days and stayed for two months, went home on Mon-day. Today they wheel in a boy with dark hair, a nice smile and what look like zipper marks across his forehead. "Seven and a half hours of surgery," his mother tells us. As Jill and I wait, the room clicks and whizzes with the noises of bags being unpacked. Drawers slide open. I watch a mom from Jersey pause over her unpacked toothpaste and glance at the railings of Alex's crib. She sees the snapshots and yellowing, clipped headlines ("Alex-ander Says He'll Take Giant Step in 2000"). She sees piles of

Alex's Beanie Babies. I look at her looking at Alex and I know that she and her son will be home by the weekend.

The nurse and doctor cluster over the Indian girl brought in right after the boy with the nice smile. "You'll feel a pinch," the nurse warns her. "Now do you want to get your wheelchair?"

"Yeah," the girl says. She smiles, showing a gap the size of Letterman's in her teeth, and climbs into the wheelchair.

By one p.m. there's still no word. The nurse shrugs, and Jill says I shouldn't ask a nurse if I really want to know what's going on. An hour passes, and all at once they turn off the red numerals on Alex's oxygen monitor. Somebody tapes an oxygen tank to his bed. They tell us we will not hear about Alex's head today: the guy who takes the reading has to sit down with other guys and decide what to tell us. Can you understand our worry? we ask. They assure us they can. Jill, a doctor, and a respiratory therapist wheel Alex's crib to the elevator. There's no room for me in there so I head for the stairs, glimpsing him in the crib before the doors slide shut. His eyes roll around and occasionally lock, but they do not track anything.

The CAT scan room is chilly. The temperature has to do with operating the big plastic doughnut with the GE logo. They will slide Alex into the hole of the doughnut after placing the duck by his head and the pacifier in his mouth. They strap him in, and I ask if one of us can stay with him. "You can, Dad," the nurse says. "Mom has ovaries, but you make sperm every four days." I tell her I do my best.

"That's what I've heard," she replies.

The doughnut whirs like an extractor in a laundromat. I stand on the other side of the hole and watch the top of Alex's scalp inch toward me. He watches me upside down, his eyes going back and forth, either seeing or ignoring everything. He looks absolutely tough and self-reliant and yes, cute. His pacifier falls out, and he cranks up to cry. They have strapped me into a heavy lead vest—in case I want to make sperm sometime after the next four days—and I drop his pacifier, or "binkie," into the breast pocket. To reach in and reinsert it in his mouth now, they tell me, would ruin the test, and do Hiroshima-like things to my unshielded arm.

Back and forth, back and forth, back and forth go his eyes as he inches into the doughnut. "We're most worried about his tracking," I say to the nurse.

"Yeah," she says, "he doesn't track."

Later Jill and I stand outside the hospital, where like a bad bird hunter I'm trying to bring down a metaphor to comfort us. We all take in information, I say. In Alex's case, it's information on moving his body; in our case, it's information about the world around us. If we were out of the loop for a while, we'd be delayed, too. Jill looks at me, and absolutely nothing eases her eyebrows. I think tonight is a lesson we will often repeat—a lesson not in handling bad results, but in waiting for them.

The next day, we've still heard nothing about the tests. From work I call the office of the doctor who's supposed to tell us if Alex slid out of the big doughnut officially retarded. "The doctor hasn't forgotten you," his nurse says. "He had an emergency this morning and he hasn't forgotten." When will he get over there?

"This morning," his nurse says, apparently unaware that it is 11:30.

I call Jill, who is at Alex's bedside. "It's like an airport here," she says. Physical therapist. Doctors. Social worker trying to help run down Medicaid forms. "I gotta call you back, bye—" Jill says.

At 1:30 p.m., three new letters enter my life: PVL. I have no idea what they mean. "From online, I know it isn't good," Jill says. I chat with the doctor. Small area of damage, small patch of gray marshy matter. It won't change. It could be A or it could be B. A is normal, and could repair itself. B is not, in the strictest sense, normal, and I'd better find those Medicaid forms. This doctor leans toward B. As she talks on, I wish again that doctors would lay off phrases like "the ultimate outcome."

"We just don't know what will be," the doctor says, her voice lifting at the end of every sentence, turning statements into questions. Over the phone I hear Jill ask to see this young doctor's boss later in the day.

Near the end of the day, the boss doctor does call me. In the background, I can hear that Jill is still there. The boss doctor says he can see where his colleague thought it was B. "But I don't think it's that," he says. "I don't see evidence of that."

I think he expects me to say something, but I don't, so he continues: Three of the four ventricles (V-E-N-T-R-I-C-L-E-S) remain enlarged. But they're no bigger than they were, and there's no evidence of internal pressure on the brain common to hydrocephalus. There's nothing there that wasn't there yesterday, and won't be there tomorrow. They'll know more when they do an MRI, which they can't do until Alex's lungs can handle breathing on cannula and they can get the big vent tubes off his face. Is there any danger to Alex?

No, the boss doctor tells me. None.

Out my office window the sun kisses the top of the buildings with orange. Before I leave the office, Jill gets on the phone. She says the pulmonologists just walked in. "But I don't care what they have to say today," she says. She sounds tired and far away, as if she had just run a race.

Believing the worst will happen is her way of preparing. My way is cracking wise with nurses while they strap lead shields over my baby. I wish Jill and I prepared in the same way. But we don't. *I'll pick up champagne,* I think. "Sweetie, you've done well," I tell her. "Go home."

This afternoon, we had a conference. Almost everybody sat in a chair. I had a folder and a notebook. The subject was putting food in Alex's stomach. The doctors don't want to. We do. We think Alex does, too, though he's too young to ask.

Some of the doctors have said Alex needs a hole cut in his stomach and a tube to pump in food. They have said that for a long, long time to come, Alex won't be able to eat enough by mouth to take in the calories he needs to gain weight. "He just can't," Dr. S. has said. Gain he must, to build new lung tissue to replace the tissue scarred by the breathing tube. They have further said that Alex has reflux, basing this on the food coloring they squirted into his formula a few weeks ago and the spoonful of blue he retched up. If he refluxes food he could aspirate, they have said. Also, he has a feeding tube into his duodenum; about every forty-eight hours or so he elects to cough it out. If he coughs it out just right, they have warned, a lot of formula could flow into his lungs. They want to cut him open and twist his stomach until it serves to close the esophagus, which may not be closing properly. The procedure is called a Nissen. Dr. B. says he's never done a Nissen he's regretted.

So this afternoon we talked: doctors, nurses, therapists, Jill and I, pretty much all those important to the situation except Alex himself, all clustered around the microwave in the nurses' room. "I intend to speak bluntly, because I feel I can," I told the doctors. Jill and I have talked a lot about how much we like these doctors. They seem to care, and are proud of the work they've done on Alex's lungs. Most of the doctors nodded. One said they were sorry they were going so slowly with him.

"You don't know what slow is," I said. "You've worked wonders."

At this point one doctor who really thinks Alex needs a hole cut in his stomach began to speak. This doctor had not taken a chair, but perched on a desktop and swung her legs, her eyes scanning whatever was on the walls that was more engaging than what Jill and I had to say: nursing schedules, baby pictures, photocopied notices of upcoming employee-appreciation days. With her leg swinging swinging swinging in the corner of my eye, I tell the story of the counselor who arranged my brother's kidney transplant years ago. This counselor told me that kidney transplants from live donors were rare phenomena in medicine, in that one body was "mutilated" to make another healthy. Dr. Leg Swinger tears herself away from the flyer of an upcoming blood drive to say, "Well I should hope that counselor is no longer working with patients! Look at the attitude he left you with!"

As I look at Dr. Leg Swinger not looking at me, I try to remember all the good stuff that can come from talk. Alex came out of having a talk, at least initially. Three months ago, after much talk, we transferred him to this hospital. If we always listened to what doctors said, we never would have met these doctors. That would have been too bad, because here they've transformed him from a boy with a tube down his throat on Super Bowl Sunday to a boy with a pink smile on the first day of spring.

But testing for reflux can be just as dangerous for Alex as eating with reflux. And if we examine Alex's esophagus with any kind of tiny tube and camera, it still means anesthesia, and that means intubation, Dr. Leg Swinger warns. It doesn't seem to matter that Alex is pushing a year old and hasn't eaten a drop of food by mouth since a week before Christmas. Back then, Jill and I used to talk a lot about how Alex would wail until we stuck the bottle in his lips, how I'd twirl that bottle between his lips and rub that nipple against the roof of his mouth, and how he'd suck and I'd watch the bubbles come up in the bottle. How it was good to watch him eat.

Something screams to me to veto surgery without more tests. One of the briefest talks Jill and I have had was about following our instincts. This talk was about a month ago, when we were looking at him squirming in the crib, and Jill announced, "I'm going to pick him up!" And she did. Since then his eyes wobble less and his limbs are starting to move with more purpose.

Today, the conference ends. One of the doctors stays behind to talk to Jill, and with Alex I go into our new game of Baby Helicopter, where I take him under the arms and go *thip thip thip thip* with my tongue until he smiles. Then I lower him until his feet touch the tops of my legs. I hoist him over my face and say, *"Wheee!"* Then I lie as flat as I can in the old hospital rocker and put him on my chest. His legs began to kick like one of those foot-long wind-up infantrymen, and he makes determined *irks*.

"You should see his face," Jill says. "He looks like he's thinking, 'I'm doing this. This is guy time, and I'm *doing* this!'"

He is. I lie him back in the crib and put my face next to his. We chat. "Al-ex-an-der," I say to him, "Al-ex-an-der." His fingers tug his lower lip. Drool slides down his cheek. *"Ai-ahh,"* he says. *"Eh-ah-aa."*

Jill and I have developed a relationship with doctors, a relationship where the power rests in one hand and the decision in another. It's a doomed imbalance, particularly when entered into by two parents who, once upon a time, knew as much about premature babies and neonatology as an infant knows about being a grown-up.

This second relationship with doctors is better than our first. That relationship we entered blind a year ago, as the buds came out and the birds twittered like doctors' promises. By last Halloween, the promises had shriveled to mere comments from the medical staff, such as "You've been crying for five months!"

We have sought a fresh start and second opinions. We found our current hospital: clean, high-tech, nice carpet, a staff that asked questions and bedside furniture that accommodated our fatigue. The new pulmonologist said wise things like, "It's not a matter of a good hand. It's a matter of a bad hand played well." Dr. S. gave him baby steps toward breathing, and then Dr. B. came in and plowed Alex onto cannula. Jill cried again over the question of whether to give Alex surgery for a feeding tube; one day, she had to come to the hospital wearing sunglasses to hide her swollen red eyes. She ran into Dr. K.

"How are you?" she recalls him asking. She told him she'd been better.

"Don't feel bad about having a hard time making this decision," he said.

When Alex's IV popped out, he had just two days to go on intravenous antibiotics. We didn't want an IV. Who would? I had moved toward the doctor to ask if they could please just give Alex a shot of antibiotics and not go fishing for a fresh vein. I was about to open my mouth when the doctor turned to me and said, "We're not going to do another IV. We'll just give him a shot tonight and tomorrow night."

When Alex couldn't keep his blood-oxygen level up while on cannula, Dr. S. emphasized that trying was not a failure. Another doctor had to help stick Alex three times for a blood sample and kept saying, "We're sorry, we're sorry." Another doctor once got on the phone with Jill and said, "I was told that if I didn't speak with you tonight, I'd hear about it tomorrow morning!" Silly phone talk.

The bloom began to fade, however, when the docs watched Alex spit up and decided he had reflux. For that, they insisted, he must have surgery. Yet, because his lungs remain fragile, they could not test for reflux. So trust them.

Which we were prepared to do, except they stopped meeting our eyes. They were in a hurry when we were around. They came in at odd hours. We understood a dwindling amount of what they were saying and how they acted. They couldn't allow a barium swallow or a PH probe, which would have tested how well he swallows and how well his stomach could hold food, but when we held out they finally did agree to the probe, as if giving in and going to our cousin's wedding. But they tested in a half-hearted way, as if going to the reception too but just sitting in the corner getting quietly drunk. When the probe report came back with the results they expected, they seemed to screech *Told ya!*

Jill and I believe Alex simply doesn't fit the profile for a fundoplication and G tube. These are dramatic procedures, requiring a sort of twisting of the stomach and surgical closing of the esophagus, among other things. We have planted our heels. "I hope to God you're right," Dr. B. says, warning of kids who spent years "trashing" their lungs microscopically, time bombs whose childhoods later petered out in intensive care. The respect has evaporated from their questions. "What exactly is it that you and your wife are objecting to?" Dr. Q. asks. "That you would risk possibly putting him back on the vent, back in intensive care? Possibly something fatal?" Their pressure came in waves, no two the same: the simple shock and emotion of two departments recommending surgery without a test; then financial thumbscrews ("Sooner or later your insurance company is going to start giving you a hard time because nothing is being done for Alex . . .").

I'm still willing to talk it out. "I have no objection to any procedure that Alex needs," I tell Dr. Q. "But I have to see that it's necessary. That's common sense." While they acted as if our motives were incomprehensible, Jill decided she could start eating all the ice cream she wanted.

Next week the doctors will present their final recommendations about Alex and surgery. Accept them, or not? We don't know how we'll play that hand. Most parents probably think we're the ones who should be giving *them* ultimatums! I know. I also know that knowing what is best is a tricky thing. I guess for now, we'll all try to work it out.

## MAY AND JUNE, 1999

THE NIGHT AFTER ALEX sees his first pinball machine, I phone my brother, Lee. "Tell Alex his uncle is very, very good at that game," my brother says.

Lee and I used to slaughter pinball machines. All those Christmas mornings when we'd unwrap the roll of quarters from Aunt Yvonne and climb into his truck to find an open bowling alley. In we'd go to the dark game rooms, past the bums on the video games to the back walls where the cool people were and the billion bulbs flickered with a midway's promise. My brother and I had the flippers and the English, and we thought nothing meant life was good like a replay's single hard *cluck*.

Pinball is out of my life now. Recently my in-laws told me they'd played a terrific pinball machine in the Pittsburgh airport. They said it was called "The Addams Family." "Oh yeah!" I said. "Where the hand comes out and steals the ball!" Jill gave her stepfather an "Isn't-he-something" smile.

Nobody's interested in pinball anymore, except maybe Alex, who insists we get a closer look at the pinball machine in the hospital game room. I had wheeled him first to the playroom, but the music was loud in there, and he didn't even glance at the Barbie keyboard or the tropical fish. After a few minutes he began to get that expression of drooling daze that he and his parents reserve for listening to doctors. So I spun the carriage and headed into the hallway, past the open door of the playroom. He did turn his head first, his eyes caught I think by the playroom shades, which were dark green like the leaves in the hospital garden. On nice days lately we take him out there and park him under a tree so he can gaze at the bright canopy and listen to Dad point out the beauty of nature. "Leaves, Alex, those are leaves."

The name of the game in the hospital is "Ice Fury." I wheel Alex around until he has a clear view of the cartoons of hockey players and the green numerals of the scoreboard. I lock the carriage wheels and watch him flick his eyes over the blinking lights. "Look, Alex, look," I say, pointing at more of the world's beauty. "Thirteen credits!"

Credits are games, and this machine—placed here to cheer up sick kids and repressed fathers—doesn't take quarters. To get credits, you just punch a red button on the front. I punch. I play, and make the numerals of the score change while Alex follows the dings of the bumpers. He moves his head—no girlie Barbie keyboard here—and starts to whap his big soft block toy with his right arm. In the last month that's become a sign that he likes what's going on.

"Light the extra ball, Alex!"

Jill and Grandma discover us on my third ball. Jill and I take Alex back to the playroom. Grandma is still playing when we leave her.

I'm all in favor of my baby hanging around arcades, but he doesn't get much of a chance. Yesterday he spat up and some go-getter resident got the bright idea, which I've been pitching for a week, to have the spit-up analyzed in lieu of putting a tube and food in his stomach. So we call a pediatrician in the hope that someone can play air traffic controller for Alex's bewildering radar screen. I ask the nurse for recommendations, and get three. I call. A doctor calls back and says he or his partner will be by on Sunday. Jill and I come in early on Sunday and sure enough, the partner is there. She asks a few questions about Alex, then says one problem with Alex's situation is the rotation system of hospital-based doctors. Just when you get somebody you like, they go off duty.

"How much credence would hospital doctors in a conference be likely to give a pediatrician in a conference, as opposed
to how much they'd give parents?"

"Probably more than they'd give parents," she admits. She
seems good with kids, too: a toddler visiting his preemie brother
in another bed comes over with the remote and gestures to the
TV, which is right behind us. He says something I can't understand. The doctor levels her glasses on him. "No, not right now,"
she says, "no TV right now. Where's your brother? Where's
your brother?"

She tells me she'll talk to her boss about taking our case.

I call her boss on Tuesday. No callback. I call her on Wednesday. She gets back to me within a couple of hours. First of all,
let her explain that her voicemail-less, cell phone-less boss hasn't
returned to the office where my message was left. Second, her
boss no longer does GI work and cannot take Alex's case in
that capacity. Third, they were talking it over and they feel that
as pediatricians, interfering with Alex's current treatment would
be "resented" by the hospital doctors. They'd be happy to follow up with Alex after he's released, though.

Sometimes you have to ask doctors to speak in English; this
isn't one of those times. She's saying, or her boss has dumped it
upon her to say, that Alex is not worth ruffling the feathers of
the hospital in which this pediatric practice makes most of its
money. They'll be happy, however, to cash our checks months
from now, when the only ones resentful of Alex's medical situation will probably be Alex and his parents.

Such conversations make me think more and more about
those times when I knew where I stood by looking at the score
in the backglass. When "Game Over" just meant dig for another quarter, or hit up my brother.

I tell him what the doctors say. "Oh yeah, I'd have to have
numbers. They'd have to prove to me surgery was necessary,"
my brother says. He moans when he hears about our reflux
dilemma. Last fall, when I told him about Alex's lung crash, he

moaned. My brother is backwoods stock from Maine; he does not moan with abandon. He also doesn't like babies. But he likes Alex, though they've never met. "Jeez he's a happy little guy!" my brother says, about photos.

He is, and I hope some day he has a quarter to hold. And I hope he gets to drop it into some machine in some place that's dark with excitement and promise, and where the games are not given away.

It's red-poppy weekend: Memorial Day. On Saturday we drive in: streets are deserted; parking spaces abound. We stop at Jill's sister's apartment to feed her cats—she's out of town—and then we duck over to Riverside Drive. Also deserted. We get to the hospital in fifteen minutes. Between Labor Day and Memorial Day that drive would take about an hour. Along the way the WCBS disc jockey says he doesn't know if we're headed for the beach or the mountains or the backyard barbecue, but he hopes we'll take him along.

Alex's hospital room, which holds four patients, is empty except for him. "We're not expecting anybody until Tuesday," the nurse says. Alex naps. Jill naps. We're both down, and I don't even want to wheel him outside in the carriage to the little park in back of the hospital. But we do. We also follow the suggestion of Jill's mother and spread a blanket on the ground and give Alex his first feel of the earth. He likes it. He lies on his side and we give him his big soft block with the bell, and he brings it to his mouth.

Jill lies down and faces him and that's the way I leave them as I go in to the vending machines for chips and a bottle of water. When I come back they're still there. I sit down, and the grass tickles my leg. There are three other people out there, hospital employees in scrubs, sunning themselves on break and probably thinking of the bonus days off they'll earn by working today.

It's about ninety degrees, but we're in the shade. I look around. "We should have a picnic out here tomorrow," I say to Jill.

"Yes!" she says. We plan to pick up a barbecued chicken, bread and some grapes that night after we get home. "We still have the picnic basket, right?" she asks.

We wheel Alex back to his room and give him a bath in the sink. We know that between the bath and the fresh air he will pass out for the night. By 4:30 he's making his new helpless baby chimp noise; we tuck him in with his pacifier. He presses it into his face by hugging the light-blue stuffed elephant my boss Howard gave him. In a minute or two the pacifier drops out of his lips, and his eyes are softly, surely closed. We whisper good night and head home.

Back in our neighborhood, we buy a roasted chicken, bread and grapes. They say tomorrow will be warm, too.

At 10:30 on Sunday morning, at the hospital, I set out to find a newspaper; when I do, of course, it's holiday-thin. I come back to learn from Jill that Alex coughed out his feeding tube. Then we have to wait for the holiday-thin x-ray staff to get here to take the picture. Then we can resume feeding him with the tube. Then we can maybe take him outside. Jill and I go to the vending area—I press the button for iced tea and two cans come down!—and we decide to leave the chicken in the hospital fridge. Maybe we'll do a picnic tomorrow.

Monday dawns murky. We decide to cab it in because it's going to be ninety degrees again, and by five p.m. traffic from the three-day weekend will be snarled. Jill and I hail a cab on Queens Boulevard. The driver doesn't have the air conditioning on this morning; the back windows are down. We leave them down. By the time we get to the Queensboro Bridge, Jill is worried about her hair.

"You look fine," I say. "You look like you've been on a boat."

Today they have decided to test the acid in Alex's stomach. This means a probe down his nose and another taped to his belly, the wires leading to a monitor that's a little smaller than a Gameboy. It's in a black sling case and is completely portable, they assure us. They just get it hooked up, though, when the nurse spies Jill giving Alex a few drops of water with a bottle.

Alex's nurses are excellent; they let you know how things stand. How they stand on this hot day, however, is that the pulmonologists overseeing Alex do not want him fed by mouth. "Jackie," says Jill, "I am his mother and if I want to feed him a few drops of water, I can."

Jackie stands her ground behind the stainless steel railing of a nearby empty bed. "Jill, I'm just telling you what they said and what they want. I'm just in the middle here," she says.

Alex's medical care is stuck in a holiday loop; we've wanted tests for a while and they've finally begun to do them—but in a half-hearted way, determined that, whatever the results, they're going to recommend surgery. We've been checking around, and between the parents on the Internet and the pediatricians in Jill's family we're not sold on Alex needing stomach surgery.

Memorial Day afternoon passes: We set him in the sink for a bath, and he doesn't seem to hate it. He naps, then about five he wakes up and Jill and I try to calm him. We can't. Jackie comes over and pats him and talks to him. Somehow I don't feel she likes us much anymore, but as long as she likes Alex that's enough. Jackie taught Alex to dance. Jill and I go home.

The next day is Tuesday. I go to work and realize that I never did see a red poppy. I have no idea what I'll see come the Fourth of July.

On the night before they are to install the J-tube, our take-out Chinese is terrible. I tried this hole-in-the-wall a couple of weeks ago and got a stupendous egg roll. But tonight, when I talk Jill into trying the place, the mu shu comes out tasting like somebody fried it in Karo syrup. In our living room, I watch Jill spit a mouthful back onto her plate.

"The one night we want a good meal," I tell her.

The J-tube is a thin feeding line leading into the jejunum in the small intestine. As Alex now weighs just seventeen pounds, his is a particularly small intestine. Into his body, just above the navel, they will put a little plastic tunnel for the tube, with a little manhole cover for when we want to give him a bath. He will have this for months. Last of the procedures before he comes home, they say.

Jill and I eat about half the dinner. It's a heavy bag of leftovers I lug to the garbage chute. I mean to go to bed early. But the Knicks surge in the third quarter against the Spurs, *Zulu* is on the History Channel, and pretty soon it's 11:30. That's when Jill comes out from her latest three hours on eBay and announces, "You're in a dogfight for Dogfight!" Dogfight is a Milton Bradley board game from my childhood. I'm bidding for a supposedly complete set. We're up to $76 so far.

Alex is scheduled for surgery at one p.m. on June 25, eleven days after his first birthday. We had a nice little party on his birthday. We had him dressed in red, white and blue, since it was Flag Day. He put his fist in the chocolate cake and pried the bows off the presents. We had strung stars-and-stripes banners and American flags around the bars of his hospital crib.

I stay up late monitoring eBay, and then wake up early. I'm bleary, and nothing much happens over the morning coffee on this last Friday in June. We call the hospital. Surgery will be at one o'clock, but it could be later, could be earlier. OR timeslots don't mean much, the doctors tell us. Despite this, I feel that the surgery is a sound idea, that we're at least on a dim, twisty road, and off the black dead-end of this past year. Maggie, the nurse, says over the phone that she hasn't received the OR schedule yet. "We get that surgery sheet every day," she marvels. "Wouldn't you know, today we wouldn't!" Jill and I like Maggie, who gave Alex a Fisher-Price gym for his birthday. Maggie has two boys. Once, when one of them missed the bus and asked her to drive him, she refused and walked with him all the way instead. Jill wants to be a mother like Maggie.

"You'll never be alone," we tell Alex when we get to the hospital. "Mommy and Daddy will be there when you go to sleep, and when you wake up." I think of the cats I've talked to before their surgeries. I remember their deep green eyes and blinks of comprehension. Alex, who has brown eyes, is busy having a Calvin-and-Hobbes-kind of fantasy bout with his red Beanie Baby. To enable his crib to fit in the elevator, I strip off the Mylar balloons: the happy face; the green heart; Tickle Me Elmo; the deeply-dimpled "Happy Birthday!" I peel the medical tape off the bars; I wrap up the flags. We also make sure we have a pacifier.

"Okay, they want Alex to get ready," says Maggie.

The elevator's full by the time they finagle Alex's crib inside, and I take the stairs down to the fourth floor, where the doctors come up to us. We've talked to them before, but they look like different people in scrubs and hair caps. It's white paper jump suits, light blue caps and footies for me and Jill, an orange blood-pressure band and green IV board for Alex. We help wheel him to the OR, down the tan tiled hallway that for a lot of people must look like the end of the road. We pass a room called "Separation." Jill asks the anesthesiologist if that's where they take the Siamese twins apart. The doctor says she has a dirty mind. In the OR we spot a chart of the heart on the wall. "You wouldn't think they'd need that," Jill says.

Somebody slips the binkie into a "Biohazard" bag. Alex lies face-up on the table and is going bananas. The light is right in his eyes; his cries are muffled under the anesthesia mask. Jill squeezes my hand. They ask us to leave.

By mid-afternoon we're back in Alex's room, sitting in the rocker in the space where his crib should be. We have ice-cream sodas and split a bowl of cherries with the mother of another Alex in the ward, talking about cats and about all her male ancestors named Alexander. I re-read about Midway in Keegan's *The Price of Admiralty*. We watch *Fantasia*. The mother of the other Alex wants to watch, too, but her doctor keeps coming in and interrupting. And so we spend three hours, two parents eating cherries and trying to not look at the clock. At 3:30 the intern whizzes by, and the happy face balloon bows where I tethered it. I make myself a sandwich.

"Are you eating peanut butter?" Jill asks. I say yes. "I just didn't expect that," she says.

At 4:30 we're still waiting. Maggie calls down. "The recovery nurse said he just came through the door," she reports. We go down to Recovery. We find Ellen, a nurse who knows Alex. I walk in after Jill and find her hugging Ellen. Alex has a mask over his tiny nose and mouth, a green elastic strap holding it snug and a fat plastic air tube making him look like a toy fighter pilot. He's draped with a blanket and a mile of cables and tubes. "Anesthesia loves tubes," Ellen says.

He opens his eyes. "Bunny rabbit," Jill says softly. Above his head, on the crib headboard, is still taped the yellowing headline: "Alexander Says He Will Take Step For 2000." Through the curtain that separates us from the next recovery-room bay, I hear a girl crying.

I call Howard. He says he was thinking about Alex all day, and that Jill and I should celebrate. I say a cheeseburger at the coffee shop on Queens Boulevard.

Jill gets to hold Alex in her lap, where he passes out with no ceremony. He keeps slipping lower and lower on her lap, but never wakes up even when we all learn he's going back to his old floor and not to Intensive Care. I ask the doctor how Alex did getting off the vent right after the operation. "Better than we expected," the doctor admits.

For reasons I'll never discover, we need an x ray before Alex can go back, well, home. By seven or so, we get back to Alex's floor, with Maggie. I ask about morphine. "For you?" Maggie says. "You look tired," adds Elizabeth, the night nurse who's just coming on.

After a while it all just feels like a thousand years. Jill and I go home. We have Chinese food; she picks the restaurant. Good mu shu, good broccoli in garlic sauce. I am tired. I walk the streets knowing that I look like that painting of the Marine on

Guadalcanal, gray under my eyes, the lids rimmed in red. I think that painting is called "The Thousand Yard Stare." I don't know if that Marine is still alive, but I promise to tell you about the good mu shu some other time.

The other day Jill and I got the latest hospital bill for Alex. The bill was $289,000.

About four months ago, I was talking about the bill with a nurse, and at that time I guessed that the total bill would come in at around a couple hundred thousand. The nurse rolled her eyes as if I'd tried to rent a luxury apartment using postage stamps. "Try a million," she said. "Easy."

When you make $38,000 a year, that kind of easy means a lot of insurance. Jill and I assault Alex's plump rack of bills. These bills use lots of "ology" words: Cardiology. Pulmonology. Pathology. There are fancy words like "endotracheal," and easy words like "Routine EKG." Though I do wonder if anyone who's ever needed an EKG himself would call any kind of EKG "routine."

Just as every snowflake is different, every medical department has a bill design of its own. Cardiology, for instance, uses a border of sky-blue lines, and toward the middle of the page just a hint of rose. Infectious Disease spruces up the corner of their bill with fine logos of MasterCard and Visa, precisely printed works in miniature. Radiology uses a dash of kelly green. Opthalmology sends black typewriting on white paper.

My insurance company has paid well so far; of the thickening stack of "Patients' Benefits Reports," Jill and I are constantly fascinated by two things. One, that the insurance company consistently takes a doctor's bill for $200, which was earned by scribbling half a line in Alex's record book ("Patient resting. Parents surly.") and bargains it to $40. The second fascinating thing comes at the bottom of the page, after all the columns and the sums and the deductions. It usually reads, "Patient's Portion: $0."

Jill and I initially had a start-of-the-school-year enthusiasm for these forms. She pre-labeled a dozen No. 10 envelopes, and we divided the load into files for "Submitted," "Forms," "Alex," and "Paid." We vowed to fan the folders out on the living room table, VCR whirring with a rented movie, every couple of weeks.

I think we did it once in August, and filled out half a dozen bills. Then we got around to it again about Labor Day. Jill began tracking what bills had been sent to what insurance company. As the bills came to the mailbox, like chocolates coming to Lucy on the conveyor belt, I slid them into the rack.

I seem to recall we next did bills just before Halloween, and, as the hospital *volksstrum* didn't kick in our door, we next opened the folders toward the end of November. Somewhere in there, Jill had the brainstorm of photocopying almost-complete forms so all we'd have to add would be the date and signature. She also decided that we should do bills on weekend mornings. I usually jump to fetch an insurance card or an envelope or glasses of water while Jill fills the too-small boxes with the answers to the questions: *Name, as shown on ID Card? Is patient employed? If claim is for a laboratory test, what is the nature of the illness? Is claim related to an accident? Is claim related to employment? Relationship to employee?*

"How come I have to do all this?" Jill asks.

As the total ticks toward an easy million, I see that my baby will continue this fight until long after he stops being a baby. I see he and I will lose a lot, and that I'll probably hear his "Da!" between the rasps of a doctor's pager. At least now, finally, Alex outweighs the file of bills.

Yesterday morning we put stamps on thirteen claims; I pitch them into the mailbox on the way to see Alex. I let the box lid go with a satisfying slam, and think of the questions I'd put on a form: *What could we have done differently? Will we ever stop asking ourselves that question? If they know so much, why is he still sick? What form do I use to file the most important claims of all?*

People have called us "incredible" and "special." Insurance wrangling aside, Jill thinks we deserve a medal. For?

"For not running out of toilet paper *once* during all this!"

Our house isn't in bad shape. We haven't seen the remote control in a couple of months. But periodically Jill sweeps the forms off the dining room table, and I, who have always loved doing laundry, never let the mound of dirty clothes get big. The sink is clear of dishes, the inside of the microwave white. There are only a few old pieces of macaroni on the kitchen floor, almost but not quite under the refrigerator. No more than two or three newspapers are fanned across our couches. Jill reads the Sunday *Times* and buys the Sunday *Daily News* for the TV section. I don't read newspapers, because I don't care what's going on.

About the worst room is our study. This is where we check our e-mail and Jill reads the preemie websites. This is where I play Duke Nukem and try not to glance at the "It's a Boy!" Mylar balloons, which are slowly deflating. The other night I opened a drawer of his dresser and found nipples still in their packages and a bottle of iron supplement, almost full. The last time I'd laid eyes on them was Thursday, Dec. 17, 1998, the night before a bad day. On the dresser sits a canister of pop-up wipies, the wipie that popped up before Christmas now untouched and brown. Each night the dimples cut deeper into the balloons.

But it is a boy. These days, the lucky parent can be swept away by the smile that splits his face. He started kicking his legs just minutes after the physical therapist told him it would be a good idea. The feeding therapist said we should give him a taste of a lemon lollipop, and after just two days he's clamping his lips around the candy and smiling while drool trickles down his cheek. Lately, Alex's lungs have to be helped by two thick plastic tubes and a clear pipeline known as BiPAP, but his settings are low, and day to day his oxygen needs meager. Pretty soon he'll be eating something besides lemon Charms pops again, and at least three people at this hospital have used the word "home."

Jill is starting to want things again. I'm still scared of wanting anything, and the stuff I used to like seems changed for
good. I've always thought laundry and I were old pals, but just
the other day a washing machine I was using in our basement
slammed shut and wouldn't finish its cycle.

I threw my baseball hat, clawed my clothes out of the other
two washers, tossed an inhumanely big load into one dryer, and
ran upstairs for a hammer. I came back with a hammer and
another guy doing laundry saw me. I don't remember what happened next, officer, but in a little while Jill came down.

She gripped the handle of the jammed machine, and the
plastic crumbled in her hand. Rusty ball bearings chattered
across the cement. "Did you hit it with a hammer?" she said.

"Don't ask me that," I said.

"Did you hit it with a *hammer*?"

That night I went down to the basement and tried the knob
of the handle with my bare fingers, because that's what I thought
somebody would do if he had his life under control. Somehow
the washer door opened. I wrestled the sopping clothes into
plastic grocery bags, threw away the shards of the machine's
handle, and scuttled from the basement. Cheap machine, built
by somebody with healthy kids.

Jill and I end most days at home watching TV. Every night
we watch "All In the Family." Sometimes we watch "Larry Sanders" on tape, but most of what we have are the final episodes,
and they're sad.

What do I do for fun? This question came from one of my
oldest friends, who, because he agrees with me a lot, I consider one
of the smartest people I know. I'd just told him about Alex being
two and a half months premature and living in neonatal intensive
care, and about how nurses and doctors comforted me and Jill
with phrases like "Some kids recover; some kids don't." Wow, my
friend said, then asked what I still think is a good question.

He wasn't trying to pry or needle. What I suspect he really
wanted to know was, how do I manage to survive months of

having my baby's life depend on a plastic tube? Months of Jill crying on park benches until her shoulders shake? Months of wondering if I died on the day Alex was born, and everything since has been a nightmare rendition of "Occurrence at Owl Creek Bridge"?

I try to not answer the phone. Friends and relatives, bless 'em, keep trying, but one by one they seem to realize that Jill and I are hardening. The smart ones admit they're giving up. "I have absolutely no idea what to say to you," my brother said. I wish others would say that.

Jill and I can choose one of two ways to look at this time:

1) How can we take any more? This is how we feel each night before going to bed, and we're realizing that we're not looking forward to falling asleep and we're not looking forward to waking up. Or—

2) We know we can take it.

I don't know which way is more fun. I do know that lately I'm trying to run up a muddy hill in the rain. All Jill ate yesterday was oatmeal and Valium. I haven't been eating well, either. I'm starving before lunch, but when I get out there on the sidewalk my stomach starts thinking, "What's the point?" I spend my lunch hour sitting on a piece of concrete where I won't have to talk to anyone and can stare at the tops of my sneakers. This rarely takes a full hour, and that's good because lately I'm getting to work late.

Later in the afternoon I steal a few minutes to type words like these, and that gets me through until five. I read the Patrick O'Brian books again except the last one, which hasn't come out in paperback. I read Churchill's account of the war in the Sudan, re-read *A Tale of Two Cities*, and re-read some E.B. White and Robert A. Heinlein's *Starship Troopers*. A lot of re-reading of unworthy books, some might say. Those people can get their own goddamn premature baby.

A couple of weeks ago I went to an exhibit of sailing ship models. I had fun in a preoccupied way, but I felt I had dragged

Jill along and later in the afternoon it started to rain. Neither of us had umbrellas. We took Valium before going to the hospital. Jill likes to buy clothes but I don't. I don't go to ball games, and TV programs suddenly seem like a bunch of people pretending they have a problem. I did catch *The Great Escape* again the other night, and that was fun because I too have been digging an escape tunnel for a long time. Also, the Gestapo interrogator who fondles a dagger and says, "Vat haf you done vith your papers?" reminded me of one of Alex's nurses.

I get the most fun out of a computer game called Duke Nukem. I play this in the evenings, in the study where Alex slept for those four nights. In the game I carry a machine gun and a bazooka. Other weapons include pipe bombs, a shotgun, a pistol and a freeze ray. Finding the correct weapon to beat each monster keeps my mind and eyes off Alex's bassinet. When I find ammo the game says, "Come get some." . . When I pause too long the game says, "Wha'cha waitin' for? Christmas?" Nobody in the game is my friend. They're pigcops, lizardmen or aliens with Gatling guns. Sometimes I also imagine a doctor.

I spot Alex's first two teeth on Sunday. On Wednesday I see a flash of white on the lower gum. On Thursday, he bites me. I had been warned. "We have a biting bear," says Jill. "You stick your finger in his mouth and it hurts!"

The teeth start as two translucent gobs on the ridge of his lower gum. A day later, I see white. A few days after, I see a similar gob on the top, then another next to it. In a few days, the bottom teeth look like tiny white railroad cars. Teeth. In a blink, I guess, Alex will have his own mouthful of bills. But before then come some tests. Like this morning, when we both got up at 6:30 to go to the hospital and watch them stick a camera rod the width of a cigarette down Alex's nose. This test is to see how food goes down Alex's throat when he swallows. He isn't eating yet, unless you count pressing fingerloads of rice cereal into his bedclothes.

So we got to the hospital and found our way into this room, where they had me sit in a dead-ringer for a dentist's chair and hold Alex on my lap. The doctor opened a black case filled with gray styrofoam. Tucked into cut-out shapes in the foam were the components of the camera, like the parts of a sniper's rifle. When the black tip of the camera disappeared up his nostril, Alex's eyes clamped shut and his pink mouth erupted. Jill turned away and pressed the heel of her hand to her lips.

"Mrs. Stimpson, if you'd rather wait outside?" the doctor said. "I don't need two patients . . ."

In the corner, the feeding therapist was busy dyeing a cup of rice cereal bright green. The camera snaked down Alex like a National Geographic probe looking for the *Titanic*, bathing his glistening larynx in unnatural white light while Jill struggled to push her own fingertip of rice cereal somewhere past the wails. She succeeded; on the video monitor, the glistening wet flesh inside Alex twitched and jumped until the bright green mound vanished down a nearby hole.

This went on for ten minutes in my lap, Alex's back against my chest, as his leg hammered my thigh and he screamed his insistence that this damned doctor find *something* else to do this morning.

They were trying to figure out if the green mound slides down the right hole, the one that leads to Alex's stomach, or the hole that leads to Alex's lungs. The test should have been done months ago.

"I see no evidence of aspiration," the doctor said, "and, more important, when I put the camera in his mouth, I saw no pools of saliva there, as if he hadn't been swallowing." The doctor left.

"You know he just had a baby, a boy," Jill said. "And I resented that 'two patient' remark. I should have told him that I've been through things that would have made his head explode."

So we have some teeth and we have a video that proclaims Alex can eat without dying. Later on, from my office, I call Jill.

She says she's "feeding" Alex by giving him a small spoon heaped with non-green rice cereal. "Up come the hands, into the mouth goes the spoon," she narrates. "And all over everything goes the cereal." I picture him, head back, mouth agape, pawing the spoon deeper and deeper. The spoon is coated with rubber, and must feel as solid as the world against those new teeth.

The most significant smiling development recently has been Great-Aunt Judie's blocks. They are second-hand and spongy, decorated in fading orange, yellow and green. Each block has a bell inside. "I washed them and I was afraid about the bells," said Judie. Alex went bananas for the blocks. I came into the hospital room to find his grandma and great-aunt sitting him up and him holding one of the blocks. I had never seen him hold anything while sitting up before.

Soon the blocks became Alex's first love. If his eyes were roaming we'd shake the bell and he would fix on the block. We'd move the block to the left and his eyes would move left. We'd move it to the right and his eyes would move right. We'd shake it so the bell tinkled and he'd burst into a smile, whapping the mattress of the hospital crib with all four limbs. Just bananas. Pretty soon he'd hiss with delight, because he doesn't laugh yet. "Ah ah ah," Alex would say. Whap whap whap.

One of his early favorite games was "Baby Adding Machine." I'd sit him on my lap and touch my finger to one side of his lips, then to the other side, then to his chin. Then I'd pull down his arm and go "Cha-ching." It killed. Then came rubbing his gums and lips with my finger, then tossing him about a quarter of an inch and catching him under the arms, and then tapping the theme song of "Jonny Quest" on his chest.

I can't remember the first time I saw Alex smile. I do know that I have to keep coming up with new stuff: Today's big hit quickly becomes yesterday's dud to the new, seventeen-pound Alex. A week ago I tried Baby Adding Machine and got nothing but drool.

I'd better come up with something good before he comes home, which may be soon. I could read him one of the funnier applications sent by Social Security. SSI interviewed me a few months ago, and mailed back a series of statements about Alex and his life, which I was to sign:

"JILL STIMPSON is interested in ALEXANDER LEE STIMPSON." Agreed.

"ALEXANDER LEE STIMPSON does not owe me any money." Ha.

"He never was married."

"He does not own any type of resource."

Not true. He has Bully the Beanie Baby, the purple Teletubby, the crinkly stuffed chicken, and most recently a squeezable red dog with a bell in it. It seems like yesterday when the hit of the season was holding Tinky Winky up to Alex's face and saying, "Eh-oh, Awecks, eh-oh." Now, just drool. We laughed over the SSI statements until we realized that they may unlock federal money, and what it could mean that our son has a chance at that kind of federal money.

If the government paid babies for standing around, as it does some adults, then Alex would be happy and loaded. In the last couple of days he's taken to loving the sensation of stiffening his legs under his hips. I hold him upright under the arms and watch the knees lock into place and the toes dig in, and once he gets the hang of it he can even swing his hands around to play in the spitty shine of his lips. Alex's career in stand-up comedy started with nurse Jackie, who spends a lot of time with Alex—more than I do—and one afternoon not long ago I came in to find her tossing him gently into the air. Jackie taught him to fly. Joann is a nurse.

"ALEXANDER LEE STIMPSON lives in AN INSTITUTION."

That's not funny. Nor is it as true as it used to be. They prop him semi-upright in his crib, while a machine drips in food. If he can hold it down, the gastroenterologists tell us, they'll try more. Maybe they'll give him a barium test.

They do, and on that morning Alex smiles up a storm on the x-ray table. His fingers scrabble at the camera, then he looks at me upside down and hugs Bully into his mouth. He smiles when he looks at you; he smiles when he doesn't look at you. He also passes the x ray. Soon we'll talk to the doctors about the last steps before bringing him home. In the meantime we still live in the INSTITUTION, brush his lips with the blocks and watch the corners of his mouth fly apart until he's nothing but pink wet gum. The tip of the wet tongue peeks out and he begins to wiggle. Wiggle wiggle wiggle. Whap whap whap goes the arm on the crib mattress. This afternoon Jill gave him plastic keys and he lost all control. He'll laugh soon, the doctors say.

Lately Alex grabs the red dog with the bell when it's time to sleep. He hugs it and licks it. We rock him and pat him until his long, black eyelashes go down. This often happens around seven on a weeknight. Jill and I take that moment to go home again.

## JULY TO NOVEMBER, 1999

ALEX IS HOME, and it's been a strange week:

—Throughout the July Fourth weekend, New York City is 100 degrees and smothered in humidity. A few minutes after ten p.m. on July sixth, the night before Alex comes home, our lights dim. On the eleven o'clock news we hear that upper Manhattan, including the neighborhood of Alex's hospital, is blacked out. No traffic lights, no subways, no feeding pumps or air conditioning except that allowed by a grumpy hospital generator. Jill and I go to bed hoping Alex is asleep.

At midnight we hear yelling on our street, words of warning ricocheting up the hot sides of the apartment buildings. Something pops and sizzles in the ninety-degree night air. Cops in reflective yellow vests herd knots of people up the sidewalk through thickening smoke. I hear the cops warn us all to get inside and close our windows. "It's poison!" I hear a cop say. A transformer has overheated under our street. The resulting buildup of gas has blown a manhole cover through a car and set it on fire.

In our bedroom, I turn on the air conditioner and it wheezes—Con Ed has turned down the power, and all I can think is, "Alex's breathing equipment runs on electricity, and he can't sleep on a night like this without air conditioning. A good father would be able to give him these things."

Jill invites one of the neighbors, a big guy named Ruben, into our dark apartment. "Nobody will get any sleep tonight,"

Ruben says. Later I do my best to prove him right, lying on my moist sheets and listening to the air conditioner grind and suck for electricity.

—On the afternoon Alex is discharged, the nurses order pizza. They order it from Jersey, because the power is still off in the hospital and the surrounding neighborhood. The lights are dark; a single fan moves the air. But it's cool. The nursing supervisor, who is also named Jill, tells us things her grandfather used to scream when they tried to take him to the hospital, like "My leg is dead!" and "Your nuts have nuts!"

About four o'clock, the big ambulance guys show up. They strap my seventeen-pound baby into a simply enormous stretcher and wheel him out to the one working elevator, which is operated by a guy named Walter. "You'll get an express ride!" Walter says as he drops us all the way from the eleventh to the first floor, even though people are waiting on the ninth. When we pass the ninth floor, somebody bangs on the other side of the door.

—That first night, our circuit breakers keep cutting out. Alex's oxygen concentrator—a machine the size of a baby carriage that filters the nitrogen from room air—takes too much juice for our apartment, apparently. Around eleven p.m. we hook him up to a green oxygen tank. As Alex gets some kind of treatment or medication every two hours, we have twenty-four-hour nursing. At three a.m. the night nurse knocks on our bedroom door and says the tank has run out and she doesn't know how to change it. At three a.m. we call the equipment company and get the salesman on Long Island who says, yeah, okay, he'll bring us a few extra tanks and he'll be there in a few hours.

When he reaches our apartment around five, he does not shake my hand. We maneuver the tanks around the crib, and he notes that we had one of the flow valves on too loose. He goes away. Next morning he and I speak around nine and I ask him how he is. "Tired," he says. But he does give us a tank of liquid oxygen that will provide a few days' backup air. He also brings us a long cannula tube that will reach anywhere in the apartment. In time we discover that the tubing will reach to the kitchen sink, for it's there we will bathe Alex while he scans our cupboards, calendar, and fridge magnets with eyes wide and brown.

—When he lived in the hospital, I got a hint of Alex's schedule from the nurses. If he didn't nap during the day he'd crash about seven p.m. and sleep through the night. If he did nap he might stay up as late as eleven, arms and legs kicking, gurgling into his pacifier and really just happy to be here. At home, I should demand that he go to sleep earlier, but I don't.

—Thursday and Friday we all begin to settle down. I give two twenties and a ten to an electrician who stalks our home with what looks like a tuning fork and a piece of wire until he finds an outlet that can accommodate Alex's concentrator. Turns out our whole apartment—which is owned by a guy who had a lot of money about the time I was working twelve hours a day at an upstate newspaper—was wired through only two of our five circuit breakers. Why would anyone wire an apartment like that?

"Who knows?" the electrician says.

Around this time, a nurse criticizes us for having no sterile water and later, as we sleep, she tears the mattress of our changing table. Still later we learn that she complains, "There's no place to put my feet up in their house!"

—On Saturday afternoon we begin to teach Alex how to applaud. The day nurse, a Jamaican giantess, has a lovely singing voice, and claps her big hands softly in front of Alex's face. His eyes track the sound. In the living room we spread an afghan and lie Alex down. I clap for him as he watches. Then he brings his own hands together. His fingers tangle on his first try, but the next time the palms meet and there's a tiny slap.

—Our friends Heidi and Teddy drop by on Saturday night. We decide we want pizza and I go to get it. The pizza place is closed, however, and I head back thinking that we'll order Chinese food. Back in my building I step from the elevator and hear hammering. I wonder which loony neighbor would be driving a nail when my baby has to go to sleep. I open my front door and there sits Alex, in Jill's lap at the dining room table, clutching his silver rattle and banging it on the table. *Bang bang bang* on the table. Later we put Alex to bed with his nurse to watch over him, and settle in the living room to eat egg foo yung and watch *The Shawshank Redemption*. "This night has been a long time coming," I whisper to Jill. She nods.

—Nothing much happens on Sunday, except Alex and I snooze on the couch. He lies on my chest and I listen to the unbroken whiz whiz whiz of his breaths through the cannula. When he stirs, I pat his back until his eyes close again. This is the first weekend in sixty that Jill and I did not have to go to a hospital.

—Monday is busy. I return to work. Jill calls in mid-afternoon. "I'm having a luxurious day," Jill says, "after all these months. Know how he gets wild in bed with his arms and his legs? He got hysterical. He was like laughing and crying at the same time."

The tired home-equipment guy calls to say that we are not covered for having both the liquid oxygen and the concentrator. He says we can call our insurance company, and that sometimes insurance companies pay attention to parents, but maybe Jill and I should decide which we want to keep. He says the mayor of New York surely won't let Con Ed get away with another bad blackout. He says he's ramming his head against the wall for our case. He says we should let things calm down for a couple of days and then he'll get back to us on Wednesday. I get the feeling that he wants some of our equipment for another client.

Monday is the first night I come home from work to my son. Jill goes to an infant CPR class and the night nurse is a little late, so I put a plate of turkey and cold chicken and bread on the living room table, and cart out Alex and his tubes and clap him in the highchair. He raps on the wipies box and watches me eat as we listen to Scott Joplin. "A lot of people are rooting for you, Alex," I tell him. I finish my chicken and before you know it, it's time for his eight o'clock meds.

Monday night we have a new nurse, Katherine. Jill thinks some of our home nurses are idiots, but Katherine is excellent. She puts Alex to sleep by putting him face down on a blanket across her lap. Jill comes home from CPR and tells me about the other parents there. They talked about falls and scrapes and about how terrifying it is to see your child bleed. Jill briefed the instructor before class not to ask her how old Alex was or what he's doing now. "We are really on a planet all by ourselves," Jill says.

—On Tuesday I call the insurance company. Absolutely you're covered, the woman says, adding that our home equipment company is not the one to tell us what is and isn't covered. I ask Jill if she knows the best cure for a nervous breakdown. She asks me a couple of times what's happening, but I never really do answer and we get on to something else. I look at Alex and marvel that my mother, who died of cancer last September, will never meet him.

—On Tuesday night Alex passes out at 6:30. Jill and I rent *Rushmore*, in which Bill Murray plays a businessman who can't believe his teenage sons are wrestler jocks. They lock him out of the family limo and ignore him while he dives drunk into the family pool. I think how Alex will never have a limo or a pool— he'll be lucky to make it to Labor Day with the lights on. It's okay with me if he wants to be a wrestler.

—It's cool all week—I'm surprised how well I sleep—but it's supposed to get hot again on Friday. On Wednesday, I call Con Ed to arrange for a backup generator to power Alex's concentrator. Jill waits at home for a carrying case for Alex's feeding pump, a delivery due earlier in the week. The Con Ed rep says our pediatrician has to send a note to some back room in Flatbush to get a utility inspector to our apartment sometime, and as the English of the customer service rep sizzles and pops and finally goes out on my phone, I realize maybe we'll get what we need by Labor Day.

The week has given me the impression that beneath the hospital level of healthcare sits a substratum of drivers, salesmen, and moonlighters who, if I held a pistol to their heads, would admit that they don't care what happens to Alex. Other than that, there's not much of a conclusion to the week. Jill calls me at work to say she's spending twenty minutes cleaning up "a little flood" caused by a nurse who for some reason dumped Alex's bath water in the kitchen trash can. It takes me six phone calls to confirm the ambulance needed to take Alex to his doctors' appointments on Thursday morning. I tell our pediatrician about Con Ed needing a letter. He has three offices and everybody in Manhattan seems to know him. He says he already sent one letter but can kick out another in a couple minutes, that's no problem. It isn't a problem if you're in the real world. I guess I thought I'd be there by now.

I spend Alex's second week home worrying about electricity. I run the air conditioners in rotation. Jill turns on a light, and for half an hour I watch for the flicker. The blanket of gray-brown haze attests to how New York is wrapping up its third heat wave of this summer. Today it was ninety-seven. Yesterday it was ninety-eight. Saturday it was ninety-nine. The Weather Channel—suddenly my favorite—said that with the humidity it was closer to 105. "Heat Means High Tension" says the *New York Post*. "All eyes are on Con Edison today as sweltering temperatures bake the Big Apple for a fourth consecutive day."

"No relief in sight," adds the National Weather Service.

I live where heat waves are infamous, where heat seeps in around June. By July, usually around the Fourth, a high pressure system parks off Bermuda and twirls the atmosphere clockwise, picking up tropical stuff in the bayou. For the next eight weeks the air entwines New York buildings, apartments and lives. The cheeks of subway riders shine. The air turns to sludge.

The kiss of air conditioning as you walk past the door of a nice apartment building teaches you the hard way how the Hamptons came to be. Every hour you survive is an hour closer to September, and you look forward to another hour passing.

The blackout when Alex came home was amazing: no traffic lights, no storefront neon, no feeding pumps or respirators driven by public power. The largely poor populace opened hydrants and sat down on sidewalks to joke for TV crews. The mayor threatened to sue the power company. Con Ed trucked in ice.

"I think that I'd prefer to have the city not in the kind of precarious position that we're in now, where whenever we have a hot day we have to worry whether there's going to be a cut-down in electricity or a blackout," said the mayor of New York. I agree.

I call Con Ed. They ask me how much reserve we have if the power goes off. I say eight hours. "That's a lot," the guy replies. They'll call us ahead of time if there's going to be a blackout. They promise.

Jill says my concern is good and normal. I feel that whatever life I can give Alex comes through a wall outlet. I tell Jill to take it easy on the halogens until the heat breaks. I ask her not to use the microwave while the TV's running. We won't run both air conditioners on high. I touch the plug of the concentrator to see if it's warm. I think about a nurse who probably still doesn't know how to change a flow value, let alone change one in the dark.

Before he left, the electrician pointed to our living room halogen lamps and said that they use a lot of power. He pointed to our overhead lights, neon that can bathe half our apartment in the kind of glow enjoyed by jail inmates or students in crowded high schools. "Those ceiling lights, those are good lights," the electrician said. They're also the kind of lights no Con Ed exec would be caught pale under, I bet. I bet that the sons of Con Ed execs sleep in air-conditioned bedrooms. I bet they have air, and I bet they have power.

Each night now, I get myself home around six o'clock. Jill has spent the day with Alex, usually in the apartment because before we can go out with Alex we have to secure a yard-long oxygen tank to the bottom of the carriage and make sure he's not sitting on any of his tubes. Sometimes Jill has the energy to get him set up; other times she rents a movie and plays with him in the living room. When I get home, Jill goes out for a walk.

I set about giving Alex his six p.m. cocktail of medications. He gets a dozen or so meds at six—just as he does at eight and ten p.m., and two, six, eight and ten a.m. At six, he gets .3 ccs of Simethicone and two ccs of Cisapride, plus a "neb." The neb is given with mist from a nebulizer and consists of three liquids: half a vial of Intal, 0.2 ccs of Albuterol from the tiny white bottle that looks like a cookie jar from a doll house, and three ccs of saline water. I lay out the syringes and the "acorn" of Alex's nebulizer and put his feeding pump on "pause." Then I pop the cap on his feeding tube and stick in the Cisapride and the Simethicone and turn the pump back on. As the meds snake through the tube toward his stomach, I take the plastic "acorn" with the Albuterol and screw on the top of the mister and hold it in front of his face. If Alex is asleep, I prop the neb in front of him using Beanie Babies and play Fuji Golf at the computer.

When the neb ends, I take the little padded thing and whack Alex on the chest and back. I think he regards this as a massage, but it's to clear crap out of his lungs. He likes when I sing to him and whack him in time to the song. His favorite song seems to be the 1974 hit "The Night Chicago Died."

"You just have to get into a routine," says Howard, who has a grown son and daughter. Howard has said a lot of cute things about Alex. Once, when Alex was still in the hospital, I told Howard I was leaving work early to give Alex a bath. "Oh no," Howard said. "He's going to give you a bath . . ."

Bath time is next. Verifying that the meds have run through, I unplug the feeding tube from his stomach, close the little catch—sometimes a drop of yellow formula oozes out—and peel the pulse ox probe off his toe. The probe is an inch-long strip of wire and thin plastic attached to about three inches of bandage. The pulse ox monitor gives perfect readings until Alex's foot moves or he sweats. I peel off the diaper—wet? feel? oh yeah—and place him in the tub on Jill's legs. The one therapist we've managed to dig up to visit him so far said that this position was great to teach him to stand. "Splashy!" I say, pouring bath water from one of Jill's old yogurt cups. Sometimes Alex tries to grab the stream, which is cute.

After the bath it's back to the crib. I take out the sheet of Duoderm, a sticky bandage, and cut off a square. Using the baby scissors that you could run with and not get hurt, I cut a slit in the square, and then, at the head of the slit, I cut a tiny hole. This hole goes under the "button" of the tube we use to feed him directly into the jejunum. I press down the Duoderm and insert the head of the tube into the button. As I try to push the tube using no pressure at all, into my mind comes the image of doctor after doctor saying Alex would like this tube (he doesn't). When the tube is in, I cover the head of it with an X of clear tape, fix the feeding tube to his diaper with another piece of tape, and go to work on the pulse ox probe. The probe wraps around his toe, further anchored by white paper tape around his foot.

From the spaghetti in his plastic dresser drawer I draw out the probe, and work it around his big toe. Which toe had the probe before the bath? Fine flakes of skin are turning white on his toes from the constant tightness of the monitors. I wrap the probe as loosely as possible and plug it in, press the button and watch the little red line catch up to his heartbeats. For a moment, the red numbers tell me that he is dead. By 7:30 Jill is in the kitchen making dinner, and I'm starting to give him his eight p.m. meds. First he gets a shot of Flovent. This involves attaching the metal vial, similar to that used by asthmatics, to the top of the plastic accordion thing with the purple plastic mask that covers his nose and throat. I don't know who picked purple; I read that plastic model kits in the 1960s came in weird colors, like pink and baby blue, because that was the color of the scrap styrene plastic available. I cover his nose and throat and give him a squeeze. It always catches him by surprise.

He then gets 0.55 ccs of chlorothiazide, 0.5 of aldactone, which we keep in the fridge, and 1 cc of Zantac. Next comes the steroid called hydrocortisone. Preparing the hydrocortisone gives me deep faith in medical science, as I draw up a syringe of water and set aside another, empty syringe. Hydrocortisone comes in little white pills that the pharmacist thoughtfully cut into quarters for us. "You've got a cute kid," the pharmacist told me once.

I take two of the quarters and put them in a spoon. Then I put another spoon on top of that spoon and, pressing the two spoons together with my thumbs, pulverize the quarter-tablets. Often during the pulverizing tiny bits of hydrocortisone fly out from between the spoons. I set the top spoon aside and gently tip and tap the white powder into the empty syringe. Then I squirt in water, seal one end with the plunger and the other end with my finger, and shake well. When most of the white powder has dissolved, I inject it into him through his J-tube.

And then we eat dinner. Sometimes Alex "eats" with us, and watches TV. Of course he isn't really eating, just sitting in his carriage with the food pump on the table behind him. I chew my food and don't know if this is his routine, or mine.

His trip back to the hospital begins when alarms start to shatter every dinnertime, and for two nights in a row his pulse ox reading plunges to seventy as we're watching TV. He stays at seventy through uncounted commercials.

Since he came home on July 7, this is the only rough patch. Besides, in the week before this started he was seen by two specialists, and by an excellent pediatrician. They pronounced him fit.

Maybe. But on this Saturday morning in August, the numbers still deflate to 75, 80, 79. Blink, 78. Blink, 73. Blink, 73.

We call the ambulance. "Medicaid?" the dispatcher asks. I tell her what's wrong with Alex, his age, why this trip is needed this rainy morning. Okay, she says, twenty to thirty minutes.

Thirty-five minutes later, the two women of the ambulance crew appear in our house, take one look at Alex and say no, nobody told them that he was this fragile. They cannot take him. His sats are holding in the high seventies. I hear Jill say the word "fucking." This crew says a qualified ambulance crew will soon be available in Brooklyn. Do we want to just go to the nearest hospital? No.

For some reason I never learn, they decide they can take him but can't drive faster than forty miles per hour. "I'll take forty toward our hospital over an ambulance coming from Brooklyn on a rainy Saturday," I say. I still think that was eloquent.

They fumble with the key to open the tank of oxygen. They are scared. So is Alex as he watches them. His crying fades and fades and he turns the color of gum. At last they hook up the oxygen. Jill grabs some bags and I grab bags and an extra, clattering oxygen tank thinking that if I bring this tank, we won't need it.

On the ambulance ride, I slide sideways, my head swaying. The siren sounds hollow. Out of a scrap of windshield I see every car ahead put on their blinkers and swerve from Alex's path. It seems awfully hot next to Alex and Jill on the stretcher. Jill is crying, not moving except for the tears sliding down her face. My face is getting warm, and my stomach swerves with the road. I'd never make a jet pilot.

They let us off at an entrance to Alex's old hospital, but an entrance I've never seen before. They wheel us through a catacomb, the orange belt of the stretcher bright against the gray painted walls. Faces appear in the chairs and over the cots. The ER is a tent in the main lobby, a cavernous, glassy foyer that was once the sidewalk between two buildings of the best babies' hospital in New York. Somebody hands me a clipboard. Aware of how my private insurance is evaporating, I again try to pass Alex off as Medicaid.

No, replies the lady in the tent.

In the back I find Alex and Jill. Someone has spread white paper over Alex's bed in the emergency room. On the paper, the ambulance driver scribbles a cake recipe dictated by Jill. "Hope she makes that," Jill says later. A pulmonologist I have never met but have talked to several times on the phone this past week drops by. He's well into middle age but still just a fellow, not an attending physician. We get all our bills from attending physicians. "You did the right thing, bringing him in," the good fellow says.

We sit in the ER from about eleven a.m. until 3:40 p.m., when Alex is finally digested into the hospital and sent to the PICU. Old home week: I remember when they installed the stars and the speckled paneling in the elevators here. I know which men's rooms are clean and which stink. I know where the Burger King is. When the boy in the next ER bed is x-rayed, I know when and how far to stand back from the rays.

The ER staff pays sporadic attention to Alex, taking a vital here and there. That's good, of course. I've learned the hard way you never want a crowd. Alex seems much more comfortable in general today: on his side, punching his Beanie Baby, and making little sounds. He's making more and more sounds, though he doesn't talk yet. I lean in close and nuzzle his ear and it's a pleasurable moment until I pull back and catch my face in his toy mirror. A bum's pale eyes, a life draining. Forty-five if a day. Yesterday I was thirty-seven. Two years ago I was thirty-five, but I can't remember that.

Jill fetches two BLTs. Through the afternoon I also eat pretzels, two ice cream bars, ruffle chips and a cupcake. "How many ice cream bars does that make for you today?" the ER doc asks. "Seven," I say. Ha ha. A girl appears with a clipboard to admit Alex. She hands me a book called "Getting Around the Hospital." Dr. K. comes in and looks down at Alex, and he asks if Alex has been urinating less.

Jill cannot fathom the question. Has Alex been urinating less than usual? The question bounces off her, and she wears that glaze that people get when they're watching a movie just before they turn to you and ask, "What happened there? Why'd they do that?"

Dr. K. and Alex are both looking at her. I try to explain. Urinating. Less.

"Oh," Jill says. "No, I don't think so."

Alex will spend this night here, the PICU of his second hospital. Every room is private, and has a VCR and TV. Alex puts his eyes on his TV, and watches "The Simpsons." He seems amazed, and blinks. Blink blink blink. He reaches up, touching the fat CPAP air tubes that frame his face. The tubes are in the way when he tries to lie on his side, and he cries. The nurse asks how long he's been home. Amazing that there's a soul here who doesn't know the legendary Alex, for whom a trip to this hospital is like an overnight at his aunt's house.

Jill and I order from a nearby Indian place. I have beef curry. Alex goes to sleep and we leave. We come home to a vacant crib and to toys unstirred. No overnight nurse. The air conditioner in his room is silent. In the kitchen is his teething toy. In the bathroom, his fleet of rubber ducks. Jill goes on eBay, and in a few minutes I hear her announce, "I think Alex needs a sock monkey!" I stand in the bathroom, where I rinse his feeding tube and do not look at his inflatable tub stuck on the wall, next to the ducks. I rinse the tube three times.

Alex comes home four days later, pink and fine. We never learn what caused his problem, or if it might occur again.

We quickly learn that Alex likes music. Even in the isolette, he took to Chet Baker and Pete Seeger—everyone's impressed with those selections—and I would play the tapes for him while he lay there under the lights. As that year in the hospital went on, Jill sang to him. She sang "Binkie for Baby" and "Nap Time for Baby," both of which taxed her talents of ad-libbing lyrics when her eyes burned and her head was about to drop to her chest.

These days Jill performs "a lot of original material, nothing I think people will recognize," she said in a phone interview. She's still ad-libbing, mostly in "Baby Went to the Coffee Shop," which, like the flip-side hit "I'm a Little Round Bear," is sung to the tune of "Ring Around the Rosy." Alex stares in her face. "He likes it when you hum," Jill says. "He likes it when you sing to him."

I sang once, in high school, for about five endless seconds, and got through it with an affected Jim Nabors baritone. I mouth "Happy Birthday" in the office. Recently I saw a TV show about my problem. Many adults claim some teacher in grammar school told them they couldn't sing. I had no idea so many people had Mrs. Strathmore in third grade.

Mrs. Strathmore (not her real name) wrecked singing for me. She had a bum leg and walked with a crutch, which she used to whack Ricky Feldon (not his real name) just about weekly. Later Ricky went to prison. "That's because Mrs. Strathmore hit him with a crutch," some might say. Maybe. Mrs. Strathmore never used her crutch on me. Instead, once when I was next to her at the piano during "music time," she turned to me and said, "You know, if you sing, you must do it with your mouth closed!" Strathmore's remark ended my even discussing music for two decades.

I doubt I'll ever boogie, unless you count behind the wheel on the Beltway. But I want to sing to Alex, because he's one of the few musical people I've ever liked. So I sing to him when no one's around. Sometimes when I sing, the numbers on his pulse ox go up. Sometimes he actually turns over from sucking on the binkie and blinks up at me. One of his favorite songs right now is "The Night Chicago Died." Even oldies stations avoid this song now, but it was the breed of narrative, post-Beatles pop-rock that was eaten by disco. Two of the lines were:

*Daddy was a cop ... on the east side of CHI-ca-go ...*
*Back in the U-S-A ... back in the bad old days ...*

In time to the beat of this song, I whack Alex with a pad. This clears his lungs, his doctors say. Two minutes on each side, two on each shoulder blade back and front, two minutes on the side of each ribcage.

*In the heat of a summer's ni-hi-hite . . . in the land of the dol-lar bill . . . WA WA WA . . .*

Alex likes the "wa-wa-wa's."

I tried the radio, but whapping in time to a car commercial is tough. So I scrounged the corners of our living room for cassettes that I haven't used since my last job, when I found that music passed the time. One tape I found was Paul Simon's "Negotiations and Love Songs." Paul Simon has taken over the throne of "Person Or Group I Would Sing Like If Mrs. Strathmore Had Said I Could Sing." This crown has been owned by Bo Donaldson and the Heywoods (1974–75), John Denver (1976–77), jointly by Neil Diamond and Gordon Lightfoot (1978–80), and by Billy Joel and Bruce Springsteen (1981–). Simon's reign began in my college months with a roommate who would stare out the dorm window with a guitar and play "Paul Simon Live" on the boombox.

"Negotiations and Love Songs" begins with "Mother and Child Reunion." The song doesn't have the lung-clearing beat of some tunes, but it does make Alex look into Daddy's face as Daddy's voice elongates into: *I would not give you faaallse hope, on this strange and mourn-ful day, but the mother and child re-union is on-ly a motion a-way-hey . . .* Maybe it's "moment away."

Paul Simon has written many songs about mothers; Alex seems to have taken a shine to "Loves Me Like a Rock:" *O my momma loves me, she loves me . . . she gets down on her knees and hugs me and she—loves—me—like—a—ROCK!* Whap whap whap whap whap WHAP! Alex's affection for the song has reached the point where I don't even have to play the tape, just sing it to his face, eye to eye, my mouth open.

*When I was grown to be a man (grooown to be a MAN), hmmm, and the Devil would call my name . . .* Grown to be a man.

Peaceful moments of song aside, Jill and I haven't escaped nurses. We have several home care people involved in our life now, including Nurses, Therapists, and Home-Equipment Guys From Long Island. Many times Alex has been in the clutches of a home care somebody, and lifted his brows and seemed to ask, "Daddy, why don't you just hit these guys?!"

Because, Alex, they are in our home to care for you by:

—leaving Pepsi cans under chairs;

—asking that we please not drain oxygen tanks so fast;

—losing our doctors' orders;

—snapping the legs off furniture.

We've whittled the nursing from twenty-four hours, to twelve, to eight. I stay up to let the nurse in, and Jill gets up in the morning to let her out. Often the nurse will come through the door and say something like, "Hello, good night." One of the more enormous nurses used to screech in Alex's face, though she did also teach him to clap. She walked in bare feet and left a broadening smudge of black footprints on our bathroom floor. "Letting me look at her painted toenails," noted Jill. We never liked having a nurse during the day. Overnight nursing allowed us to sleep. Alex sleeps like a professional baby, lips parted, one arm nestling a stuffed bull and the other, numb to this world, crooked like a lone tree on a prairie. His sats hover around ninety-nine and now and then he'll flip over, lips smick-smicking, seeking another binkie. Jill and I need the nursing.

"You know, I just peeked in there," Jill said to me, climbing into bed one night. "The nurse was snoring."

As if drilling us for the evening when Jill and I can make it through a night without listening for a nurse's snore, the overnight people sometimes don't show. This has happened five times in eight weeks, often on a weekend. The agency usually doesn't call, and when they do it's usually to explain that weekends in the summer are tough and it's tough to find help these days. Lately our case has disintegrated faster: five nights out of the past twelve. Last night we got a call at 9:30 to say our nurse wouldn't be there at eleven o'clock, though the agency "had calls out" for a replacement. The next day we heard she had a car accident. She's all right. She fell asleep at the wheel. I call around to find another nursing agency.

"Well, thirty-three percent coverage by the parents is the industry standard," says one place. I reply that nobody ever told me that.

"Of course they didn't," is the reply.

Of course. And our home-oxygen company makes me feel like a bedroom-window busybody who phones the cops too often. "Yes, Mr. Stimpson?" says our rep, a Long Island guy who expected to make more money out of a job that instead gets him phoned at four in the morning. He's a young parent. I think young parents look at Alex and his cannula and the undergrowth-green oxygen tank and think either: "Poor guy. Can I help?" or "Thank Christ that's not my kid." Then again, Jill and I have both yelled at this guy, like the time he called to say he was taking away the reserve tank of liquid oxygen.

"But don't freak out, don't freak out! I'm bringing you an H tank." An H tank of oxygen looks like the torpedo Humphrey Bogart stuck out the bow of the *African Queen*. Since I promised not to use names, let's say I screamed, "Long Island Guy! Listen to me! You are not coming to take that tank, or if you do you're bringing a replacement! It's what we want and you have one and our insurance says we can have it!"

Long Island Guy folds if you yell at him over the phone. "Okay, okay," he panted. "I'm sorry. I'm sorry. It's just been a lousy week . . ."

Most of these people keep claiming they know what a lousy week is. "Been a rough one," says the guy who was going to be late getting us the feeding tubes to ram into Alex's tummy. "It's very, very hard, but we all have to work together," says the service coordinator who let a month drag on without therapy for Alex.

Social work crawls with people who fulfill the same role as literary agents. Nobody grows up saying they want to be a literary agent; they grow up saying they want to be a novelist. No-body grows up saying they want to be the social worker who arranges for social workers to actually come to your house and work with your baby. Because of one of these literary agents of social work, Alex is without any therapy until almost Labor Day. They claim they haven't got the faxes from the doctors. I've talked with the doctors and I've tried to talk with these people, and I know who lost the faxes.

Eventually, therapists begin showing up. One is a special-education teacher, a middle-aged guy with salt-and-pepper hair who keeps calling Alex "delicious." Pretty soon he has Alex stretching and watching soap bubbles float across our hardwood floors. Teacher dangles plastic links in front of Alex, who snatches them. "Oh, he tracks better," teacher says. "He's looking up and processing the information a lot faster in just this past week." Another therapist also has a good word: "I owe Alex some time," she says. She's the first medical professional to say that.

Jill and I aren't delighted that Alex needs any kind of therapy. We're trying to help him catch up. I've taught him how to give me five. He helps me play golf on the computer. I tickle him and make noises like a strafing fighter plane. When he has a cold, I make a game out of cleaning his nose with a Q-tip.

One morning I calculate that Jill and I have suddenly soloed overnight for six of the preceding nine nights. Not long after, the one remaining nurse says she has to start leaving at six in the morning. A few days later, the agency calls and asks did I know that this coming Friday was going to be that nurse's last day, as she had taken another job? Her potential replacements include the nurse who once complained there was nowhere to put her feet up in our house.

So I say thank you anyway, and we begin choosing our own sleep schedule. This has included skirmishing in the wee hours with Alex's pulse ox. The makers of the pulse ox call it "move-ment sensitive." I call it "movement insensitive." If Alex rolls over or, frankly, just wiggles his toe, the pulse ox cracks our sleep with a beeping alarm somewhat like a smoke detector. Actually it cracks Jill's sleep, and she eventually cracks mine. I wear one earplug—pre-fatherhood, I wore two—and she often hears the pulse ox first. She says I sleep in a Flintstones-like state, where I have something that wakes up so it can wake me up.

We've had three or four disputes in the dark of the night.

"I've gotten up three times already!"

"I have to work tomorrow!" Once we talked about divorce. Then we went back to sleep.

Now my family has been able to sleep alone for a month. Alex comes to appreciate our schedule. He used to fall asleep around eight p.m.; now between nine and 10:30 I look into the crib and find that his eyes are closed. Sometimes he has an arm in the air. And I have learned that when Alex falls asleep, I should hit the hay no more than an hour later after filling Alex's bag of formula and wrapping the probe around his toe.

Middle of the night: "Can you get this one?"

"Can't you?"

"I've been up three times already!" Has a pillow ever been this soft?

Tonight when I come home we will fix Alex up with another probe, and in the wee hours of tomorrow I will scurry to find Alex immobile with his hand in the air. If Alex will be doing anything in the middle of the night, it's rolling around and smiling before he goes back to sleep.

Jill and I will try to go back to sleep. But sometimes we will lie in the dark and think, What's wrong with his left eye? When will he talk? How come he has that bald patch on the back of his head? How can any little kid stay alive in New York City? What about cancer? Hard questions, at hard hours. But I remember my kind of sleep in those first thirteen months, and I'll take this new kind of tired.

Alex starts from on his back. There he lies and flaps his arms until my face looms over his and I clap my hands once and say, "Wanna come up?" He hooks his fingers on my hand. I tug scarcely hard enough to move a sheet of paper but he'll none-theless sail to a sitting position. After a few minutes there he'll start rocking on his hips, curling his toes and chattering like a bird in a pet shop.

Last night, while sitting in his little inflatable tub, he wanted the bath sponge bobbing in the water in front of him. He leaned forward, grabbed the sponge and sprang back to a sitting posi-tion in a way I haven't been able to do since I started manhan-dling a twenty-pound baby. The night before last he held the jingly toy in his left hand while he pivoted to the right to reach back and steady himself.

Therapists have helped his hands to discover his feet, which we tell him are two expensive toys we just bought him. Another of his therapists used squeaky blocks to help Alex understand how to knock over a stack of blocks. Seeing what the therapist was up to, I fetched Alex's own stacking cups, and the session soared. One day later, Alex was knocking over stack after stack of his cups, and afterwards unfailingly picking up the orange one. Pretty neat. When Alex encounters a new toy from a per-son who's more unfamiliar than known, his chin hits his chest and his arms drop like a robot whose power has been turned off. Some of the therapists claim he has "sensory issues." One suggested "adaptive seating" for his carriage. But Aunt Julie notes, "You don't have to lift him at all anymore."

Alex laughs a lot, considering all those big needles. He is engaging and attentive, and polite to his parents when they show him something new in toy departments.

So what's up with the cough? It occurs most when he wakes up, and it sometimes strikes him when he's drifting to sleep and trying to cram the horns of Bully in his mouth. It seems to start in his chest, his lips forming a tall zero and the sounds popping up in his throat and mouth. Often two or three coughs; if it's more, they turn into a retch you can hear start from farther down Alex's twenty-eight inches. Then they ricochet out to us in the living room where we hunch over our dinner, shattering the illusion that he's gone to sleep, and any idea that he's out of the woods.

We dash in, snatch Bully from his face and heft him up. I try to hold him horizontally over my shoulder. Sometimes I can feel his mid-section cave in as the cough takes him: the last thing to torture him, the last thing doctors can't figure out. The monitors start complaining that they've lost their reading as he settles down. Sometimes it's because we've calmed him. Sometimes it's because his throat and mouth have deposited a wet spot on my shoulder and I realize I heard a sticky spatter on the wood floor. I bring him to me face-to-face; his eyes are often closed as his head moves side to side. Sometimes from deep in his face we hear the hitch of air around mucus. Jill claims she's seen white bobbing up the back of his throat.

Side to side, eyes closed. "Just give me a binkie and put me back," he seems to say.

So what's up with the cough? "I don't know. I really don't know," Jill says. "I think it's getting a little better. I think when Alex has a cough it takes him a while to get over it. And when he coughs, he vomits."

Sometimes Alex has a bedtime from which you'd never deduce that he's known so many doctors or lived with a tube down his throat. I jiggle the crib or read him *Goodnight Moon* or *Mr. Midshipman Hornblower*. He studies his fingers until Bully and binkie appear from nowhere. The lashes descend, the binkie goes snick-snick, and he rolls over. His face goes soft in new sleep, and I go to the other room for dinner.

Despite the coughs and somewhere between the feeding pump and the oxygen torpedo, Alex starts to acquire normal kids' stuff, such as hair. In the hospital, he never seemed to sprout more than a fuzz that kissed your cheek but which, on one occasion, made the neonatologist remark: "It'd be nice if he got some hair." That neo was apparently as good at growing hair as he was at growing babies, because Alex's head began to darken shortly after we transferred to the new hospital.

Now Alex's hair has shaded his whole scalp, turning it from the color of the eastern sky at sunset to more of a full night tone. In person, Alex's hair is Jill's brown; in snapshots or bright sunlight it's a replica of my own reddish-blond. In the very back, at the peak, he has a swirl like a satellite picture of a hurricane, and as I plug his feeding tube into his stomach I remark to myself how my son almost needs a comb. Earlier this week I noticed a single hair sticking up, and last night I was even treated to a genuine sprig. The spot above his fine-crafted ear grows darker and darker with each passing evening, as I lean over and tape the nozzle of the feeding tube in the hole they made in his stomach, as I listen to his breathing through the cannula, as I watch the red glow of the pulse ox probe on his toe. I look forward to his first haircut.

Earlier this week, Alex went to the pediatrician for shots. Three shots; he howled. I didn't hear him, because he was in the examination room with Jill and I was out by the front desk prepared to do my own howling. We owed the pediatrician—a calm man who seems partial to the phrase, "We'll work something out . . ."—$1,430. This doctor does not take insurance.

Turns out this was a good appointment, because the woman behind the desk told me that my insurance company should send me a check providing I hand her a check first. Sounded fair.

Not all of Alex's insurance needs are fair. The federal government, for instance, doesn't seem to like Alex. They recently determined that he's entitled to no (0) Social Security benefits. Not only that, they claim to have overpaid Alex $35 in benefits this year, and could he please reimburse this money, making his check payable to "United States Treasury."

"Gaa," replies Alex.

So I take to the keyboard: "This letter is in response to a recent notification that my son Alexander (DOB 6/14/98) was overpaid SSI benefits in the month of August in the amount of $35.00. As directed in your letter, I contest this finding." Every time I write like this, I'm astonished at how easily I slip into another species of English. "Alexander was born premature in June of 1998, and his course has not gone smoothly. He came home for a few days in December, but was readmitted under emergency conditions. Out-of-pocket medical expenses for Alexander continue to be pressing. Alex's medical needs and expenses continue to mount even as his private insurance is all but exhausted. I cannot believe that, under these circumstances, the Social Security Administration would find that he had been overpaid."

The shell is in the breech, the gun is aimed, and with a grunt I jerk the lanyard:

"In fact, I find it surprising that his benefits have been discontinued at all. If I may also appeal the decision to rescind his benefits, please instruct me how to do so immediately." Immediately, do you hear! Now begone!

I have not heard back from the feds, except for a generic Social Security brochure that told me that if I work until I'm seventy I may receive $1,500 a month.

Hospitals, however, bill us about every other day. I no longer return these calls: There's no legal record of a phone call, plus half the billing people I phone return my call about three weeks later, to say I never called them back. I saw on "60 Minutes" that a lot of these collections departments are work programs in prisons.

The longer I field the pop flys of Alex's insurance, the more I wonder if any provider, bill collector or convict truly expects me to write a check. I think they would rather I just keep the paper moving.

"To Whom It May Concern: Attached please find documentation regarding recent medical services rendered to my son, Alexander L. Stimpson. Your letter indicates that you cannot process the claim because you lack evidence of a referral from our primary care physician. Therefore please find enclosed a copy of that referral."

"To Whom It May Concern: Attached please find documentation regarding recent medical services rendered to my son, Alexander L. Stimpson . . ."

". . . Your letters indicate that you cannot pay these claims because you lack information on other coverage. My son and wife were covered during the period in question by my insurance policy. A sample medical benefits request form is enclosed, as well as a photocopy of my insurance card. I hope the enclosed information answers your questions."

"Attached please find documentation regarding recent medical services rendered to my son. Your letters indicate that you cannot process these claims because you lack evidence of a medical emergency. Therefore please also find copies of my son's Neonatal ICU and Pediatric ICU summaries, which both state that he needed emergency hospitalization and treatment immediately after his birth. Thank you." Thank you as well for making me once again set eyes on these documents, mention of which makes most other parents avert their eyes.

"To Whom It May Concern: Attached please find billing documentation for services rendered to my wife. I wish to submit this bill for payment. Please be advised that these are advanced-notice billings, so your prompt attention is appreciated."

Jill reads this one. "'Advanced-notice billings?' What does that mean?" she asks. It doesn't mean anything. It just moves.

I'VE BEEN WRITING about Alex for a year and a half, but only in the past month have I been trying to get them to more people. I submitted an article about Alex's birth to a magazine and the editor e-mailed a response:

"I'm so sorry what you and your wife have had to go through. These next stories I will not be able to use for I don't want to scare expecting parents. I don't want to downplay the hardship your family has gone through but we will need to edit some articles . . . I hope you can understand that we will have to eliminate any mention of his illness or hospital stay since we will not be covering that. I hope I haven't totally offended you."

I replied that I understood that expectant parents would be bothered by Alex's birth and the aftermath, and that I appreciated the editor's concern. "I hope," I wrote, "you can appreciate that I can't edit references to the conditions, medical equipment and special care under and with which Alex lives. I feel that for me to do so wouldn't be fair to him. It wouldn't tell the same story." I was not offended. I don't know what I felt.

Nor was I offended a month ago, when two kids watched us wheeling Alex down the sidewalk and we heard one of them say, "Hey, what happened to that guy?"

They called him *guy*! we thought. They called Alex a guy! "'Guy' is a peer thing," Jill said.

She spends most of the time with Alex on the street. Last week the local 99-cent store refused to let her and Alex in because he required a carriage (to carry his oxygen tank). Yesterday a man helped her and my son and his carriage and his oxygen up the stairs, and when he was done he touched her shoulder and said, "Bless you." Not long ago on the sidewalk a woman zeroed in and demanded, "He's gonna be okay, right?!"

I wheel Alex through the grocery store, and people glance at the cannula and at the oxygen torpedo. Some smile. Some move. The couple who run the laundromat are nice; they have a baby about the same age, who is always snoozing under a mound of blankets. At the toy store, Alex's carriage and tank won't fit through the fencing they have to contain shopping carts, and once the handicapped entrance was blocked by a chained-up bike. The manager had it moved.

"How old was his mother?" a woman on the playground asked me. (None of her fucking business, is Jill's answer.) Is he breathing through that? people wonder. "What's he got under his nose?" asked a woman at a church sale. I said a cannula. "Oh I thought he had some kind of toy," she said.

People generally get out of your way, Jill reports. "Because they don't want to catch what they think he's got," Aunt Julie points out.

A lot has assaulted my faith in human kindness. Doctors who yelled at us. Nurses who told us to get over it. Friends and relatives who couldn't believe doctors or nurses really behaved that way, and what was the exact date when we could expect Alex to just get better, anyway? Editors who demanded "a plateau" in his progress. Other parents who thought it did me good to hear that because of my family, they were going home that night and hug their kids. Attempts at kindness came to feel like slaps.

Now we wheel around the streets, a family on oxygen, Alex looking around, me looking at the people looking at him. I can see them wonder: How long will he have that? Should I forget the sight of this? I too once wondered how people got through their lives with wheelchairs, crutches, bodies that aren't what most bodies are supposed to be. With every wobble and slanted thump of a foot not under control, every jerk of a neck or unsummoned grunt I used to wonder, How does your family live with this?

Things happen to people, sometimes people you love, and pretty soon medical gear all over your house seems no more odd than the wallpaper of a neighbor's kitchen. "Offended" is the wrong word. I am angry not that the world has chosen one more way to make me feel different, but that it has chosen to make my son and wife pay for my difference. That is the story I live with as I unknot tubes and change a diaper and bash a pulse ox monitor, as I prime a feeding pump and screw a gauge onto a fresh torpedo of air. I can even feel sorry for parents who don't do those things and who see only medical gear when they look at Alex.

Santa's back in the window of an apartment up the street. The Santa, which lights up, is about twenty inches tall. His arm moves up and down, up and down, and his head tilts back and forth as he wishes us a Merry Christmas from behind dirty glass. I noticed this Santa a year ago.

I expect that this year, I won't be coming from a hospital on Christmas afternoon. I will instead, I hope, just be unplugging our Christmas tree and balling up the wrapping paper for Alex to twist through his fingers. This holiday should be Thanksgiving and New Year's and Christmas in one. We've been disconnecting his feeding tube for longer and longer periods, and last night he lunged forward, lips apart, for four spoonfuls of blueberry-apple baby glop. Jill has him drinking from a bottle at the end of the day, a cut of Pediasure and water which he sucks down while she softly sings, "The bear went in the woods today, all day long, thirsty bear . . ." He looks into her face, the yellow formula bubbling around his lips.

We take him into the living room with us for dinner each night (ours, not his); last night he kept chattering and hopping on his haunches in the carriage. He wags his head "No!" and goes "dee dee dee." Twice last night he curved his tongue around an "L" sound. Several times in his crib he said what I'm convinced was "Da!" Leave him alone and he'll explore a new toy. Every day around 5:30 the hungry bear gets cranky. When he wants to be picked up he makes what Jill calls "the sad monkey" sound. When he makes this sound and you stand him up, he'll head right for the metal support of the crib rail and grab it, and across his face comes an expression of deep concentration. I have to speak to Alex to recapture his attention.

In the crib he doesn't so much crawl yet as lurch, often pitching forward face-first onto the mattress. I used to check him every time after these crash-landings; since I always found him smiling I don't check anymore. Last weekend he started turning the boom box over and over in his crib (with a little help from Dad). He bounces and flaps his arms and gurgles, and a few times he's trembled on the brink of saying, "Da da!" Last night Jill made him giggle a real little-boy giggle that he didn't have three days ago. When I stepped back from the corner a little past ten, Jill called me into his room. She was holding him.

Why wasn't he asleep?

"Jeff, he can pull himself up to standing now," Jill said.

I woke up at 5:30 this Christmas morning, eager for the day. That hasn't happened in three years. We have a rotund, two-foot-high potted tree. We took it home and, while Alex stared at a tape of "A Charlie Brown Christmas," draped it with stuff from the year. The beads and plastic chain links he plays with; a binkie; one of our old passes from the hospital. The star at the top is the July Fourth pinwheel we bought for his first birthday.

"Strange little tree," I said to Jill when we'd finished.

"Strange little year," she replied.

Earlier this week his pediatrician—whose bill we just erased using a generous holiday check from Alex's grandparents—said Alex looked great. Doing what he should be doing, drooling when he should be drooling, getting into what he should be getting into. "Pretty soon you'll have to kid-proof," the ped said. They say you must first kid-proof the cabinets under the kitchen sink. Then electrical outlets, then everything else. It must be a sad day when you don't have to kid-proof anymore.

This strange little year will be over in a few days, and a strange new time will begin. By next Christmas we'll have kid-proofed all the cabinets, only to find that he can get into other things.

We're feeding Alex because we're sick of the feeding pump. The pump, about the size of a paperback, puts 60 ccs an hour of formula into Alex through a plug in his midsection. The blue plastic nozzle of the tube slides in and locks into place; we cover it with a long strip of paper tape and anchor the tube with more tape to the front of Alex's diaper. Every night we throw out the feeding bag and tubing that hangs beside the pump, and wash out the nozzle end with hot water and white vinegar. Fifteen to sixteen hours of nibbles per day rather than three meals—the contraption seems at once sophisticated and crude.

This tube and tip and "lock" business was never built for a baby who's learning to stand, crawl, and in general move into the world. More and more often we find the tip has silently dislodged. We discover Alex's tummy, navel, diaper and clothing slimy and sticky from formula that the pump has stupidly continued to drip.

This happens now. "God, I'm sick of this thing!" I say, stripping the tube and nozzle—my son has a nozzle!—off his diaper and flinging it to the floor. Jill fetches the Mop & Glo and gets on hands and knees to wipe the yellow dots. The pump remains Velcroed to the side of the crib. Alex is also learning how to undo Velcro.

I work with a tiny bottle of Gerber's No. 2 blueberry-apple stuff usually between six and 6:30 at night, just before his bath. Jill oversees beverages after the bath. The blueberry-apple stuff smells, feels and tastes like applesauce but is the color of grape gum. We keep it in the fridge. I take half a tablespoon of the

stuff and put it in one of Jill's coffee cups and give it five seconds in the microwave. I take it out, add another half-table-
spoon of the cold stuff, swish it together and head to Alex's
room. I sit him facing me, spread a towel across his knees, and
whip out the dry baby spoon. He takes it. The feeding therapist
has recommended we scrub his cheeks first with a cool, wet
washcloth, but I never do this. He takes the spoon and puts the
rubber part between his teeth. He's gotten good at holding it.
Sometimes the handle angles up and he looks like FDR with a
cigarette holder.

He slaps at the spoon, quickly turning the handle slimy with
food. When we started this exercise months ago, he would often turn the spoon over and over and about half the time tuck
the metal end between his teeth. Now he never misses: always
the rubber end. "A-di-ah!" constitutes his dinnertime chat. He
drops the spoon and claps, spraying his face and forehead with
pinhead spots of purple food. I bob my head back and forth
and go, "Boop, boop, boop."

But life isn't made up of jaunty angles as you try to reac-
quaint your baby son with a sense of taste. I take the spoon back.
This goes on and on until most of a tablespoon of lukewarm
blueberry-apple stuff is inside Alex, or smearing his fingers, or
dappling his blanket and bib. Or all three. A couple of weeks ago
he routinely downed five or six baby spoonfuls of the food, opening his mouth and keeping his hands down where they belonged.
Lately though he's been grabbing the spoon, yanking it away to
one side then mashing his fingers in the contents before finally
bringing the whole mess to somewhere near his mouth.

Lately our spoon-feeding sessions disintegrate into sessions
of Whap the Night Stand. This passes time until I strip him for
his bath. Later I bring him back and Jill has mixed a bottle of
water and Pediasure, a yellow formula. Through the past several weeks Alex has come to expect this bottle, lolling on his
back and popping his mouth wide. He sucks down about half
the bottle, sometimes all of it. When he drinks all of it I like to

peer through the bottom of the plastic bottle and watch the last yellow drops vanish out of the end of the nipple, and into Alex. We've tried to get him to eat sitting up, but angling the bottle is tough for him. He loves to drink lying down.

As with chest PT, we sing to Alex during feeding. I sing a man's songs.

I sing like a hinge, but Alex doesn't seem to mind and everyone says singing is a good way to distract a baby. Only distracted babies eat. "You can feed him anything," the pediatric nurse says, "anything we could eat." In addition to the bottles, we give him minuscule spoonloads of tomato soup, cheese and eggs, and mashed potato, which of course he doesn't so much eat as smear. Refreshingly normal.

Alex's GI, Dr. L., thinks "anything we could eat" also includes Pediasure in strawberry, vanilla, banana cream and chocolate. We've tried to spice things up with cinnamon and lemon curd. Our Instant Breakfast Initiative fizzled; I bring the packets into my office to have in the afternoon instead of all those vending machine bags of Ruffles.

Alex drinks up to seventeen ounces a day now, four to four and a half a feeding. We try to feed Alex four times a day. Sometimes we hit it, but Jill's notebook shows a ragged day-to-day history of slurping: 16 ounces, 14 ounces, 9 ounces, 11 ounces, 15, 11, 9. Dr. L. says Alex needs 24 ounces by mouth per day before we can pack the pump away. Jill feeds him during the day, while I'm at work. "It's a struggle," she often reports.

She likes to sing "Working on the Railroad" and "What Should We Do With a Drunken Sailor?" She holds Alex looser when she's feeding him. I'm not sure about the title of that "Drunken Sailor" song because I don't sing it to him. I curl my arm under his back, his head resting on my biceps, and I mold his legs into a little diamond on my thigh and tip up the bottle:

Nothing goes down like pink, pink strawberry. Alex has learned hunger, I think. Now we're trying to teach him about meals. For a while singing was my best weapon. Lately I've added toys to the arsenal. He likes the caps of baby bottles, pieces of the crib mobile long-since stripped, and big syringes (no needles). Wooden blocks are good but he tries to put them in his mouth. The baby sunglasses are good for at least an ounce and a half.

"Alex!" I say. "That's just three ounces. C'mon. You can do four—c'mon, be the bottle! Where are your sunglasses?"

The right toy is good for two ounces. If the toy is too small he'll chew it and ignore the nipple. If it's too big he'll drop it to crash on the uncarpeted wooden floor. The right toy is never the same toy two days in a row. Last weekend's Baby Boombox made way Monday night for the Giant Keys. Grandma's String and Bell Thing and Mom's Old Yogurt Cup are dependable, but both got the gentle release of little fingers (*crash!*) last night in favor of the Farm Motif Abacus.

Within a week, we're able to get about twenty-five ounces a day into him from a bottle, mostly canned formula and instant breakfast. Last night we sat him in the high chair and Jill gave him baby spoons of Cool Whip while I packed away the feeding pump, yanking the zipper closed. The shucking of the machines continues.

First to get the zipper way back was the home suction machine, basically a medical vacuum cleaner with a thin catheter that slipped down Alex's nose or throat and sucked out mucus. Alex hated the thing, which sounded loud as a lawn mower even before it located any mucus; then it sounded like a boot being pulled out of mud. I hated it because the reservoir for the suctioned mucus was see-through. Jill plain hated it.

Alex is also kicking drugs. Now he gets three injections through his feeding tube in the evening and three in the morning. Jill and I have quietly discontinued his noon Zantac, another checkmark in our campaign to end all his medications and machines by summer. The other day at the hospital for a checkup we asked the GI if we could officially shuck the noon Zantac. "Why would you want to do that?" Dr. L. asked. "You want him to suffer?" He added that if Alex ever failed to drink down all the formula needed at a meal, we could "squirt" the remainder into his button.

Alex still has some machines. An air concentrator broadcasts a wall of white noise across our living room. Once or twice a day we fill a tiny vial with liquids that once upon a time we couldn't spell and turn on the nebulizer, which sends a mist over Alex's nose and mouth. Every night we wrap a monitor on his big toe and turn on the pulse ox. "We're the parents of a pulse ox," Jill said in the middle of one endless night. "What about being done with everything by June? July at the latest?"

Alex himself has hinted that he might dump all the machines and medicines someday. The first hint came late last summer, when he was checked back into the hospital and they took away his cannula and replaced it with fat tubes called CPAP. "I'm not impressed with his need for CPAP," a doctor said. That doctor should see Alex now. When he came home, he needed a liter and a half of oxygen from the portable air tanks. Now we wheel him out in his carriage on a quarter of a liter; we know he's getting the air he needs because he twists around against the straps until he's facing backward. In the grocery store he tried to knock over a $10 cake, and you can't do that if you're short of air.

The other day Alex was napping in his crib, wearing a monitor, when I slipped the cannula out of his nostrils. His numbers dripped, steadied, then rose and took to the sky. They held for an hour, or so another machine told me. The next day we tried it and his numbers held again. I'd never seen him longer than a few minutes without some tentacle of a machine on his face.

"I'm not impressed with his need for oxygen," says Jill.

A week after the pump was packed away, Alex drinks about half the formula he needs for breakfast. I squirt the rest into the button, and in a few minutes he begins to retch. "I don't like the sound of that," Jill says from our bedroom, and he spits up a puddle of sour pink and then coughs for half an hour. Done with everything four months from now?

One of the last of his incoming teeth is taking its time, and it has turned his lower right gum into a red bulge. We think it must hurt. Jill and I give him Tylenol and tell ourselves that our son has been conditioned to have a high threshold of pain. Neither of us mention that you don't really want your child conditioned to have a high threshold of pain.

We bring in a feeding therapist. She's in our house for a couple of hours, shoveling opinions about Alex's neck muscles and brain before she gets down to the feeding. She watches him with a bottle and declares his suck "weak." She says we should throw out the special purees—Jill had liquefied some take-out Chinese from the night before—and skip right to solids. "Twizzlers and cheese doodles," the therapist says, "and put the Twizzlers in the fridge for a while first." She charges $330.

I eat the Twizzlers, which Alex uniformly turns down. Cheese doodles seem headed for a similar fate one Sunday afternoon in the high chair, when suddenly Alex accidentally bites off a florescent orange chunk no bigger than you might brush off your pants. His face begins to fall apart; his tongue squirms and his fingers fly for his mouth.

"Alex NO! Alex LOOK!"

I think Alex has figured out when a hard voice is trying to help. He does look, and I put my mouth and tongue though deliberate, slow convulsions of chewing and swallowing. He watches me, then tries to do it. The orange bit appears on his lip. He bites the doodle again. Not bites, exactly, but lays his teeth on the cheesy crust until there is a soft rasp. Then he brings the doodle down and chews nothing. His face looks grave.

Within three weeks, Alex is pretty smooth with a cheese doodle. Up, in, rasp, chew. The doodles disappear. I haven't checked the floor, though.

We're still trying to drizzle formula into him, still counting the bubbles while the GI doctors stand in the background. His gum gets bigger and redder, and in the notebook his daily total of ounces of formula steadily falls: 21, 22, 20, 19. Seven ounces of strawberry at a meal become an achievement for a boy who should be demolishing packs of Arrowroots. Give it a week, Dr. L. says.

I tell Jill that I can't be the one to hook him back up to the pump. I say to Alex that breakfast is the most important cheese doodle of the day.

On Friday, March 3, I order cannulas for Alex. We have let the stockpile in our home dwindle to none, but I'm confident we can get more from our home-equipment supplier within one or two business days. I order four or so pediatric cannulas, two humidifier bottles for Alex's air concentrator, and as many pulse ox probes as the Home Equipment Gods decide we deserve.

The cannulas are critical. We're down to one that was giving out in cannulas' Achilles' Heel: the little plastic thing that plugs onto the air tubing that runs from the concentrator, and the little plastic thing at the back that tightens the cannula and keeps the prongs in the nostrils of a crazy, active, unreasonable baby. "I'll send them out today," says the supplier's phone rep, Tori (not her real name), on March 3.

March 7 rolls around with no shipment. I grab the phone. "Okay," says Tori, "I see they went out on the sixth. And you don't have anything?"

I don't have anything.

"Should be there tomorrow," she says.

Isn't. Next day, the mail guy does hand me a UPS envelope that's suspiciously thin. I open it. Two probes and a one-page invoice done on an old dot-matrix printer in crying need of toner. Two probes, ten bucks each. Yup. In the sections describing the humidifier bottles and the cannulas, someone had drawn a big black "X." I've learned that it takes 4.5 phone conversations to convince a home-equipment supplier that what they happen to need to clear out of their warehouse may or may not be the equipment your child needs.

I tell Tori about the X. "Does it also say 'BO?'" she asks.

No, I reply, there's no indication that anything's been back-ordered. I think she dislikes that I knew what "BO" meant.

"I'll look into it," she says.

March 9, March 10, another weekend. Jill finds an unopened cannula in a bottom drawer, and we carefully coil the old one and put it in the drawer where we can find it in an emergency. Nothing has ever happened to a cannula Alex was wearing—no breaks, cuts, or rips in the plastic—but why wait?

Still waiting I am, however, after the UPS delivery of Monday the 13th. I call Tori's supervisor. He's a friendly and helpful man with a German first name but no trace of anything but a Long Island accent. I tell him the tale so far, ending with the X. "I will ship you the rest out today," Franz (not his real name) says.

March 15: The contents that spill from the UPS box late that morning include two humidifier bottles with brown tops instead of the blue I was used to; I guess they might work. From behind the bottles tumble just two coils of air tubing.

"Franz!" I say into the phone. Where are the cannulas? I can't even use the tubing because it's only seven feet long, hardly enough for a crazy, active, unreasonable baby.

"So even if the order had been right, it would've been wrong," Franz marvels.

Gosh, that's true! Get me the right stuff by tomorrow. "We will have a delivery there tomorrow at your office!" Franz says. "No charge."

In the nuances of home-equipment supply, "a" delivery is not the same as "the" delivery. On Thursday morning out tumble four pediatric cannulas. The prongs are green and flared, and you couldn't get them into Alex's nose without surgery. I leave a message for Franz. So does Jill. I call him an hour later. Out to lunch. Jill calls Franz's boss. Later she reports that the boss personally picked out the order and it would be at my office Monday. "Tori said she was going to send whatever she had on hand," Jill adds. "I told her to feel free, but if it wasn't what we needed we would just throw it away."

It's Sunday the 19th. I just screwed one of the brown-top bottles onto the concentrator, and it seems to work. When I re-attach Alex's cannula, the last good one we have, the little plastic thing that plugs into the air tubing feels decidedly loose. While Alex naps I disconnect him to test how long he can breathe on his own now. Fifteen minutes, then his numbers drop, and I reconnect the tube.

ALEX IS STANDING.

That's a generous way to put it, maybe. But I just turned around and found him upright and holding onto the railing of the crib. I never put him there.

"He *does* stand," proclaims Jill. "I wouldn't say it's a 'generous' way to put it at all." She's seen him pull himself up. I have seen him grab the railings as if about to demand to see the warden. Then he rests his elbows on the railing and holds with his arms while you raise the railing and, viola!: standing. Often he wobbles like a cute drunk, his legs sliding into a V. He makes his way hand over hand, lift of the leg by lift of the leg, around about a third of the perimeter of the crib. He bows his back and looks up. Sometimes the knees buckle. Then he goes plop.

Whatever the outcome, the look on his face is electric. "Incredulous, amazed, proud—a big smile of accomplishment," says Jill.

Accomplishment, that variety of milestone most parents mention in their later years with sweet loss for the passing of their own lives. We don't have time for such stuff. There's eating, breathing and standing to be done.

He's trying to learn all three, but he's furthest ahead in standing. Close behind is crawling. Jill discovered this by placing Alex on the floor, on a spotless mat and watching him wiggle without hesitation toward the dusty radiator. She turned him around. He broke for the electrical outlets under the crib. I came home that night to "Jeff we have to babyproof!"

Alex's movement doesn't surprise me. At birth, he came out squirming. I've wondered what he saw at that moment, looking up at the three faces in green masks, three wise men who wanted wires on him and a tube down his throat. He fought the wires they glued to his chest and the air tube they slid past his lips. Preemies' milestones are different from the milestones for most kids; loss has no place in what I feel when watching Alex inch around the railing. Knees thick and stiffening as they take his twenty pounds. Babble trembling on words. These are moments instantly gone for me, true. But they're also moments a lot of people tried to tell me I'd never have. "Who said Alex would never walk?" Jill asks.

I don't remember. Somebody did, apparently not caring that tough people, no matter their size, tend to move around. I remember a neonatologist leaning against the wall on Alex's second day of life and saying we were "getting ahead of ourselves" talking about learning disabilities, which that doctor had brought up in the first place. Later they said they'd "hoped Alex would do better" with weight gain.

Some people never doubted. I wish John could see Alex stand. John was an orderly in our first hospital. John was a happy guy, with a beard and glasses and salt-and-pepper hair. His grandson had been a preemie, and at the time of our hospitalization his grandson weighed eighteen pounds. John would always put his arm around Jill and tell us Alex was going to be all right.

"Who said he'd never walk?" Jill asks.

I think of some hospitals, some doctors, the way an exile thinks about the police back home. I should just forget, should turn around to see those thick knees stiffen and see the world at last where it belongs. Under my son's feet.

He shoots upright in the crib without a thought or a pause. Tilt him over and he pops up. In a blink he's at the crib railing. The smart little toy! In a blink he is at the railing, and he's begun to climb. I see his feet are not on the mattress. One is flat against the vertical bars of the crib, the other scrambling for purchase anywhere higher. He makes his industrious noise: "A goy goy goy . . ."

Jill and I have dropped the mattress of the crib to the last rung. "You know," says Jill, "my mother says she came into my room when I was a baby and found me crawling along the edge of the crib railing . . ." We have shelving near the head of his crib. We keep the binkies in there. It used to be beyond his reach. Last night he hooked his arms over the railing—lot of hooking going on—and as his feet shot three inches off the mattress he began to trample the bumpers, the blankets, anything that stood between him and Up. I think he grunted.

"Alex, no!" I pried him off the railing and cast him down on the mattress—in a gentle, fatherly way—and then, as now, he popped up and started climbing again. Smart little toy, with die-hard batteries. He seized the railing and started flexing back and forth. I heard the wood creak. "A goy goy goy." He is fit and solid, as much cat as human.

If his cannula comes out of his nose, he's often the one who puts it back. I see his little fingers test the entrance of the little nostril, and marvel. I take his hands and he'll waddle between my legs all the way to the lower cupboards of the kitchen, which always arrest his attention. He lifts his foot over his air tube without a glance. Put him on all fours in the living room and he will crawl, slow and unswerving, into the bedroom, where he will reach up with both hands and try to climb aboard the bed. Up there is Fluffy Blanket. And he knows that Mom and Dad will wrap him and help him swing. He gallops the slipping wooden horse from the front of the entertainment unit all the way back to the rattan couch. Every night he hauls back and forth on the crib railing.

"A goy goy goy." We're all climbing away from what we were. Fluffy Blanket is perpetually rumpled; our apartment has been redone in Early 21st Century Plastic Baby Toy; the mobile, long ago stripped to its stump, remains screwed to the head of the crib. I should buy him a new mobile, I think night after night as I tuck him in, plug the feeding tube into his stomach and wrap the oxygen monitor on his toe. This morning, I woke to find him still asleep but the cannula out of his nose. On the monitor, his numbers stayed high for twenty minutes.

Last night I looked in expecting to find him asleep and instead found him tugging his weight from side to side on the crib rail. He spied me in the doorway and said, "Ha!" Then he reached up and grabbed the stump of the mobile with both hands, and jerked it to one side and then the other. His legs came off the mattress, and hung in the air. My feeling grows that soon nothing will be safe.

Jill and I got up late this morning and talked about exhaustion. It was past eight a.m., Alex was still asleep. Jill and I sat on the couch, where we never sit for coffee anymore. The clock crawled to 8:25 and Alex slept on. He's supposed to have eaten by 8:30. I'm supposed to have fed him.

That is the deal Jill and I have. I do the waking and the morning feed. By 7:30, I should have started prying Alex awake, gently jiggling him and calling his name until he broke into a stiff stretch and his mouth turned down in a stifled yawn.

"It's the past two years, Jill," I said on the couch, thoughts coming clearer with the coffee. "It all started even further back than that. I'm afraid we're just going to get Alex squared away when this is all going to catch up to one of us." I ask her if she'll make me a sandwich for lunch. She says yes, but can I please wake Alex?

He's perpendicular to how I last saw him, at three a.m. To wake him, I use my favorite tactic of checking the diaper. His eyes open, and as the sticky straps of the new diaper take hold he rolls to all fours and pops up. It's 8:30. I have to leave. I don't like these days when I don't see him in the morning.

I head to work, leaving Jill coaxing Alex on her lap, the bottle in his lips. I place his feet in a little diamond shape on her lap. She says that isn't important. I should just go, so she can try to get six ounces or so into him. I ride the train into Manhattan. It's an old train, rattling and with lights that wink out. We stop twice in the tunnels. At Times Square I transfer to the Broadway line for one stop downtown to Penn Station. There I weave through the mobs of Long Island commuters on my way to the escalator to the street. The loudspeaker tells me, "Welcome to Amtrak's Pennsylvania Station. Please use caution when riding the escalators. Welcome to Amtrak's Pennsylvania Station. Please use caution . . ." I board the escalator leading up to 7th Avenue. I have been doing this for two years. I no longer hear the loudspeaker.

What if he doesn't take six ounces? Will I reach my office to find the stabbing red message light lit on my phone? Or will it be an e-mail? "Baby just took 3. Couldn't do more. Very tired and depressed. Really need you to do the morning feed."

But in my office there's no red light, no e-mail. I try to plunge into work. I want a desk without a phone. But at a new job, I bet I'd never get out by five. I can also come in at 9:30 on those days when my morning routine staggers under the weight of the last two years. I phone Bernie, my father-in-law, who says that he'll get the papers for what will soon be our new apartment by ten a.m. and get them to Jill to sign, then run them by my office for me to sign. Does Jill know this? I consider calling her. The hum of the fan in my computer sounds like the ripple of quiet water. I phone Jill. Bernie is there.

"We're signin'!" Jill says. "Can I call you later?" At 2:30, Jill calls. Did Bernie drop by my office? Yes, and we have a week to apply for a mortgage. How's Alex? I ask. "He didn't like the feel of the mashed banana," Jill says, "but he does like the Cheetos, and you know that in the beginning he didn't eat them. Let's see how the sippy cup goes." Pause. "He is drinking from the sippy cup, I think. But he's only getting a few drops. His table manners are so crappy." In the background he sounds like a monkey swinging on an old hinge.

I swore I wouldn't ask, but I do. How much has he eaten today?

"Oh, eight ounces," Jill says. "I decided we were just going for an eight-ounce breakfast." How much since then? Two Cheetos, so Jill signs off to feed him.

Soon she calls again. "He's taken . . . two and half ounces in fifteen minutes!" she says. "He squirms, he fusses, he jerks his head away and it gets all over his shirt!" Halfway through our talk, Jill starts crying. Not a shoulder-shaker, just a sob or two. "That makes, what, eleven ounces for the day?" she says. "That's not even half of what he needs!"

No, it isn't. I hang up and take a call from Microsoft. I don't know what they want. When the woman is finished talking to me, I still don't know. A few minutes later Jill sends me an e-mail: "Alex took 4 1/2. Includes a bit of spillage. Why oh why does this have to be so hard? Feeling bitter. Call me if you have time this afternoon. We have to talk about dinner." I call her. I say four to five ounces is pretty good, and maybe some of the physical therapists coming this afternoon can offer tips on positioning Alex during feeding. After all, he's about three inches longer these days than last summer, and Jill isn't. "You're what, five-four?" I ask her.

"I love you," she says.

"I know you do."

I go home, riding the winking train and walking the familiar sidewalk. I have no other memory of getting home, but when I arrive Alex is asleep. So is Jill. The evening begins. Later, in two sittings that night, broken by a bath, a gallop on the rocking horse and a nosh of Cheetos, Alex takes nine ounces. I hold him while he drinks. He still fits well in my arms, though I feel that I missed his day.

Headlines from Alex at home:

—Opening and shutting cabinets. Mostly in the kitchen. Stands up, grasps, pulls one open and then the other, peers inside, closes doors. Over and over. Earlier this spring, needed two hands on the cabinet handles to keep standing. No more.

Agitated when he can't get to the cabinets because we're using the portable dishwasher. Would like to figure out how to open dishwasher, preferably while it's running. Also likes the drawers on the entertainment unit. Careful to keep his fingers clear (last night he did catch them closing the napkin drawer; howled in the bathroom). Always closes whatever he opens.

—No cannula during changing of shirts. Bathing without cannula. A lot easier to scrub his cheeks and under his nose. Bare face looks striking and mature.

—Waving with both arms at once, then clapping. Then making Grandpa wave.

—Moving furniture. Grandma was over on Sunday and asked, "Does he get any exercise?" That night he pushed the living room table across the floor until it was flush against the bookcase. Alignment took several tries, from many different angles. Daddy watched from couch. Daddy does not get any exercise.

—Trying to tip over the playpen. Just starting to do this. Not sure where it's going.

—Doing that thing with his finger that the little boy does in *The Shining*. Bearing in mind what happened to Jack Nicholson at the end of the movie, Daddy tells Alex to stop.

—Sharing. Other night while Alex was munching a Cheeto, Daddy put his face close and asked if Daddy could have some. Alex held it out toward Daddy's mouth. Daddy took little nibble, Alex took little nibble, Daddy took another little nibble and so on until Cheeto was tiny and Daddy was almost melting. Alex held out last Cheeto nub for Daddy, who tried to put all of remaining Cheeto into his mouth. Alex quickly pulled back Cheeto nub and ate it.

—Falling with less impact to skull, more plopping on his butt and reassessing situation. Rode in Mom's handcart, then started pushing it. Grabs the handles and just shoves. He may have discovered what the front door is for. Still crawling when there are miles to be made.

—Dismounting sideways off the rocking horse and getting stuck between the seat and safety bar.

—Twisting out of his seat in the carriage. Followed by standing up and facing backwards.

—Reaching for stuff. Yellow flowers in a pot on 7th Avenue. Precariously stacked items in the grocery store.

—Pounding at the computer with Mom or Daddy. Pounds with a ferocity Daddy used to reserve for tight spots in Duke Nukem. Disconnected decoy keyboard is a failure. Chats online with Aunt Julie, who answers him in twenty-point type.

—Tugging J-tube until almost an inch of clear tubing worms out of the hole in his stomach. Daddy asks him to stop, but why should he? He didn't ask for the damned thing.

—Understanding words. "Push" and "pull" mean help Daddy get the tray off the high chair. "Story" means he doesn't have to go to sleep.

—Trilling. Loud. Loudest when tired. Reminds Mom of a lemur. Daddy can't make this sound, unless you count gargling. Mom can do this. So can Daddy's big brother, who used to call it "the chipmunk noise" and pestered Daddy with it through the 1960s. Alex needs a little brother.

—Setting the pulse ox off at night again. Nothing wrong with Alex's breathing. Suspect he's getting too big for the probes. E-mailed manufacturer about adjusting the sensitivity to movement. Answer came back saying buy one of their newer, more expensive machines.

—Not going to sleep.

Then there's his weight. Today we see the GI. Last night I told Jill that we're just going to get his opinion and realize that we're not going to change it. We think Alex still weighs about twenty pounds. Nineteen, maybe. We see Dr. L., whose instructions we've ignored for so long that to go back and follow them now would be an impossible backtrack. We're not using the feeding tube. We're sure Dr. L. will order us to. We will then refuse and have to find another doctor. Jill and I have one goal at this meeting, and only one question which was recommended by one of Alex's therapists: What does Alex have to do to get rid of the feeding tube?

Gain weight, obviously. But we feed him all he'll take—sweet potatoes, bananas, prunes, applesauce spiked with heavy cream, cereal and maple syrup, Pediasure and fortified babies' yogurt. It totals about thirty ounces a day. I've stopped counting. I have no clue how many ounces of Spam I had for lunch yesterday, how many milligrams of spaghetti pie I downed for dinner last night. Counting the ounces made me feel as if Alex still belonged to the hospital.

In Dr. L.'s office, we unhitch Alex from the carriage. He takes off, crawling to the receptionist's desk. Slap slap slap go his palms on the tile floor. I trail after him with the small oxygen tank. He crawls up to strangers and tries to crawl into the back hall of examination rooms. I go to remove his cannula.

"Don't do that!" Jill says. "I don't want him to burn calories. Ever."

He's still burning them, though, when Dr. L. appears. He has glasses, a gray goatee, a soft voice and light-blue eyes. A year ago, when other doctors wanted to do an even more severe surgery on Alex, Dr. L. was the only one who said we did the right thing by just getting the feeding tube.

We go into his office; all the grown-ups take a seat. Dr. L. asks me if I have a cold. I say I caught it from Alex. He asks if Alex has been retching, coughing, or choking? No, no, not at all. What is he eating? We tell him.

"All by mouth?" he asks. Jill answers most of the questions as Alex twists and scrambles in my arms. He needs a change; it takes three of us, a binkie, and a plastic toy. Then he's weighed. Remember that number, Dr. L. says, wrapping a tape measure around Alex's skull, and tries to get Alex to lie flat for a length measurement. Alex won't even lie flat to get a diaper change anymore. The measurements show that since his last appointment eight weeks ago, Alex is shorter by about ten percent.

That would be like me waking up tomorrow and being 5'4". That's the kind of measurement you get when you try to measure a boy who's moving the furniture.

Dr. L. puts pencil to graph, however, to draw a dot marking the spot of Alex's new weight. Strung together, the dots make a curve that flattens and is drawing farther and farther from the big blue shaded area marked "normal." Once dots on a graph start looking like that, doctors can do one of two things. Most will hold up the chart, hold up the pencil, and use the two props to let you have it. Or they can do something else.

Dr. L. lets a short silence linger before saying, "Well, you know as well as I what has to be done. What is preventing him from taking thirty-five or thirty-six ounces a day?"

I don't know. Alex just always turns away after an inscrutable and insufficient number of spoonloads and bubbles in the bottle.

"I don't mind him being a little thin, as long as his brain continues to grow," Dr. L. says. He used that phrase two appointments ago, to Jill's terror. He goes on to say that as Alex's metabolism increases, he will burn more energy and need more food. Won't Alex get hungrier as a consequence? I ask. "Not necessarily," Dr. L. says. "Boy, look at him. He reminds me of a perpetual motion mobile."

I listen to Dr. L. *Get to the point,* I think. We are to go home, feed him as much as possible, and check in with Dr. L. again in two weeks. Boy, we think, it pays to dread the worst!

That night, after Alex's bath, before I can get the diaper on him, he urinates on the floor. Our disgusting little animal, our dear little son. I get a diaper on him and it seems loose. Then we feed him yogurt, applesauce with cream, bananas, and formula. He takes twenty-nine ounces.

We turn to powerful foods. One of Alex's therapists reports that when he was about two, all he'd take was milk until he tried bacon, and thereafter his mom's kosher household was ruined. Bacon is powerful. And this morning I smelled the smell.

This really started yesterday, when Jill exclaimed, "Guess who ate bacon!" Alex did, in a Queens Boulevard diner, a scrap from Jill's sandwich. "He just grew so *quiet*," Jill said. "There was a lot for him to think about all of a sudden . . ."

In his high chair we've administered a combo of bottle, baby yogurt, and jars of mush made out of peas, sweet potatoes, carrots, prunes, chicken, applesauce, and anything else that would lend itself to cereal thickener, heavy cream, and a squirt of Log Cabin syrup. We'd buckle him in and coat a baby spoon with the stuff, make him look up by rattling a toy, and slip it in. Sweet potatoes went over best. They still do, followed by peach mush as Daddy, who's getting weary of singing "Battle of New Orleans" and "Working on the Railroad," tries to impersonate Billy Joel. But Alex is getting bigger and more aware of what a good singer should sound like and what food should feel like. I think he wearies of having small spoonloads of softness slid into his mouth while enduring Daddy's rendition of "Honesty."

We're trying new food. Cheetos continue their reign: he nibbles them with contented grunts, and holds them out to let us take a bite. Yesterday, Jill made a milk shake of vanilla ice cream, vanilla instant breakfast and whole milk. Down Alex's hatch. We hope prune mush and baby yogurt have little chance once bacon and milk shakes hit town.

I fry up four slices, eat the two chewiest myself and crumble the other two for Alex. After he's taken almost a jar of sweet potato baby food, I set the plate of scrumptious dark crumbs in front of him. He picks up two and throws one on the floor. The other he puts on his tongue, closes his mouth, and chews like a big boy. Sort of. His chin sticks out and I see his jaw moving shallowly up and down, but after a minute it appears that something's wrong. His mouth forms a perilous little red "O" and he coughs as pink floods his cheeks. I spin in my own chair looking for any container that I don't value highly, and have nearly found one when the yellow spurt shoots from the O.

The yellow comes twice, leaving a single dribble down his chin, a flush in his cheeks, a tear under one of his eyes, and a mess somewhere in the seat of the chair to be attacked later with 409. I clean him up, hand him his green toy clock, and mix another batch of sweet potatoes. He takes most of that.

One night, I crouched down with the canister of Pringles. If you rattle a can of Pringles, Alex is on you as fast as he can come. He jammed his right arm down the canister and pulled out a Pringle (nacho-flavored, orange as a life vest). I expected him to start cramming the chip into his mouth, letting it disintegrate against his lips, letting the fragments flutter down and letting whatever made it to his mouth make it to his mouth. Instead, he brought the Pringle up, placed one edge between his teeth, and bit daintily, as if enjoying a teacake.

In lieu of pounds, we're hoping for daily progress in chewing. He's since carried the biting thing to other foods. But he inspects, carefully pinches, winces at and heaves from the high chair every other food. Feeding him is like feeding a mad king who's scared of poisoning.

*Oh my god! Oh my god! Scrape off my tongue!*

Recently I hit upon the brainstorm of mimicking a real meal when I feed him. Nibble. Nibble. Nibble. Drink.

*Juice? What kind of juice? No.*

I place one pretzel stick, one Tato Skin, and one strip of bacon on the tray of the high chair. I let him select what to eat in what order. I put my hand over his to control the depth of his bite, and when he's finished chomping all three I offer him a bottle. He still drinks from a bottle, through a big nipple into which we slashed an X with a paring knife. We've tried other beverages, in methods of delivery from sippy cup to shot glass.

*That's not a straw! It's a serpent from Hell! Serpent from Hell! Serpent from Hell!*

Oat Bran Squares don't really belong on the list yet, as they've only been in field use for a week and have suffered almost a fifty percent casualty rate, bouncing across the floor tiles for later pick-up by the bottom of an adult bare foot or, when swept up, to bounce back out of the dustpan. Life cereal recently failed a similar test spectacularly. Tato Skins were introduced because my vending machine at work happens to have them this week.

*New? Overboard!*

You must sneak in new stuff after priming Alex with pretzels or Cheerios. Even the Cheerios have gone sailing lately if they're used too soon. (I was surprised to learn about the entertainment empire that's been built on two-year-olds eating Cheerios. In a Manhattan Barnes & Noble, I saw shelves of puzzles, books and games. But where's the book and board game with Mom and Dad picking about a hundred Cheerios off the kitchen floor?) Cheerios I use chiefly for breakfast, or as filler between strips of bacon, the way steak houses use baskets of bread.

*Sigh.*

What's he got to sigh about? He gets to eat bacon every day. Crisp bacon: 2:20 in the microwave, on high. Any less and he might not chew it, but sort of gum it around into a wad destined for any feet that miss the Cheerios. Or the bacon might head to the floor, where I race Jill for possession. Since we've been feeding Alex, my diet has come to include, well, let's see, Cheerios, Oat Bran Squares, Tato Skins, pretzel sticks, and bacon. Also Stouffer's macaroni and cheese, an almost nightly yellow mound of hope that Alex still disdains.

*No! No bib! And put on a white shirt.*

The feeding therapist told us to "just put food on the tray and give him a spoon, and see what happens." Anybody who's ever been in a Spencer Gifts and seen that poster of the baby with the bowl of spaghetti on his head knows what happens. But Alex is dexterous with the spoon when we use Gerber Sweet Potatoes, which he once adored, and chocolate pudding. He will bash the bottom of the bowl with the spoon, then slowly bring it up between his lips. He seems to understand that the spoon has something to do with his future. He also understands that pudding makes outstanding hair conditioner.

*A dish? Of food? Let me see it. There!*

I beat Jill to what hits the floor. Scrumptious. I've gained nine pounds.

We're on the playground when we run into a neighbor. The neighbor has a little girl with what I think is a enormous, melon-sized head and legs like sausages. She's around nine months old. "She's about normal for nine months," Jill says. The girl inches up to Alex as he tries to relax in his stroller, and just keeps touching his toes. Grope grope grope. She's also a screecher. Alex is late for a nap, so I don't blame him when his face dissolves and he begins that deep wail that reminds you of the sound of a lost cat.

Alex's therapists say that he's in the stage of "parallel play." It was explained to me as when new toddlers run around in their own little world, seeing nothing ahead of the walker but their own imbalance and stumbling, shifting weight. They can play side-by-side with another person and never acknowledge or even see them. Sounds like my social life in high school.

It looks like a fun little world. On the playground, he assaults the baby gym glancing neither right nor left, or tools away on all fours until he's a speck. He flings himself on the Fisher-Price walker or Mom's pull-cart, thin legs pumping with abandon, his head down and sometimes the tip of his tongue out. From his perch in the baby swings, Alex sees only our faces swooping back and forth, back and forth, and of course we see only his. The other parents glance at the green aluminum oxygen tank and the swinging tubing. Some smile; some don't.

Older kids have been noticing Alex. What happened to the baby? one little girl asked, and another time in a grocery store I heard a girl say, "What happened? He's so cute!" The therapists say that around age four, kids grow out of parallel play. Alex may grow out of it faster. Recently on the playground Alex toddled right up and took hold of another little kid. I wasn't there, but from what Jill said it sounded cool. When we take him out in the carriage his head has started to be on a constant swivel from kid to kid, with a hard craning at a particularly interesting little person.

The other day in the doctor's waiting room, Alex was tooling, palms slapping the floor, as his late grandmother used to say, "just as tight's he can travel!" when a father brought in a little boy. The boy took one look at Alex; Alex took no looks at him. Later when we were coming out after Alex's exam, another little boy wanted to touch his cannula. Alex assumes a Douglas MacArthur stance for these kids: brown eyes level and unstirring, mouth fixed and unsmiling, chin slightly up. I think Alex doesn't know yet what to make of these confrontations. The boy's fingertip was almost on the cannula when his Dad pulled it away. Alex didn't wave bye. As we were wheeling out, a little girl in a dark short haircut and a blue dress went by, and Alex swiveled around to stare after her.

Soon he will be doing this all the time, and he will start to notice what's in front of him. The brown eyes will be upraised and scanning back and forth, and the legs will pump with a fraction less abandon. That will be too bad. Twilight will fade between toddler and boy, and suddenly Alex will know how to look around, and when to look away.

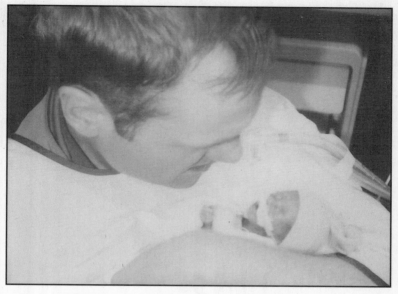

Jeff Stimpson and his son a few days after Alex was born.

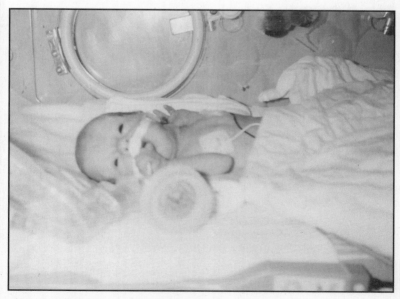

Alex, at about two weeks old.

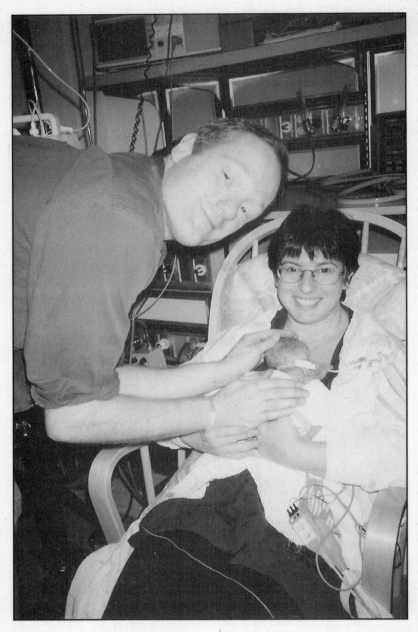

The Stimpsons and their son. Alex is about a month old here. Jill is wearing what she will later recall as her "big fake smile" *(Photo by Eric Hegedus)*.

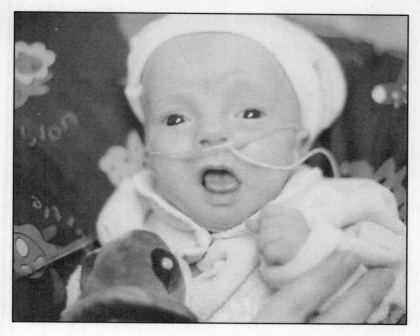

ABOVE: Fall, 1998. On Alex's face is a naso-gastric feeding tube, and a cannula to deliver oxygen. BELOW: Alex in December of 1998, about the time he came home for a week.

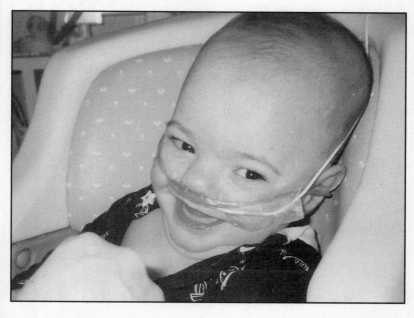

With dad on his first birthday, in the hospital, June, 1999.

Alex, after coming home, summer, 1999.

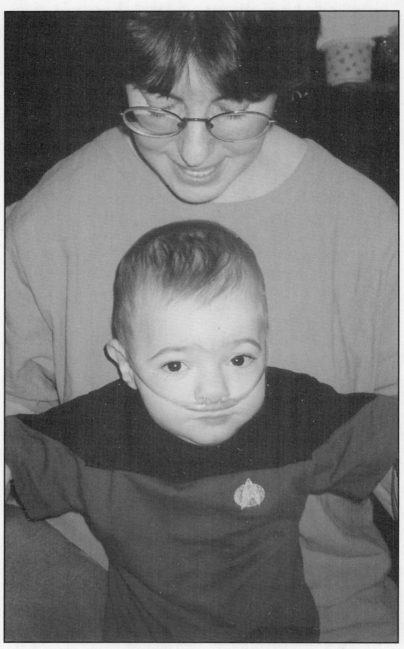

Alex and Jill on his first Halloween out of the hospital, 1999.

ABOVE: The first photo of Alex with no breathing apparatus on his face, summer, 2000. BELOW: With his newborn brother Ned, January, 2001.

On his third birthday, Alex tries chocolate cake and ice cream for the first time, June, 2001.

First trip to the ocean, summer, 2001.

Alex just before entering kindergarten, 2003.

THESE EVENTS TAKE place during a typical day:

7:30 to 7:45 a.m.: I lumber into his bedroom and find Alex either asleep or sitting up and tugging at his pulse ox probe. I think Alex looks sad doing this, so I flip him on his back and change his diaper. Then he sits quietly while I go to the kitchen to mix his breakfast and turn on the coffee.

7:45 to 8:30 a.m.: I buckle Alex into the high chair, get my coffee and a couple of towels. We get something going with toys, and I try to shovel the stuff in fast before he realizes he isn't chewing something and starts fussing. He likes to chew Cheerios. I put a few on the tray for him to munch whenever I get up to rinse the spoon or put the empty baby food bottle in the sink. I don't sing to him during breakfast; he doesn't seem to miss it.

8:45: On weekdays, I leave for work as Jill is usually wriggling him into the day's clothes. She prefers coveralls, a T-shirt, and matching socks. This is subject to the restrictions of our laundry pile. I tell him to have a good day, kiss him on the forehead, and try to leave him smiling.

9 to 10:45 a.m.: Somewhere in here, three days a week, his speech therapist shows up for half an hour. She digs beeping toys out of her bag, gets him interested, then takes them away and tries to make him ask for more by putting his fists together. When the therapist isn't there, Alex is rocking on his rocking horse, or toddling over to open cabinets, closets and the dishwasher. Walking

for him seems to be coming slower than for most kids, but he's going faster and straighter with each passing day.

11 a.m.: A snack. Two or three ounces of baby food and formula. Shifting these days to just Cheerios.

11:30 a.m. to 2 p.m. Maybe to the park or grocery (baby food) shopping with Jill. More closets and cupboards. Somewhere in here is about a ninety-minute nap, which Jill regards as a lifesaver.

2 to 2:30 p.m.: Lunch, about eight ounces of baby food, some with meat, plus Cheerios. Followed by a scrub by Jill.

3 p.m.: Occupational therapy. Crawling around.

4 p.m.: Physical therapy. Crawling around.

5 to 6:15 p.m.: The exhausted, cranky baby naps. So does her son.

6:15 p.m.: Daddy's home! I'm not sure Alex would put an exclamation point here, but I do.

6:15 to 6:30 p.m.: Waking Alex for the evening while taking care not to wake Jill.

6:30 to 7:30 p.m.: Dinner. This is the big meal that makes or breaks the day of feeding. Sweet potatoes, Cheetos, baby meats, peaches, prunes, cereal, cream, Cheerios, toys, songs, conversation, instant breakfast, anything that he'll sit still for. Last night we tried chicken rings from White Castle. Ten ounces is acceptable, thirteen, great. Scrubbing of all surfaces organic and plastic afterward.

7:30 p.m.: Bath time, after a stop at the mirror, at which he laughs and licks. Favorite games in the water include holding hands in the trickle, high-level bombing by rubber ducks, singing the "Gilligan's Island" theme while sinking the toy boat, standing up, and closing the shower door and looking at the blurry image of each other's face through the frosted glass.

7:45 p.m.: Drying, diaper application, change into nightclothes. Sits still for none of these.

7:45 to 8:15 p.m.: Dinnertime for us while Alex plays in the crib with the Disney music thing.

8:15 p.m.: Clearing of dinner dishes. Highly advisable before next activity.

8:15 to 9:15 p.m.: Tooling time around the living room and kitchen. Vehicles include rocking horse and Fisher-Price walker. More cabinets and closets, plus whapping of TV screen and moving of coffee table. Some time on couch crawling on parents.

9:15 to 9:30 p.m.: Snack. Sometimes just formula, often lately nothing, as he stiffens his back and cries at the first touch of the plastic of the high chair seat. Routine scrub afterward.

9:30 p.m.: Bed, stage one. Removal of socks and toys, dimming of light, issuing of sock for him to contemplate. First attempt to lie him flat.

9:31 p.m.: Second attempt to lie him flat. Storybook, usually *Good Night Moon* or *Spilt Milk*. When I get to the mitten page in *Milk*, Alex usually pats his hand on the page to see if the mitten would fit. Return to crib for "Bear in a Bear Cave" game under the fluffy blanket.

10 p.m.: Bed, stage two. Burrowing forehead into blankets, butt high in air, falling on side.

10:15 to 10:45 p.m.: Sleep. Wrap pulse ox probe on foot. Bed bed bed for Mom and Dad! Exclamation point here definitely needed.

All times approximate and subject to change.

Soon after, we get a letter saying that our power company, Con Edison, may not be able to continue to provide us special protections for Alex. "Like what?" I ask. I ask no one this question, figuring that would be about as effective as asking Con Ed.

When last fall finally arrived, I'd learned that Con Ed no longer sends out inspectors and hasn't provided generators in years. Around that time, the *Times* ran a story that Con Ed had known for months about the strong possibility of a blackout in Upper Manhattan and had done nothing. Last summer it took four phone calls to get the address from them even to send Alex's medical "certification." There was no fax number, nor was I ever given a phone number. The address had something to do with a room in Brooklyn.

Now, snow has come and melted, knuckles have ached and warmed, puddles have swelled and drained. Smoky streets and news stories behind us, Con Ed seems to want to make a fresh start, at least with me:

"The required certification that a resident of your household is suffering from a serious illness or medical condition that severely affects his or her well-being has expired," reads the letter. Though I question the taste of saying "expired" in a letter to the parents of a kid who needs home medical equipment, the letter quickly shifts to the warm breeziness of advice. "We encourage you to have your doctor or local board of health send in a note describing the circumstances so that we can offer special protections to you." The letter is signed by a woman named Bogus.

Dear Ms. Bogus: You and Con Ed will have an easier summer if you realize that my son may have been born into a special population, but I have nonetheless never felt specially protected. This summer drapes its haze on a father who's learned on whom he can depend for protection.

Trouble starts late on Thursday afternoon. I call Jill from Queens Boulevard about picking up salad for dinner, and she says Alex is not well. "I put him on the swings this afternoon and he was not happy," Jill says. "It was like a light went out. It was like a cloudy day."

Alex's feeding tube leaks. We discovered this last night, the second night in a row we'd resorted to using the tube to feed him because he's been running a 100-degree fever and hasn't eaten right for two days. First we noticed a mushy yellowness around the button of the tube, then twin rivulets down his belly. On the mattress was a three-inch-wide wet spot, with another the same size on his nightclothes. This was food and medicine that was meant for him and that wound up on the mattress and his clothes.

We called the hospital and paged the GI and surgical doctors on call. Both called back quickly. Neither knew us, though they knew Alex by reputation. This fever, now in its third day, convinced us to plug his belly in again. I tick off the medical history, condensing one of the biggest years of my life to less than two minutes and capping off the narrative with the seepage on this, the first night of the first Memorial Day weekend. Halfway through my words I think, "Who in God's name *lives* like this?"

"Describe the leak," the doctors say. Both say we should stop using the tube. The surgery guy keeps mentioning the emergency room. "You can bring him in to the ER," he keeps saying. I get the feeling this doctor spends a lot of time in the ER. "Is the site leaking when you're *not* feeding him through the tube?" the doctor asks.

There is no immediate danger, as long as we can get Alex to eat and drink somewhat normally, and keep him hydrated until the first big holiday of summer is past and we can cart him to the hospital on Tuesday.

On Saturday, we're supposed to see friends, a naming ceremony for their nine-month-old daughter. Instead it's 11:30 a.m. before Alex even has his pants on. He drifts in and out of his routine, one minute trilling at the rail of his crib and the next lying limp on his side and quietly fingering a soft toy. His head feels like a skillet half an hour after the burner has been turned off. That afternoon he eats four ounces, sleeps thirty minutes, and wakes up with a 103-degree temperature.

We—actually, Jill, does a rectal. One hundred and four. We page the pediatrician. We tell him the temperatures. "Wow," he says. No parent wants to hear "wow" from a pediatrician. The doc, who I think is calling back from a restaurant, says feed Alex whenever the Motrin and Tylenol kick in. He adds that Alex doesn't sound like a candidate for emergency surgery this weekend.

"It will be different next Memorial Day, and even Labor Day," Jill says. The Motrin kicks in, and soon Alex is babbling into his blanket.

On Sunday he's up and at 'em: eleven ounces for breakfast, more chattering in the chair. I wriggle him into a fresh T-shirt and pants and he's all over the house, opening cupboards, playing on the dirty kitchen floor, gallivanting on the rocking horse, tooling around the living room coffee table. "How's he feeling today?" ask Grandma and Grandpa. Alex scampers to Grandpa and tugs at his pants leg. "Hello sir," says Grandpa, lifting him. "Good exercise," notes Grandpa.

At 12:30, Alex won't nap, walks around in his crib instead, clapping his hands and mumbling. He lies on his side and flips through a board book. "What's he doing?" Jill asks. "Reading," I say. We let the Motrin kick in. He feels pretty good and comes out to the living room, where he plays with big yellow boxes. I put one of the boxes over my head and say "None shall pass," like the Black Knight in *Monty Python and the Holy Grail*. Alex loves this. Later I'm walking to the camera store to pick up Alex reprints and I think how on Memorial Day 1999 it was ninety degrees, and he coughed out his feeding tube and we spent that holiday waiting for an x ray. Today it's cloudy, about sixty-seven. I think that our friend Linda is coming to baby-sit tomorrow and may still salvage this weekend.

Sunday we use the tube only for an injection of Motrin. Late in the day we notice a yellow dribble around the hole. In my mind I see what's going on inside him, stitches snapping loose like cables on the smokestacks of the sinking *Titanic* as his fever climbs. Nothing helps, we hear him whimper, and each moment we let it go on is another moment he isn't on the way to the ER.

Monday we see no seepage, and Linda comes over. Jill and I go out for a sandwich. We think we'll have a movie and some time away. All the movies are sold out, so we walk for a few minutes discussing how it's cooler than last Memorial Day and how we'll handle tomorrow. We buy a few groceries in what Jill later calls a "pathetic" shopping trip. That evening Alex passes out by 9:45.

Next morning Jill calls me at work to say we have an appointment with the surgeon on Thursday. The holiday ends.

The illness passes, but another surgery looms, and the week before it is busy. Doctors want to see Alex Monday and Tuesday. We close on an apartment on Thursday. We must be at the hospital at 6:30 a.m. on Friday. Busy. Jill says she feels almost nauseous.

They're taking out the feeding tube. On Monday afternoon, Jill has to take him to the hospital for an EKG and a blood test. I get there about 4:30. He's asleep, hands behind his head, his T-shirt up under his arms, shiny clear jelly smeared on his chest. The technician goes click click click on the sonogram keyboard. This machine shows part of his heart in color; every pump makes something orange flame up in the middle. The sonogram drags past five o'clock. He wakes up. Click click click. About 5:15 the doctor comes in. The upshot is Alex, who developed a heart problem in the NICU, has apparently gotten a little better and at least no worse.

Next day at noon, Alex has to go to the pediatrician. I go, too, because the pediatrician wants to take blood, and Jill is sick of being the one who has to listen to Alex scream in a small room. Jill arrives at 12:25, and we get an abridged appointment. No blood, but the ped does weigh Alex—nineteen pounds, twelve ounces—and whips out that blue chart. This upshot is that Alex's weight-gain line is flattening, but his height line is curving up. Maybe his body has made up its mind to be a slender two-year-old, the ped says. If his weight gain line doesn't rise soon, we could be looking at installing another tube.

I feel the old loops closing around my ankles. I fire questions past the ped's bow: is this chart for ex-preemies or full-termers? Is Alex's J-tube interfering with his eating? Isn't it possible his body has had to devote resources to repairing the lung damage inflicted when he was born? Aren't his current oxygen needs dropping below half a liter? The ped sends us to Rite Aid with a prescription for liquid hydrocortisone over which our pharmacist only scratches her head.

Wednesday is Alex's second birthday. We're waiting to have the real celebration after the hospital stay, but on this day I get him a pop-up phone toy, we order Chinese food, and give him a cake with two candles. We take off his cannula and place the $O_2$ connection far, far away. Because of the oxygen, of course, Alex has had little experience with flame. Jill brings the glowing cake into the living room. "Wonderment," she says later of his face, "like when you take someone to a science museum and they're old enough to understand. It was Alex's first 'wow!'" Alex eats the carrots out of the chicken and cashews; he turns down the applesauce with his hydrocortisone in it. I look at the button on his stomach—Aunt Julie has told people it looks like the pop-top of a sports water bottle—and wonder what will be there Friday night.

The last night home for Alex begins with phone trouble: clicks and whirrs, overlapping dial tones, neighbors' conversations when we're trying to make calls. His respite nurse gives him a pirate ship for the bath and wishes us luck. Jill holds Alex while he types at the keyboard. She sets him down. "I just hope this isn't a huge setback for him," she says. Later, in the bath, he chews the heads of the little pirates. *Bye Bye Birdie* is on TV. We order bad pizza. Alex has a taste of sauce, and goes to sleep about nine. I abandon the movie after "Put on a Happy Face" and go for a walk. It's a short walk, because the taxi is coming at a quarter to six. Tomorrow it will be over. Jill wants to take a picture of the button in his stomach.

The surgery goes well. After about half the time we thought it would take, the surgeon comes out to us in the waiting room with a cheery "Hey I know you two!" Alex bounces back that afternoon on mere Tylenol. We go home and sleep ten hours; we haven't planned to spend the first night with him in the hospital because we thought he'd be too doped up.

"He woke up and I think he was apprehensive," the nurse tells me on the phone Saturday morning. "I think he was apprehensive at waking up in a strange place and not knowing anybody." But he's in the wing he lived in for half of 1999, where the nurses are practically his aunts!

"He was sad," the mother of another patient, from Utah, tells us when we get there. "He wasn't in pain or anything, but wailing, kind of sad. I thought you'd want to know. I thought I wouldn't spare your feelings."

Alex fingers a toy in his crib and will only glance at us. He smiles once or twice behind the binkie. He will only fall asleep on Jill, as she clears his wires and tubes, including leads and a stitched-in central line for hydration. The surgeon comes by and thinks Alex looks good. So good, in fact, that the nothing-by-mouth order falls in a day and a half. That afternoon he sips chicken broth. A few hours later, I go out to get myself a Hungry Man dinner and when I come back Jill says he passed gas.

Could be a big night!

5:30 p.m.: Alex finally asleep in his crib. Jill reading, still here, curled in a chair. I'm drowsy. The kid with the heart problem in the next bed refuses to eat his burger. Alex wakes, and I pick him up.

5:45: "That doesn't look right," Jill says. On Alex's shoulder, the bandage over the stitches of the central line has turned bright red. "Look," Jill says, finding the end of Alex's line on his bed, still dripping solution. The nurse says she's never seen this happen before. Will they have to do an IV? She talks to surgery, and finagles a chance for Alex to eat enough by mouth to avoid getting his ankles or wrists pricked. She says he has until nine. Such a reprieve might not have been granted on most wings; there are advantages to being in the hospital with your aunts.

6:15 p.m.: The microwave in the back is weak, and my Hungry Man Salisbury steak comes out half frozen. I just eat it and glare at Jill, who suggested a TV dinner and now suggests putting it back in the microwave, until the nurse comes by and says, "Don't be ridiculous. Put it back in!"

8 p.m.: Jill left an hour ago. I've been trying to get Alex to drink water or cranberry juice from the bottle. I scrounge a cherry Jell-O—astounding how hard it is to find one—and, since I lack a baby spoon, I feed him using the end of a plastic knife handle, the red of the Jell-O brilliant against the snow-white of the knife. Soon it's time for his medicines, and what formerly went through the central line must now be wheedled and squirted into Alex's mouth. He presses his lips together and wags his head. No no no. I take a syringe, offer him the binkie, and when his lips part I slip the syringe in and press the plunger. I do this with two medicines and then with water. It's a trick, but it's also better than some exhausted resident pricking his vein for an IV.

8:30: "If he'll take liquid from the syringe like that, I don't see why he needs an IV," says the night nurse.

8:45: The woman from Utah and her son hang around the kid next door. They all talk like buddies in the barracks. They've all been here for a week. They don't know that Alex lived for months on almost the spot they're standing. I don't tell them. This isn't a contest. But it was right where they're standing.

9:15 p.m.: Alex finally goes on his back, puts his paws in the air, and sleeps. I brush my teeth at the hospital sink, and wash using the soap from the dispenser on the wall. (There's a parent shower down the hall, but I don't remember this until later.) Beside Alex's crib, I press flat the "recliner" chair-bed and get ready to settle in when the mom from Utah comes out and says, "Why don't you close these?" She grabs the partition curtains and sweeps them closed with a crashing rattle. Alex stirs but doesn't wake. She finds me a fitted sheet, then finds her way out through the curtains like a talk-show guest. Some-how, I never would have thought of closing the curtains.

11 p.m.: The kid and his mom in the next bed are watching a monster movie with the sound low. I see Godzilla flickering through the curtains.

Midnight: The nurse touches my arm to wake me. She whispers to me, holding a syringe. It takes me a moment to understand she's saying that she sees no need to give Alex painkiller. Okay, whatever.

2:15 a.m.: He's sitting up. No no, baby.

4 a.m.: He drinks from the bottle. He shifts around. He's sweaty, crying. He drinks.

6 a.m.: I forget what happened at six. Later the nurse will show me an empty bottle.

7 a.m.: Up and out for coffee. It's a cool day, Father's Day. It was ninety yesterday. All I have with me are shorts.

7:45 a.m.: The kid next door is already up and watching "Barney." Alex is still asleep. As I wait for Jill and her family to arrive for Father's Day, it dawns on me that this was my first peek at what made up a lot of my son's life for a year. I don't know how he did it.

I'm not sure how we did it, either. But the tube is gone. This is a moment. Alex gets out of the hospital in four days, and returns to what is, slowly, becoming his normal life.

Alex likes the toy cell phone that a reader of my website sent him for his birthday. He likes books and his pop-up farm. He likes real toys like old phones, and remote controls old, new, and still in use. He likes his Fisher-Price walker, though he can walk pretty well without it now. He likes his toys. He doesn't take care of any of them.

I come home from work and find fragments of toys all over the house. The mainmast of the bathtub pirate ship under the sink, one of the pirates on top of the TV. Bell blocks in one box, the pig's head from the pop-up farm on the entertainment unit. Wooden blocks in every corner of every room, apparently doomed never to reunite and spell anything. On the counter near where he eats, it looks like a scrap pile: bits and pieces at every angle, bell toys and building bricks, the ringing ball skewered with the plastic rod from the mobile that hung over his PICU crib. And there's the treasure chest from the pirate ship.

Not that he's bored, easily distracted, or dislikes play. Alex will sail across a room to secure his Teletubby, then wobble away a moment later and drop the doll like garbage off a freighter. He will waddle and scamper across the kitchen tiles after a binkie he's spied from over near the sink, like a cat spotting an ant. One stacking block here, another there. A Sassy ring in front of the bathroom door, where lately Alex stands and swings the door open and closed, open and closed, and laughs. Someday he will learn a door is not a toy.

"I just want to say that I'm the one who tries to keep all the sets together," says Jill. "The stacking cups, the stacking rings. I try to keep everything together." That's because Jill is a girl.

Someday Alex will look back at the period he's entering now and recognize it as Prime Toy Time. Mine lasted until I was eleven. All those years I had cardboard-carton toy boxes, one under a table and another behind a door, and another upstairs in the ancient ark of a Maine house where I grew up. Every toy found its way into those boxes; most found their way into all three. Rarely did I find a complete set of toys in any one box; with a combination of self-discipline and laziness I'd limit myself to playing only with the contents of the nearest box. That policy made for some odd pairings, but it did hone my imagination to the point where I can survive in an office cubicle.

The point is that when I was young, almost all my toys came with a lot of crap to scatter among three toy boxes. A dive and a rattle of plastic might turn up GI Joe's scuba tank, a Major Matt Mason moon cart, the steering box of my brother's old red remote-control Cadillac (my brother had all the cool toys first; I inherited the pieces). Look sharp for the plastic knight, the wooden paintbrush, a phaser made of pieces of an old fence, and, in the bottom with the spiders, marbles and scraps of playtime I can still see but not identify.

"What's so important about having all the damned bits of toys everywhere?" Jill wants to know. What's important is that you never knew what was in the bottom of the carton, never knew when you plunged your arm in what shape that day would take. What's Johnny West going to do with scuba tanks? Will the spy doll's briefcase go off prematurely? I would play until I found out what happened, because after that day Johnny West might never have those tanks or that briefcase in his hands again.

The last time I saw Po was when I jammed him into the carriage seat behind Alex on Thursday. I returned to my office after escorting Jill to the doctor's and soon got a call from her saying, "Jeff, where is Alex's red Teletubby?"

Jill and I first saw the "Teletubbies" show in a suburban London home in 1997. We were staying with a couple who had two boys, ages one and three. One morning we came down to tea to find both of them on their stomachs in front of the screen. I watched for a minute, and found the show lulling: a simplistic fifteen-minute story, sometimes interspersed with live action and told twice in a half-hour. "They just love the show," their mum told us. Jill vowed no toddler of hers would wind up worshipping TV characters.

"Jeff, you have to find another Po!" Jill says.

Alex had a pair of Tinky Winkys a year ago, back in the hospital. We used the smaller one to prop up his IV boards when he went to sleep. We used to stand up the big one in the hospital bed and pretend it said, "Eh-ho, Awecks, eh-ho." Alex couldn't sit up by himself then. He couldn't walk, either, but Tinky made him smile.

I work a block away from a Toys"R"Us, a Kids"R"Us, the world-famous Macy's, and a seven-story shopping mall. Last year, you couldn't swing a toddler without knocking over a Teletubbies display. Lamps, mobiles, play sets, toothbrushes, bags. And dolls. Dolls that talked or walked, dolls of plastic firm or soft, plush or hard, from key-chain size to some as big as a family dog. This year, however, I strike out at Toys"R"Us, Kids"R"Us, the world-famous Macy's and the KB toys in the seven-story shopping mall. Two other stores lousy with Tinky Winky last year have closed. Through Hallmark stores and retail video outlets, I hunt uselessly. Even the Kmart lets me down as the third lunch hour of this mission evaporates amid the stacks of CatDog and Cookie Monster. Rugrats and Dragon Tales. Pooh and Bull Frog and Rolie Polie Olie. Blue's Clues and Barney. Powerpuff beanbags and tricycles. Pokemon card games, pencil sharpeners, pens, dolls, notebooks and a talking calculator. Even the merchandise of duds like *Rocky and Bullwinkle* claim more shelf now than yesterday's Teletubbies. Last year is an eon ago in kids' retail, if not in the life of kids Alex's age. I sought a toy store ghost. My boy's in love with a cold fad.

But there they are at last, stacked in a corner ghetto and topped by a six-inch Laa-Laa, in a ripped box, a smudge on his yellow arm and a clearance price on his tag of ninety cents. Under Laa-Laa, I find a box of all four Tubbies for $25.99—no clearance tag there, boy—and grab it without even checking for smudges on the nose.

On the phone to Jill I say that I had no luck finding one Teletubbies doll. Jill started to say that was all right when I chopped her off: "I found all four!"

"Are they nice?" she asks. "Do they have the little rubber things on the bottom of the feet? If they aren't nice, we're taking them back." When I get them home, Jill calls them cheesy. Alex examines them one at a time as if searching his memory, holding each close to his face before letting it hit the floor with a soft thud and trotting back to the bedroom to play with our surge suppressor.

Generally, Alex is getting better with clothes. Before bath time, for instance, he'll wiggle and squirm out of his T-shirt if I get him started. He will lift one foot and then the other when I put his sweatpants on him. This seems to indicate he's moving forward mentally. By no means was that always a given.

But good things started a few months ago in front of the dishwasher. On top of the dishwasher sat a tube of Pringles. In front of the dishwasher stood Alex. The dishwasher was closed but unlocked. Alex likes Pringles. "Just a minute, Alex," I told him as I left the kitchen. I returned a minute later and found him standing on the opened and flat dishwasher door. He stretched up and took the Pringles.

Soon after, I was giving him a bath. Alex likes to pull the stopper and the strainer out of the drain. I don't like him to do this because the naked drain would be a lobster trap for his hand: just big enough to get the hand in, but too small to get it out. So whenever Alex starts fiddling with the drain, I put my finger on top of the stopper. He tugged and tugged at my finger. "No no, Alex," I said, "we've talked about this." One night in the bath, however, something must have clicked in his head. Before reaching for the drain with his right hand he reached out with his left and held my finger away from the drain.

"Wow!" remarked one of his therapists. "Problem-solving abilities!"

He's beginning to imitate. "All gone," I tell him when he eats the last piece of bacon. "Awn ga," he replies. "Door," I tell him when he's in one of his swinging moods with the bedroom door. "Knock on the door, Alex." He does, obedient taps with his fine knuckles, then he says, "Daw." "Bath time, Alex," I say. He helps me wrangle his T-shirt off over his head and starts saying, "Bat, bat." Two nights ago he said "bat bat" right after dinner, and ran straight from the high chair to the bathroom. Last night, he threw a ball.

If he wants you to read to him, he opens the book, carries it over and lays it on your thigh with insistent and growing force. He likes to slam the sliding shower door. I don't like him to do this, so I check the door with my hand. He saddles over and tries to pry off my hand. Then Jill says that the other day Alex pulled a diaper from the drawer and brought it to her. She checked. He was wet. Problem solving.

It's dawned on him that the front door is more than just a movable wall that sometimes reveals beloved therapists and babysitters (to squeals of delight never squandered on Jill or me). Let him out that door and he finds a straight and empty corridor that I think is dingy but that he finds custom-built for a first halting run. He scales into the high chair when hungry. He grasps the big hand from above when crossing the street.

"It's true," says Jill. "If he finds one part of a toy, he looks around for the other parts."

I wish one thing he'd put together is who Mom and Dad are. I pick him up and he squirms and wiggles and tries to press his elbow into my neck. He likes the hugs that turn into flip-flops and games of Upside Down Boy. There are toys he clearly loves, chairs he likes to climb, and when I got back from a business trip last night I swore he'd grown an inch in three days. But how come when I came home, he didn't scamper to the door and screech in delight? "He has cuddly moments," Jill says, "but not many. You just have to get used to that with boys." He studies books, murmurs to himself in a broadening range of sounds while fingering a toy, moves with increasing smoothness from couch to ottoman to dining room table.

This is the first July Fourth that Alex spends entirely with his parents. There is a family event in the morning. Four kids are there, and a lot of adults. We wheel in Alex, regal in his new featherweight stroller—a fraction of the weight of his previous, heavier carriage with the oxygen tank wedged in the bottom. A glance around the room tells me that few people at this party have had experience hefting an oxygen tank or stepping over cannula tubing. "I just took him off the oxygen," I tell Jill a few minutes later. "It seemed easiest."

For weeks, it has seemed easiest to let him go without cannula and tubing. Early on we kept Alex religiously attached to the oxygen concentrator, afraid that he'd turn blue in even just a few minutes. Last fall we came in from outside and I changed him over from portable tank to concentrator, yet in a few moments he began to look tired. Half an hour later I realized I'd forgotten to turn the concentrator back on.

"Look for signs of fatigue or labored breathing," the pulmonologist taught us.

In the weeks prior to removal of his J-tube in June, we kept him on oxygen most of the time because we didn't want to tax him as he tried to gain weight, learned to eat, and continued to learn how to walk. He got better and better at walking, too: Suddenly he wasn't where we'd left him, and the tubing (we have about twenty feet of it running from the concentrator to the back of his head) was always there like an arrow. Kitchen. Bathroom. Under his crib, messing with the surge suppressor. Follow the yellow brick air tube.

But whatever claim oxygen tubing can make, it isn't made to stay out of the way of a two-year-old who's just learning that every room in a home has to be visited as many times as possible in the next hour. Sometimes we find Alex wrapped in tubing. Other times he'll be scampering along and *whang!*, he'll yank to a stop like the dog at the end of his leash in Foghorn Leghorn cartoons. We'll track the tube back and find it snared on the footrest of the rocking horse, under a chair, or around and around the dinner table. The tubing then gets a tongue lashing from me or Jill, the way we used to yell at the food pump.

The $O_2$ in the plastic tube seems to be the last hurdle; Alex looks like a kid ready to breathe. We have him off now for about two hours in the morning, and from bath time to bedtime. He circles the dinner table these evenings—we haven't progressed to where he sits in a high chair and eats with us—like a busy aunt who wants to pick from your plate. He dismounts the rocking horse and runs away. The other night he ignored *The Wizard of Oz* on TV to pull books from the bookcase. These hours are a delicious new mystery, during which the coil of plastic near the concentrator provides no clue to his whereabouts.

Before we put him back on, we always get a pulse ox reading. Last one was ninety-six. "When he's off the oxygen, the signs may be subtle," the pulmo said lately. "You may not even be able to tell that he's doing damage to his lungs." That warning was always worth the price of seeing my little son with a ring of clear plastic around his face, between his upper lip and lower nose, the kind of ring somebody with white hair wears day after day long after he's retired.

In Central Park, one crystal afternoon two days ago, he wore no cannula. He walked with me in the grass, and bent to touch it with the suspicion of any proper city boy. When strangers looked, they saw a boy and his dad on a hot day in the park. They saw the lips, the brows and the brown eyes. They saw no plastic. Independence, indeed.

A new picture sits on top of our bookcase: a close-up of Alex's face. He is crawling toward the camera. His lips are tight in concentration and his eyebrow arched. I took the picture while I was lying in the grass. I like that picture on the bookcase. I like how big his face is.

## JULY TO NOVEMBER, 2000

When I was a small baby, my mother left me in my brother's care. "Watch your baby brother!" my mother told him. Right. He was setting up a Monopoly game to play by himself. "Uh-huh," he said. My brother continued setting up his game and reportedly had no intention of misplacing me. He suddenly glanced around and saw I was nowhere in sight.

Ask him about this today and he will say his first thought was not my welfare, but terror at what our mother would do to him. He searched and searched—I don't remember him searching—and still couldn't find me. His stomach must have been a hard lump when he noticed the top of the Monopoly carton slowly crawling away.

What a cute story, burying your baby brother with a box. Soon I may see this episode replayed, for Jill is pregnant.

"I just hope he won't be too shocked," Jill says, speaking of the new guy.

I've informed Alex, holding him near and asking, "Would you like a little brother?" while he rams an elbow into my neck and tries to squirm down to his rocking horse. Right now Alex has the run of the roost. He can play with whatever he wants whenever he wants. He can open and shut every cabinet, scamper room to room unimpeded by any toys but his own. He can sneak away to fiddle with the surge protector, piles of sweepings, or the salt shaker. The only cute actions in our house are his. Aunt Julie calls him Little Piggy, and he glows. He overpowers family dinners with his charm, and banging, at the table. He sleeps in his own room. When he cries, both parents come.

Alex will look at the next baby with wonder, resentment, love, hate, indifference, affection, and every other ingredient of siblinghood. Will that really happen, though, when there's another hand on the salt shaker? "Would you like a little brother, Alex? How about a Monopoly game?"

I have a brother and a sister. They were people for me to talk with on the phone during my mom's last years, when she lost a lot of stuff before she stopped living. We were different people, but we understood. Mom died in Arizona, living with my sister. My sister tried the hardest of us. My brother is nine years older than I, my sister eighteen; growing up, I was that kind of only child. My sister was married and starting a big family of her own by the time I came along. To her I became the spoiled brat. My brother probably thought the same thing after I started rifling his room for canteens, broken BB pistols, his sword and shield built in metal shop, and other equipment for my play. As he moved further into the teen years, of course, he had only the typical uses for a little kid, such as practicing karate. As we lived far away from other kids, I played alone, acting out a library of ongoing stories that I didn't have to clear with any other kid.

I've decided to take the responsibility route with Alex and tell him that we need his help with the baby and that he can pitch in. I hope he won't be too shocked. And if he is, at least years from now, when Mom and Dad start losing things, he'll be able to pick up a phone and talk to someone who understands. I hope he finds that worth the price.

Alex becomes the first person who makes me lock my own toilet bowl. "You have to buy a toilet lock!" Jill says on the phone. "Alex, NO!" Alex has become fascinated by easily accessible water. At the same time he was nurturing this instinct, he learned the Lid Secrets of Life. Mainly that lids go up pretty easily.

I'm glad I have this problem. If I have a child, I would rather have to buy a toilet lock than not have to buy a toilet lock. And the store puts the locks right in front, as if waiting for me. Once again I'm struck by the new-parent's amazement at how when you need baby things, they're right there in the store: cabinet locks, outlet plugs, diapers, the high chair tray with the groove to catch spills, the two-piece cap for the baby bottles. I still have a hard time accepting that other people had kids before I did.

The lock is $5.99, including Spanish instructions (*"Curradura de Abrazadera para sanitarios"*). In the same trip I buy diapers so the check-out girl will be sure I have a baby and not just some problem. ("Maybe because you bought the diapers, she just thought you had an even worse problem," Jill notes later.) The lock is tan plastic, about five inches long by two wide by a half-inch thick, and comes in three pieces. It attaches to the toilet with a combination of glue strips and good old clamping. It helps keep kids, toys and hands out! Detachable when not in use. No tools required.

We'll see. I kneel in a place I don't spend a lot of time kneeling and examine the rim of our toilet bowl. The instructions say the glue on the strip will hold better if I clean the bowl and lid with alcohol, and let dry. I should do that. I don't.

"Hold the assembly in your hand," the instructions say. "Pull out the release button in the lower center of the Lid Clamp Housing and press down either one of the release tabs on either side of the Lid Clamp Housing. This will separate the Lid Clamp Housing from the Rim Clamp assembly."

Well, no, it won't, at least not until the third try. This becomes a typical home job: nothing conforming to the instructions until you've been at it a minute. Suddenly it strikes me that a balky toilet lock can become a serious situation. Fast.

"Install the Rim Clamp Assembly to the rim of the toilet bowl (Fig. 5a & 5b). Adjust interior Rim Clamp until it is firmly gripped under the interior bowl rim (Fig. 6)." It also strikes me that these instructions were written by somebody who teaches

soldiers how to take apart their rifles. "With the toilet seat and
lid in their upright position, attach the Lid Clamp assembly to
the Rim Clamp assembly by pressing the Lid Clamp housing
over the inverted Hook on the Rim Clamp (Fig. 7). Lower the
toilet seat and lid down into—"

*Alex get away from that!* God yes, *sanitarios, muy sanitarios.*

"—down into their closed position. Fold part 1B of the Lid
Clamp assembly down until it is even with the lid. Gently press
down until it rests—"

Snap.

I run my hand across my forehead, and the fingers come away
dripping with sweat. I don't regret that children are fascinated by
water. I do regret that I live in an age when what should be made
of steel is made of plastic. In some ways this is the hardest time in
history to have a child, especially in this bathroom.

I stick the clamp down on top of the lid, click the lock shut.
Look at that! The lid really won't go up! It takes only four tries
and ten minutes to unhitch the lock again. I look around for
Alex. It should be fun watching him try to open this. It should
be, except he's three rooms away, banging cabinet doors. I snap
the lock closed again, wipe away the sweat, and look up to see
Jill. "I have to go to the bathroom," she says.


Once, after baby-sitting Alex, Aunt Julie said, "Pretty good.
He only hit his head twice." Months ago, Alex's grandmother
said, "He's going to take his spills." Toddlers are aptly named
and don't always stand up. Sometimes Alex falls like Gilligan.
Other times he falls from lack of practice, his feet suddenly de-
ciding *Nah, not right now* . . .

Alex took a bad one the other night. I was in the study, Jill
was on the phone with her mother. In the seconds it takes a
skull the size of a softball to pitch forward out of control, we
weren't watching. When I last saw him before the screaming
started, Alex was sitting and murmuring on the rattan couch
that he'd discovered as a plaything. I think I heard the thud.

Then I heard him screaming. Then I heard Jill screaming. "Jeff! JEFF!"

I ran in. She was holding him. "He hit his head on the coffee table," Jill said. "And it was a bad one. Can't you help watch him?"

"He was on the couch last time I looked!"

"Well, it was a bad one."

Our coffee table is wood, with four wicked corners that look like they'd have no problem cracking—Well, never mind. We never covered the corners because Alex never seemed to fall against them.

He did this time. He was wailing to the ceiling, a siren, a full-bodied scream. He was probably marveling that somehow, after he finished a thirteen-month sentence in hospitals, pain keeps finding him.

I held him. Jill held him. He cried and cried. His tears are small; sometimes they bead like diamonds on his long, dark eyelashes. I took him to the bathroom and put a cool cloth on his head. On the mirror I saw a spot of blood; I never found out where it came from. But on the way back into the living room I banged his hand—lightly—on the wall. "Oh Alex," I said, "bam! I'm sorry."

"Who are you?" Jill said. "Emeril Lagasse?"

No, I'm Jeff—that much I remember—and I used to fall. On my right eyelid is a inch-long scar that I got when I was two, maybe three. My aunt was baby-sitting for the afternoon and I fell off her couch. *(Pretty good. He only hit his head twice.)* I had to go to the doctor for stitches. "God," Jill said when I told her this story again recently, "I bet your mother was furious with your aunt." Years later from that same aunt's house I borrowed, unseen and unsupervised, my cousin's ten-speed bike, which was far too tall for me. I weebled and wobbled and got about twenty yards down the street before tipping endlessly to the left. My kneecap and I skidded into the roadside gravel. Bam! What a scab! The following year, when my sister and her family were visiting us, my niece was about three and she wanted to come downstairs. I, her joyful but ungainly thirteen-year-old uncle, lifted her up up up, whee! high over the stairs and banged her face-first into the wall. What a thud. Like a cartoon. She didn't cry. As her brain function returned, she looked puzzled, I guess wondering what had happened and if she had the right to get mad at an apparent adult.

"Which niece was that?" Jill asked.

"The one who didn't grow up to be a lawyer," I said.

When Alex falls a million thoughts go through my head, all ending with the thud. I hug him to my face until the screaming is right in my ear, and I wonder how the future was just altered. At the end of the day, as he sleeps, I look at the faint bruise above his eye, the pink scrape on his stomach. On his wrist and upper thighs he still bears the IV scars from the hospital.

Alex brings me the book, places it against my thigh, and starts looking down at the pages in complete expectation that I will, in fact, read aloud. "Goodnight clocks, and goodnight socks."

You should read to your child so he or she gets to know your voice, digest the language, and catch the rhythms of the written word. Experts, most of whom are not children, prefer furry animals and no grown-up stories. First to hook Alex on books was his teacher, Ron. Alex would sit with Ron the whole hour, selecting the books from among a few choices, then scarcely lift his head throughout the story.

Maybe as a result of this, Alex reads to himself a lot now. He sits with the book on his own thighs and flips the pages, murmuring in his priceless, private language.

"I see a red bird looking at me."

"Bunny is eating his good supper."

Alex believes that to really know a book, you have to re-read it. He's learned to press his face on the picture of the sun in the color book. He used to like it when I flipped up the lid of the piano in *Where's Spot* and said a deep "No!" for the rhino and a tiny "No!" for the bird. He doesn't like this so much anymore. *Little Fur Family* gets the early hook, and to this day I don't know how *Runaway Bunny* ends. The copy of *Alex Alligator* I bought in Florida spent months at the bottom of a toy box, and may have missed its window.

"Peek a who? Peek a MOO!"

Jill got him engrossed in *Miss Spider's Tea Party*; I hate spiders, and "Five rubber bugs stared silently" is a nightmare line to me. One of his nurses gave him *Goodnight Moon*. Did you ever notice how the moon rises in the window as the story goes on? Or how the bookshelf contains a copy of *Runaway Bunny*, one of the author's other books? The mouse moves around the room, too. And is Pat the Bunny merely asleep or in some kind of stupor? Is that even Pat the Bunny, or a different bunny in the book within the book?

"Polly put the kettle on, Polly put the kettle on."

His feeding therapist gave him *The Cheerios Animal Play Book*. My friend Sean gave him a Spot book in Gaelic ("Bran ag obair . . ."). Our friends Tom and Naomi gave him a copy of *The Wheels on the Bus*; inside are real wheels, and you pull a tab to make the riders on the bus go in and out, in and out, make the windows on the bus go open and shut, open and shut, and make the wipers on the bus go swish swish swish. (The wipers were the first to go.) Howard gave Alex a big Richard Scarry book. I'd never heard of Richard Scarry, but apparently he's famous. Fathers learn something new every day, whether they want to or not.

"Oranges and Lemons, say the bells of St. Clements."

Those who haven't read these books don't know what it's like to have that weight on your knee, the little face fixated while the timeless, simplistic phrases tattoo themselves onto your mind. "If I have to read this damned 'Oranges and Lemons' once more . . ." says Jill, lifting Alex.

His favorite places to be read to are Mom's lap, my lap, or beside us on the couch. Often an initial request for reading delivered to your thigh will, upon lifting him, degenerate into a session of Scrambling Toward Alex's Imaginary Devil Bunny on the Wall. But often too he will sit and listen.

"And a quiet old lady, whispering 'Hush.'"

Sometimes the requests land on your thigh at a busy moment. "Oh, Alex, Mommy will read to you," I'll say. Sometimes he'll go with the secondary reader. Sometimes not. There's nothing to do then but lift him and read. I'm ashamed that I don't read to him every night. I mean to, but when I come in at nine p.m. and find him asleep, I realize that another night has slipped by without a goodnight story.

We're still in that time before he's talking. What he absorbs from the pages stays in, or at best dribbles out in his private language. But somewhere ahead, one by one, his murmurs will turn into words. He will begin to tell us what he reads, it is we who will get to know his voice, and I may never learn what happens to that runaway bunny.

The reading must be having some effect: Jill came into the living room last night and reported that Alex had just asked for a cookie. I wasn't with them when this happened, but Jill said she asked him if he wanted a cookie, and he flashed a huge smile and she gave him a cookie. "It was almost like a conversation," she said.

Leaving aside that this was past his bedtime and I'm the only one around here who eats cookies at that hour, this is remarkable. "Is he verbalizing?" people ask us. Is he saying any words? No. For weeks now he's had a speech and eating therapist who keeps him in stitches and who has achieved a lot—getting him to put a brush to his teeth, using his molars to bite a pretzel, getting him to snap the bacon flashcard into your palm whenever he wants another slice. Since his eating horizons have broadened—even internationally, with falafel and Irish black pudding—his word play has increased. Yet I can't say we've heard any words.

He can communicate, often from two or three rooms away. As when he was banging the glass on the door of the entertainment unit and I took his hand and made him stop, and he looked at me for one instant before running across the living room and burying his face in Jill's lap. Often we know what he's trying to say. Often, but not always. "You've got to learn to talk, little boy," we've told him.

For a long time Alex has trilled when concentrating. He did this in a restaurant and a Finnish woman came up to us and asked, "Do you speak English with him at home?" Turns out that children who don't make that noise in Finland are taken to speech therapists. "Turns out," I told her, "that children who do make that noise in America are taken to speech therapists."

If Jill and I try watching "Larry Sanders" in the evening without first ascertaining that Alex has dropped off, he'll screech loud enough to make the characters flinch on our TV screen. His other phrases include:

—"ub": A faint popping noise with his lips when he wants to be lifted. Seems encouraging.

—"da": Kind of a compliment to me. Means anything good or wanted. I think.

—Assorted murmurs and mumbles in the bath: Perhaps he's trying to keep up with the sounds of the water. He has figured out that "Splashy!" is Daddy's word for "Please soak my shirt!"

I've heard him say many things, sometimes sounding like Latka on "Taxi." "Good luck to me." "Ah nah." "Add doubloon." "Dracula there." "Ha." No sentences in the high school graduate sense. In the years before Alex, I always thought that one day toddlers are dribbling at the lips and the next they're speaking words, usually starting with "da" and "ma," and knowing what the words mean.

Alex does say these. For weeks he's brought his lips together for "Mama." I hope that Jill won't weep any more at the end of *Escape From the Planet of the Apes* when the smart baby chimp that Ricardo Montalban smuggles from his parents says "Mama, Mama" from behind the bars of his cage. Every now and then when I look at him, Alex says "da," following this with "dadadadadledadle," so I'm not sure that he identifies the two syllables with these big creatures with whom he lives. "That's right, Alex! Mama and Dada! Mama and Dada! Where's Dada's nose?" Often at this he reaches up and touches my face. Sometimes he beams back at us as if to say, "Isn't that cute? They're trying to talk!"

He's been getting to the top of the coffee table himself. Alex is just shy of a yard tall; the table comes to his stomach. He puts his arms out and his palms flat on the wood, then up comes the left leg as the foot searches for purchase. Finding none because its two-year-old owner isn't yet a Rockette, the leg thrusts forward the knee and the right foot leaves the floor. Sometimes I give him a little push in the behind or steady his left foot in place. An instant later Alex is propelled to the top of a new world to slap his hands, grunt once, and grin.

Up up up. "Up comes the baby!" was one of our first games. The first thing he learned to climb was his own rocking horse. And how long ago did I come into the kitchen and find him standing on the dishwasher door (which he'd opened) to better reach the can of Pringles?

Typically two, he still wants to come up. "Uppa! Uppa!" I say, taking him by his hands and tossing him into the air. This got big squeals for a while. Other times I swing him left and right, and other times he just likes me to take his hands and let him scale up my front like Batman on a building. Then he stands on my shoulders and looks at the top of the refrigerator for the can of Pringles. He knows more about the top of my fridge than I do.

Alex has charming movement. (Jill brought him to my office once and he delighted in the long, straight, carpeted hallway. "He's fast!" Howard said.) The other night I was watching him trying to mount a dining room chair. The left foot came up and hung there, so I helped it the other inch or so and held it to the seat of the chair while he rose. Alex trilled as he stood in the seat and grasped the chair back. Then he reached up, up, and hit the light switch. Then he got down, sliding off on his stomach, the way his physical therapist taught him. I turned off the light. Then he turned around and wanted to get back up. I again held his foot. Again he stood and turned on the light. Again he slid down. I went into the kitchen, and when I returned Alex was standing in the chair and again reaching for the light switch. Click.

He learned this light switch thing last week, when I was gone on a business trip. When I left, I'd never seen him handle a light switch. "Oh, yeah," said Jill, "he does that now." She says that a lot lately about Alex.

Chair, trill, stand, click, trill, click. Click, down. Away. The light is still on. Who does he think pays the light bills around here?

"I want to get him on stairs," his physical therapist says, so now no stroll to the playground is complete without an ascent on the stair/slide complex. Sometimes Alex goes up the stairs sideways, left foot always up first, as if he were climbing some old table, and sometimes he crawls frontways while I hover behind and strain to not touch him. He grabs his way along the railing at the top—it seems to me Alex could shoot through the gaps in the bars of the railing (". . . *he's fast* . . ."), but he just works his way hand over hand to the top of the slide.

Here I scoop him up. "Let's go down, Alex!" I say, and I put him on my lap and wiggle onto the shiny metal. I forget to lift my sneakers, though, and we go down herky-jerky. Then he darts for the concrete steps leading to the playground gate and the busy intersection. "You're taking my hand if you're going near the street, pal," I say, grasping his fingers. Alex tries to yank his hand away, but I take it again. As we walk away, I can feel his glance return to the gate, and I can feel the little pull down there as he wants, wants, wants to get close to the big fast cars.

"Once more on the slide, Alex?"

Jill calls next day to say he's climbing the *outside* of the shower door. "He's Spiderbaby!" she says. At home tonight, I know I'll look one minute and he'll be grinning on the coffee table. Then I'll look again and he'll be on the floor and headed my way. When did he get down? Who helped him?

Stairs are getting easier for him, too. On my way down to the subway, I'll see a little girl standing with her mother on the steps. The mother is trying to get the little girl to walk down. "C'mon. Everyone's watching," the mother says. The little girl grips the railing, smart enough to know that no one is watching and that the staircase is very, very long. Up the steps come the rumble of trains. I can't imagine how far down it must look to eyes that are, at most, four years old. It must be like a dizzying scene from a Hitchcock film, a billion steps to get her twirling before she's swallowed by a floor of cement. "I don't want to," the little girl says.

Can't blame her, but I know Alex would've had those stairs for breakfast. He's been going out of his way to walk the stairs for weeks. Take him to the playground and he flies by the swings, bolting for the steps that lead down to the street. Let him into the corridor of our apartment building, and you'd best plant yourself near the top of the stairs to stop him sailing down. Be prepared to hear some screaming when you take him back into the apartment before he's ready, too. Makes me proud.

He doesn't do stairs alone yet. I bend over and grasp his hands (though lately he has shown a predilection for the banister). When he walks down he still sort of hops, with me lifting him off one step and lowering him to the next. He walks up, however, like a big kid. None of this one-foot-on-the-next-stair-then-the-next-foot-up-to-join-it business. He moves up in the world by gobbling steps, one foot climbing in front of the other. I'm not sure he could do this if I didn't hold his hands. Still, makes me proud.

Alex comes from a long line of stair users. My mom was a nurse for many years, and at least one night a week she'd come home and talk about the whole buncha lazy young nurses who sat at the desk eating potato chips and who took the elevator to go just one flight. My mother's duties took her up and down that seven-story hospital; she unfailingly used the stairs. "Concentrate on lifting your knees, and take the steps one at a time," she advised me once when we were together on a long staircase and I was getting winded. I was sixteen at the time; she was fifty-six.

The average stair still comes up to about Alex's kneecap. Jill asks if I remember when she wondered if Alex would ever walk. Oh, yes. And for a long while the swings were the best thing at the playground in his eyes. Then his therapist began using a stepstool and our couch to teach him to climb. He tried it first on all fours, then as the therapy sessions went on, he would lift one knee, plant one foot, and smile at the fresh altitude. Soon at the playground our time was split between the swings and the half-dozen rubber-coated steps of the giant jungle gym. He took those on all fours at first, too.

The rubber play steps are giving way to the real cement ones to the street, or those that lead up to the wonderland of the big kids' basketball court. The swings he just leaves swinging empty, as if from a strong breeze.

The other day we went to a Barnes and Noble bookstore. Amid stacks of the world's most enduring thoughts, Alex went straight to the staircase. Up and down we went, up and down, up and down, while I held his hands, thought about lifting my knees and taking one step at a time, and tried to forget the ache in the small of my back. Up and down. Six times. Alex started for the stairs for the seventh trip when I picked him up and carried him back to the bookstacks. "C'mon, Alex," I said. "You look tired."

Also, he can't stop laughing. Part belly laugh, part giggle, the laugh of the extremely young for whom anything can be funny: Daddy's frown, a Cheerio on the floor, a vision seen only by those little brown eyes and fed into that little new brain. A laugh like a bubbling pot, like Mary Tyler Moore at the funeral of Chuckles the Clown.

I noticed that laugh six months ago, from another little boy on a sidewalk. Some man, I guess his father, held him high. There it came out of the boy, the giggle-laugh, heeheeheeheehee, bouncing off the buildings. Too bad we can't bottle that laugh. A special laugh, from a son to a dad, manly, wild, scarcely under control. "That sounds familiar," Jill said, as the man and boy walked by.

The first time I heard Alex gut-laugh at home was when he was in his crib, and I blew on his legs and belly after the bath and told him "Guys like air!" I still do that. Up comes the laugh. If it's going to be a really good one, sometimes Alex will growl beforehand, or squeal. Then he'll settle into that laugh, and laugh until seized with hiccups. Just like Dad.

He's laughing now. He won't stop. Or can't. When did this start? "About four o'clock," Jill replies, "in the drug store. Then he started crying. I had to hold him for an hour and a half. I have to lie down."

I trail Alex. In the bathroom he touches the toilet and staggers. Hahahahaha hic, hahahahaha hic. He reels by the cabinets under the sink, floored by the wit of a childproof lock on the handles, and he laughs and laughs and collapses like a freshman at a kegger. I laugh too. Jill, who's been around it for two hours, shuts the bedroom door in hope of some peace. I follow Alex into the living room and sit him down for some, perhaps, quiet reading. But tonight *Polar Bear, Polar Bear, What Do You Hear?* is the funniest satire since *Catch-22.* He leans back against me; I feel him shake. Some girl told me once that when a guy made her laugh, it started with the crack of her smile, then spread like an earthquake across her face until she was helpless. This is how I feel with Alex now. I feel the crack widen, my cheeks pull back and my chest start to quiver. Who cares what's funny? I drink it up from him like a gift.

In the crib, he finds the railings a riot. I fill the tub and hear him in there, idling in giggles, revving for bursts of laughter.

My smile fades as the water rises and I wonder, "Is this right?" Jill wonders if he's too young for a psychotic episode. Has his new little brain, overheated by old hospital bills, endless paperwork to secure a new apartment, the woes of jobs and sickly older relatives, at last come off its hinges?

He has never been too young for medical stuff. For thirteen months, remember, anything new that happened to Alex was often bad. Alex hasn't been to a doctor for a while, though we are dreading what his pediatrician will say about his weight.

I peel off his diaper to the sound of a tickled banshee. "Better than crying," I say to Jill. Into the water, which comes up just over the scar from his J-tube surgery. Tonight he delights in thrashing his legs and turning around and around. Laughter echoes up from the tub. Three hours now. I have stopped laughing.

Jill was talking to someone about Alex the other day and never mentioned the hospital. "First time I've done that," she said.

I mentioned the hospital just a few days ago, when I told a new co-worker about Alex. Alex spent the first thirteen months of his life in a hospital, I said. "Thirteen months? Wow," said the co-worker. "The doctors couldn't have given him much chance, huh?" When I talk about Alex in the hospital, I round the numbers: three months premature, though it was only two and a half; thirteen months in hospitals, though it was only twelve and a half.

Co-workers have said a lot of things about Alex in the past two years, even when he was in the depths of the hospital. "It will all be a memory in a few years," said one. This guy's daughter was three then, and he used to delight in her calling him at work and telling him about her day. Now he's divorced; I think there's a custody fight. I feel bad for him.

Mike, another co-worker who was there for the whole Alex in the Hospital Escapade, looked at my favorite photo of Alex and said, "You'd never know from looking at this that anything was ever wrong." No. The picture in Mike's hand is of

Alex's face close up, that one from Central Park. That photo says charm, determination, a fetching boldness that he probably started honing back in the isolette. That photo helps fade the memories: when we stopped at a red light on our drive in on the night Alex was reintubated, a beggar appeared at my car window. "Please no," I said to his face through the glass. "We have a baby in the hospital. Please no." His face faded into the night. Holding Alex past midnight, trying to keep his numbers up by pure cuddling while the robes looked on. Watching him chomp a binkie as the numbers fell. Two in the morning, a morgue-still waiting room, no one coming out of his room to tell us anything until we burst back in and made the faded robes turn gaping in the lights. Two years ago next Sunday.

The day of the spinal tap comes back to me in glimpses: the queasy blue stripe of the NICU blanket, the reflection of the neon in the clear plastic of the isolette, the fine green wires snapping as he wiggled in there. One thing I can't remember is, did Alex actually get a spinal tap? Jill says yes. "His face was creased with pain and a complete lack of comprehension," she says. "They didn't give him anesthesia. He looked like he'd been run over by a truck." She pauses. "I can see that face . . . anytime I want." Oh yes, I remember now.

To recall the day his IV sprang a leak I just have to look down, to the drop of blood, brown as old motor oil, on the toe of my boot. Alex was grinning. The nurse wiped the blood off the floor by dropping a washcloth and pushing it around with her foot. I look at that spot now and it makes me fearless. Mail from the collection agency? Loud teens in the subway? Threats from those who don't know what a threat is? Look at the spot. I hate to say it, but I'm glad that spot is there.

The thirteen months have seeped into me, and I'm not sure how to get them out, or even if I want to.

## DECEMBER, 2000, TO JUNE, 2001

"ALEX, CAN YOU say 'baby'?"

Softly: "Ba ba."

"Alex, can you say 'baby'?"

"Ba ba."

"Remember that word, Alex."

Just before Christmas, 2000, the new little brother, Edwin, comes home. I watched this birth, too, and compared with what Alex experienced Edwin went through nothing. A bored pediatrician flicked him on the foot and walked away, leaving my second son squirming under the heat lights. Edwin was calm at birth and is calm now. He does everything he's supposed to, like a well-wired new home computer. He sucks, finds his fingers, makes little irking noises like those flying creatures on the "Star Trek" episode where Kirk's brother gets killed. Edwin's eyes move over me with questions.

*And you are? . . .*

When this Little Brother is born, we are still kicking around names. I favor Edwin Joseph—the first names of Jill's father and grandfather, and Edwin would allow me to call him "Neddy," which sounds like Nettie, my late mom's name. Aunt Julie, however, suggests Douglas or perhaps the names of Manhattan stores like Zabar or Fairway.

Alex has no suggestion for a name. He comes to the hospital but doesn't seem to notice his little brother until Edwin/Douglas/Fairway cries. Then Alex half smiles and tries to touch his brother with a hand that is enormous. It is the first time Alex has looked imposing.

"Before the baby comes home," advised Howard, a wise dad, "get Alex a nice toy. When Jill brings the baby home, have Alex in another part of the house. Have Jill come in, get the baby settled in another room asleep, then she comes out to Alex. Don't let Alex see her with the baby."

This is no mere baby. This is a baby brother. For weeks, after Alex got "Mama" and "Dada" down, we coached him on "baby" and "brother." Soon he fashioned "be be" and "bru bru." "Alex, can you say 'baby'?" I kept asking him, until he was quicker with the answer than I was.

I told my older brother how I'd also coached Alex on how inestimably special and breathtaking little brothers are. "Yes," purrs my brother, who owes whatever skill he's retained in kung fu to the hours of practice on me in the late 1960s. I don't think he once let me watch "Captain America" without teasing me from the couch, where he always got to sit. My brother says that if Alex needs a toy now we could give him a little baseball bat.

By the time Alex and Ned have been home together for five days, "We've already had some interaction. Alex hit him in the face with a book," Jill says. Actually, Jill says, Alex didn't see Ned. He approached Jill and did what he's always done approaching someone when he wants to be read to: he went "dadada" and swung the book. Ned was sort of in the way, and didn't even cry. I didn't witness this.

"Alex, can you say 'Ned?'"

"Ney."

For the past two nights we've given Ned his bath in Alex's room, in part because it's less drafty and in part because it gives Alex a chance to see Ned bawling in indignation. Just now before the bath, however, I swaddled Ned and held him to the railing of the crib. Alex didn't sidle away, but instead reached out his hand with the same light stroke he's used for new dogs and flowers in the pots on 7th Avenue. "Alex: baby. Soft, Alex, soft." Ned blinked at me, seeming to ask: Who is this? Who are you? Where am I?

This is your brother and you are here, and your brother will love you.

Jill began to snarkle and blow shortly after we moved into our new apartment, which I attributed to the dust and cardboard fibers filling the air. Within a few days she was laid low.

"Don't give it to me," I said.

Jill deployed boxes of Kleenex through the apartment, and empty DayQuil capsule containers began to appear in our bathroom wastebasket. Soon her sense of taste was gone and her voice took on a rasp like Brenda Vaccarro's. She coughed a deep cough. "Every now and then I cough up something that reminds me of one of those bits of ectoplasm in *Ghostbusters*," she said. Then I got it. My hankies became my best friends, though they gradually grew stiffer in my pockets; nasal spray and Vicks became part of my bedtime routine. I took to dropping my own opened bubbles of Nyquil into the wastebasket.

Then Alex got it.

For two winters we lived in terror of colds. We'd heard stories of how colds with vicious new initials could reverse the clock for former BPDers. Last year, Alex got a drug to fight RSV—Respiratory Syncytial Virus, the leading cause of lower respiratory tract infections in infants and young children—at $1,000 a shot and worth every cent. But this year his pediatrician said he didn't need it. And Alex seemed healthy at least through four a.m. Tuesday, when he woke up crying and hungry. I held the sippy cup while he sucked down the whole thing, then I coughed and blew my heavy nose and we all went back to sleep.

On Wednesday morning, Alex began to cough. It racked him for hours on end. I could hear those little lungs try their best over and over and into the night. Eventually deep dimples began to appear under his ribs with every breath. We put on the oxygen cannula, and didn't take it off. From a sitting position in his crib, his head would pitch to the side. He seemed to sleep little, but would lie with his eyes open until he realized we were watching him, then he'd close his eyes and pretend to be asleep. He stopped eating and drinking.

Thursday we took him to the pediatrician. "There's a nasty one going around," the doctor said. Every kid's having it. For kids like Alex it can be very bad. Alex doesn't have many reserves. Old lines. Don't skimp on the oxygen, the doc advised. Give nebs every four hours. Here are your steroids and antibiotics. Without warning our evenings, which have for months trembled on the verge of normal family life, were fragmented again by stretches of time between medicines.

On Friday, Alex barely got up. We switched to grape Dimetapp, but it didn't seem to bring him around as well as children's Tylenol. (Both smelled fruity and enticing, but I tried them and they tasted like wax.) I went to work, and spent the lunch hour with my pockets stuffed with stiff handkerchiefs and the wrappers of Hall's Honey Lemon drops, and walked store to store to find Puffs tissues with lotion for Jill.

At about three in the afternoon I called Jill. "At this moment he's sitting up and eating Cheerios," Jill said. I informed the pediatrician. "Sooner or later he's going to have to turn a corner on this thing." Can we keep giving Tylenol every four hours? Of course.

Emergency oxygen round the clock. Fiddling with the probe to get a clear signal on the pulse ox that we haven't used overnight for months and were on the verge of returning. Suddenly Alex couldn't go in the carriage without being attached to a little B tank of oxygen, which is about the size of a thermos bottle. Just a few days before he'd needed only a quarter-liter— when he needed oxygen from the tank at all. Now it amazed me how fast a B tank drained on the flow Alex needed. When he rolled over in bed, the wires turned into the same knot we used to wrestle with when we brought him home. From his drawers we rooted out supplies that we haven't used in months. Syringes, tubing, tape that no longer sticks.

Sooner or later he will turn a corner on this thing. But not on Saturday, as his sats continued to dip even as we cranked the oxygen tank closer and closer to one liter. We rushed him to the pediatrician's office in late morning. "There's a nasty one out there," said the doctor who was covering for the weekend. She gave us a new antibiotic and a new neb formula and instructed us to take him home, force sugary juices in with a syringe if necessary, and whap him on the chest and back to loosen the mucus.

"Call me later," the doc says.

Yes, whap him, before the numbers sink some more and we wind up headed for the hospital and sleeping on a cot beside his bed, holding his free hand while they search for a vein for the IV, watching him watch the alarms and screens that for months were his night time companions but that now, to him, have nothing to do with home. We used to have these pads to whap him with. We inflated them with a syringe. We got home and I rooted around for them and Jill rasped that we threw them out weeks ago. In the end we just use our hands, wishing he could tell us how he's feeling.

He still needs oxygen, which poses a big problem one day on a city bus when Jill's having a crappy day, she forgot her scarf, and her mother is back in the hospital with pneumonia. We want to go sixteen blocks down 5th Avenue to a museum for a couple of hours. We can't fold up the carriage because Alex's "E" tank, the size of a scuba tank, is in the bottom.

"You want to give the driver the spiel about the carriage?" I ask her.

"Oh, can't you?" she says. "I always do it."

Jill gets on first. I lift the carriage up the steps of the bus when I notice Jill has stopped near the driver.

"This boy is on oxygen!" I hear her say. "We *can't* collapse the carriage."

"Lady, you cannot bring the stroller on the bus without collapsing it," he answers. He is a thin, sinewy young man who looks like his life hasn't exposed him to portable oxygen tanks.

"The—baby—is—on—oxygen!" Jill repeats. She stretches out every word, I guess in hopes that one of them will ring this guy's bell.

"Lady, you cannot bring that carriage on without collapsing it!"

That is the law. As Alex's oxygen needs have dropped, Jill has been known to put a cannula in his nose but not hook the cannula up to the tank, the theory being that most drivers won't know the difference and allow her to board with the stroller unfolded. Most drivers just wave her aboard. One driver put his hand over the fare box and insisted Jill not even pay. Another insisted that the stroller be belted into the slot reserved for wheelchairs. You can ride on a New York bus if you're in a wheelchair. Usually no more than a quarter of the passengers will sigh through their noses and look at their watches while the mechanical wheelchair ramp is slowly lowered, the chair comes on board and the driver straps it in, the ramp is secured and the driver strolls back to the front seat.

"We'll bring him up the back stairs if you want us to."

"Lady, you can't bring it on board without collapsing it."

I see the faces of the other passengers beyond Jill.

"Jeff, we're gettin' on!" she declares.

I pay the fare and we wheel the carriage to the rear of the quarter-full bus. But we don't pull out. Instead, the lights go dark, the engine dies, and the driver slams out the front door and walks away. The front door is also closed, and the power is off to the rear door. No one can get on or off the bus.

"Where's he going?" I hear one passenger ask.

"What is he doing?" wondered an enormous man next to me, a janitor at nearby hospital. I tell him we don't want to hold anyone up, and if the driver will open the door we'll take another bus, or a cab. The enormous man assures me that he has plenty of time. "He's gone to get his dispatcher," the man says. "Now that's just stupid!"

Alex looks around. Jill and I get up and move to wheel Alex off when the driver returns.

"You sit down," says the enormous man. "You sit down. You're in the right. You stand by your argument!"

"The baby's on oxygen," a woman up front says, as if explaining to the universe. "The baby's on oxygen and going to the hospital."

Across the aisle, two teenage girls agree that our stroller is not as big as some. While this discussion is going on, the driver returns and mutters something about how we're going to have to get on another bus.

"You stay right where you are," the enormous man says to Jill. "You sit down and stay where you are." The other passengers echo him. If we'd just pulled out, we'd be off the bus by now. I apologize to him again. "I got time," he says again.

We sit in the darkened, motionless bus, and I have the chill feeling of being in the center of a bad situation that I think is a dream but is real. I start thinking of the Americans with Disabilities Act.

"This child is disabled," Jill says. Then to me she adds, "I made a tactical error. I tried to bulldoze the driver. I shouldn't have. We should have just gotten on another bus. I've had to do that a couple of times before."

The driver has found his dispatcher. He is gargantuan, hidden behind sunglasses and about fifty pounds of beard. He lumbers from the rear of the bus toward the front door. "Take your time, turtle," one of the teenage girls calls to him through an open window.

He pokes his head in and stares at Alex's tank in the stroller, which I have spun around for him to look at. "What if the bus gets crowded?" he asks.

"Then we'll get off or fold it up," Jill replies. "This has never been a problem before."

He stares at Alex, who is still looking around. Alex likes buses, though he likes yellow taxis more. The dispatcher leaves and lumbers past the teenage girls' window again. "Thanks, turtle," one of them calls.

The driver gets back on board. He turns the lights and the engine back on, and the bus pulls out. In about ten minutes, we get off. We go to the museum, and when we're done we take another bus home. It's a different driver, and she just waves us aboard.

"—jingle all the way. Oh, what fun it is to ride in a one-horse open sleigh . . ."

If you convert all the syllables in that refrain to "de" (as in "de-de-de, de-de-de, de-de-dedede . . .") you can do a Vegas-worthy impersonation of Alex.

"De-de-de, de-de-de, de de de de de . . ."

I have no idea how or when Alex ever heard "Jingle Bells." During his second Christmas, the only song I cranked was the Royal Guardsmen's "Christmas Bells" about Snoopy and the Red Baron. ". . . or was it the bells from the village below . . ."

"De-de-de, de-de-de, de de de de de . . ."

Alex's connection with "Jingle Bells" surfaced in November, when we were all at his grandparents' and he was sitting in his stroller next to Aunt Julie. He was fiddling with some toy and he started going "de-de-de . . ." in a rhythm that was soon vaguely familiar.

"That's 'Jingle Bells!'" said Aunt Julie. "He's singing 'Jingle Bells.'" She turned to him. "'Jingle all the way . . .'"

"De-de-de."

I'm glad Alex likes "Jingle Bells." Of all the Christmas songs, it was the most magical in my childhood, and like a good sport it lent itself to variations: "Jingle Bells, Batman smells, Robin laid an egg. The Batmobile lost a wheel, and something some-thing day . . ."

Confirmation of Alex's predilection came during "A Char-lie Brown Christmas," when Schroeder plinked out the song sarcastically for Lucy. Alex, watching from the stroller, started "de-de-de"ing not only with the music, but ahead of it. "Eerie," Jill remarked.

As I often do, I experimented when he was in his bath, singing: "Dashing through the snow, in a one-horse open sleigh, o'er the fields we go, laughing all the way. Hahaha—" I rapped half the tune out on the side of the tub, and he picked right up with the rest of it. Rapraprap, "de-de-de." Rapraprap. "de-de-de—de—de." Where'd Alex learn so much about changes in tempo?

For adults, and everyone else except Alex, that song is gone for another year, like its associates "God Not the Bells!" and "Chipmunks Roasting on an Open Fire." But to revisit Christmas just once more this year, "Jingle Bells" has some arresting lyrics. Especially if you relish studying them with a two-year-old.

"Oh what fun to laugh and sing and something something night!"

"De de de, de de, de, de-de-dedede . . ."

Alex rapidly develops his own language. "Pfft pfft" for "beep beep," "Poppa" for "Grandpa." When asked, he recites "Mama" and "Dada" without fail, but ask him to say "Alex" and he replies only "ga." He's starting to say "ga" for his name with more strength and conviction, and I'm starting to wonder what the sound means in his secret language.

Alex does, however, have a clear new word. "Alex, you want more?"

"Muh."

Alex is getting lots of words. "Ba" for bath, "bebe" for baby. His talking really began when we drilled him on these words, in this order: "Mama," "Dada," and "Alex." Jill says his "Mama" is a caress. His "Dada" is sprightly (I think he means to say "fun ba dude"). Lately, he repeats and will take a stab at any word: hen, penny, okay, uncle, owl, mouse. The other day he handed me a Teddy Graham and said, "Bear."

When I say he's learned to say these words, I mean that he gets out the sound of the beginning or the end of one syllable, and the rest we sort of give him credit for. New Year's Eve, when Grandpa came over, Jill asked him if he could say "up" to Grandpa, thinking that she'd get a toddling gesture and a vague sound, and instead Alex piped out a clear "Up!"

"Muh"—okay, not "clear," exactly—is his first sound that's taking on the dimensions of a real word. It was born out of "more," and is an imperative meaning "Don't stop" or "You may continue." "Muh" may come hard or it may come soft.

If Alex is on his tiptoes at the kitchen counter and on that counter is his Flavor-of-the-Moment musical toy, "muh" means "give me the toy." If I'm swinging him around until my arms start to ache and I stop, "Muh" means "I'm not tired, Dad." Tonight two "muh"s come back to back when I try to stop the bedtime recital of *Little Lamb* at just fifteen readings.

"Muh" is a standby during "The Duke of York":

". . . and when they were up they were up . . ."

Alex: "Up!"

". . . and when they were down they were down . . ."

"Dun!"

". . . and when they were only halfway up they were neither up nor down!"

Pause. Then Alex pulls the binkie out of his mouth like the chairman of the board pulling out his cigar, and proclaims, "Muh!" Crisp, confident, bitten off. Muh. Sometimes Jill and I use it, just like we once used "ehn ehn ehn," "gaa," and "daddle daddle daddle." They were handy phrases.

"Alex, do you want another cookie?"

"Muh."

"What do you want, Alex?"

"Muh."

I guess "muh" is becoming a crutch. His first word, yes, but with so many possible meanings as to be gibberish. Jill thinks he should have moved on to other words by now. I tell her not to worry, but how's he going to get through school by replying "muh" to an undeserved poor grade? Is he going to look his boss in the eye and say "muh" to a meager raise? What will girls think?

We read about brain damage in preemies. Tomorrow he goes to his first playgroup, and those kids scream a cornucopia of words. Today we bought a potty; I get the impression that understanding the spoken word is one of the most important elements in learning to use it.

"Alex, do you want me to read to you in my lap?"

"Muh."

"No, where do you want to come? Do you want to come 'up'?"

"Up!" Crisp and bitten off. That's good to hear.

What's not so good to hear, at least initially, is his word one night when I'm changing his diaper. We're still using diapers. We shouldn't have to be, and we don't want to be, but we're still using diapers. Alex starts to twist and raise himself off the crib mattress. "Alex, diaper," I say. He has learned that when I say this, he is to lie still. But he shouldn't even be in a crib anymore. We're worried about his future and his head size, and all the stuff that both of these things might mean. I'm worrying about all this stuff when I pull the sticky tab too hard. The diaper rips.

"Damn it," I mumble.

I get one sticky tab done down there and am just starting to line up the other one over Alex's hip when from down in the crib somebody also says, softly, "Damn it."

It's like little snowflakes drifting to earth and landing in the shape of a swear word. "Alex, don't say that," I tell him.

I swore when I was three. At least that's what my big brother says, and he should know: he tripped me. My old house had railroaded rooms from the back of my parents' bedroom all the way to the sink on the far wall of the kitchen, and I was barreling down this highway when, reportedly, out came big brother's foot. I landed on my stomach and skidded three feet until my head met the base of the sink cabinet with a little *ting*. My brother says he leaned over and, between spasms of laughter, managed to ask if I was all right. I, again reportedly, rolled my eyes up at him and for the first time said the F word.

Had I known her then, maybe I could've learned that word from Jill, who grew up in New York and who is therefore as charmed as I am by Alex's new word.

"That is so cute," Jill says. "We can't let Grandma hear that."

"Damn damn damn," Alex murmurs, hand over hand along the railing of the crib. "Damn damn damn." He won't eat vegetables or cheese, but he'll say "damn it." Alex has been mimicking well and starting to string syllables together. The other night Jill got him to say the whole title of "Go Dog, Go," a new book from Uncle (Big Brother With The Foot) Lee and Aunt Diane. He walked around all night repeating the three words.

"Alex," I whisper, "don't say 'damn it.'"

"Damn it."

Two words! I just realized that's two words together!

Obviously Alex doesn't know what the words mean; they're just sounds. But he will learn what they mean, and they'll be useful to him growing up in New York. Especially if the delays he seems to have begin to deepen. Sometimes, he just cocks his head to one side and stares into space. He rarely responds to his own name. The diapers speak for themselves. He doesn't seem to understand when other kids want to play with him: Yesterday I took him to the park and a boy not much older than Alex wanted to play Follow The Leader. Alex went his own way.

Doctors have said words that are hard for me to hear. Today I got a report that sprayed words like "truncal hypotonia," "nystagmus," and "microcephalic." I think I know what these words mean, damn it, but I have no desire to look them up. One phrase in the report that I did know the meaning of was "ongoing difficulties."

As Alex goes along his own way, he's learned to be happy when the cab pulls up, to eat better in restaurants than at home, and to sleep on the subway. "Damn it" is just another survival tool to be learned by this little New Yorker. I'm afraid it's going to be a lot more useful to him than "Go Dog, Go."

We've seen three preschools: warrens with eruptions of finger-paint in the halls, above cubbyholes with children's names written in sparkles on colored construction paper. The backs of all the chairs come up just to my knees.

When he turns three in June, Alex will age out of his Early Intervention home-based therapy. These therapists have done well. He likes to read and roll his trucks across the floor. He can sort of brush his teeth. Last night he ate four fish sticks. He's getting too old to receive therapy at home. He's ready for school, and, almost bewildering to me, some part of some government is going to pay for it. But, said one social worker, some 3,000 other similar tots in New York will age into school next fall and they won't all get into a school. There aren't enough schools. Ah. We were cruising waters of entitlement in an almost socialistic care system when suddenly it's as if we're applying to Ivy League schools and rejection could come based on any reason. Or whim.

We'll no longer have therapists coming to our home with their bulging knapsacks of toys, which Alex dives into unasked. Instead he'll have to be trundled off every morning to school. I wanted to be home with Alex for a while before he's sucked into the educational system, but I guess it isn't to be. The idea of school for Alex once seemed remote as Mars, but all of a sudden we're on the tours and filling out the applications and wondering how in God's name a bus driver will ever get him to sit still.

"I just hope he doesn't have to ride the short school bus," Jill says. He's half a year or more delayed in such academic disciplines as eating, running and holding his balance. Maybe it's just because of all that time in the hospital. Maybe too it's because of something a co-worker of mine, who also had a delayed kid, called "the hardware."

I tour these schools, I meander through the scent of Play-Doh, and I hope school doesn't become another industry I learn about. I learned about prematurity, for instance. I learned that hospital care can be as much about politics as practice. What I learned about premature birth is tattooed on me. "Education" being such a behemoth in anyone's life, how can I expect it won't turn into another endless, bumpy ride, another subject I'll comprehend only after it's battered me beyond recognition?

We've been looking at schools that take "special" students. One school got a great write-up in a magazine when, according to Jill, they "turned around" an adopted Russian boy with problems. Another school is all "special," though as I peep into classrooms I see no wheelchairs or medical gear—not even oxygen tanks, which have been in my life so long it's hard for me to believe every kid doesn't have one at home.

We unleash Alex in one classroom. As he flits from tiny table to tiny table, there comes a pleasant-looking boy we're told is named Henry. Henry inches down in front of me and starts playing with a wooden train set. Alex marches over. Henry is bigger than Alex, but Henry exudes mildness. Alex is not that mild. He takes pieces of track away from Henry—not violently or in a bullying way, but I think he just doesn't notice Henry. Henry moves on. I feel a little bad for Henry.

Alex finds a rocking horse—he can find a rocking horse with the same instinct I use to find a pinball machine—and he watches the kids on trikes and on the big balls and on the plastic indoor gym. He's rocking and rocking on the horse. I watch as a little girl comes out of nowhere and starts rocking next to him. She starts moving closer and closer, and I get the impression that she too is a prospective student on a tour. She moves closer, and then Alex sees her and reaches out for her hair. (Once at a church fair Alex was climbing a chair while a year-old girl watched him; when he climbed down he needed something to hang on to, so he used her face.)

"No, Alex, touch nice," I tell him, just as I do when he reaches for Ned. The little girl moves off. Another little girl comes out of nowhere and grabs the front of the horse. She says "Hi" to Alex. I think he will be angry. But he smiles and starts to laugh. The little girl tells him good-bye and runs off. I see him watch the little girl leave and watch other kids bounce in. The next part of his education, and ours, is suddenly all around me like the smell of Play-Doh.

It isn't long before we're hoping Alex gets to ride any school bus. "Dear Mr. and Mrs. Stimpson: We are very sorry that at this time all of the openings in our classrooms have been filled for the academic year 2001–2002. We anticipate that some places may open up in the next weeks or months, and we would be pleased to keep your application active, if you so desire."

"There are definitely loopholes in the system," says one special-ed advocate. I ask if there are support groups for parents of special ed kids who are trying to get into preschools. "Maybe you'll start one, right?" she replies.

"It's sad to see what happens to some families in the process," adds a social worker. "Tell me about Alex."

Okay. He'll be three in June. He needs a hand on stairs. He doesn't point or use a spoon. He can't, or at least doesn't, respond to his name. He has maybe a dozen words, and uses half of them interchangeably. I can't imagine Alex behaving on a school bus, short or otherwise, without Jill or me beside him.

The process to get into a school is an education, its textbooks nth-generation photocopies. Few of the documents we've received had straight lines of type. Most were so old that the small Es were filled in. Some had the name of city officials on the letterhead. One read "David N. Dinkins, Mayor of New York." Dinkins left office in 1993. At least his name was crossed out.

Social workers ask if Jill and I know our rights. We read everything we receive—it's easy once you're used to the filled-in

Es—and as near as we can tell from the spaghetti of bureaucratese, Alex must be evaluated for his needs. That's underway. Then our school board will meet with us and determine what Alex is entitled to. At this meeting we're entitled to bring a battery of supporters, and even Alex himself. If we don't like what the board says, we can appeal and even have him evaluated by an independent expert. Sounds fair.

But when all the photocopies settle, Alex may be standing there, a truck in one hand and *Tom and Pippo's Day* in the other, along with 3,000 other kids. I've lived in New York long enough to know what can happen when you stand in line with 3,000 other people, all of you looking for something that's in short supply. Jill has scouted the online boards and found wails from parents whose kids applied to ten schools and were rejected by all of them. The tone reminded me of a friend in high school who applied to Cornell. He was tying his sneakers for gym class when he finally admitted, "Nah, they didn't want me."


A knee-high kid who wants a Pepperidge Farm Goldfish has few options. He just learned to say "open," but he can't open the pantry door himself because of the plastic childproofing hook we installed. Even if he could he can't reach the shelf where we keep the Goldfish. He's found a way around this, though, as long as he can reach up to take your finger. "Alex? Where we going?"

His touch around my thumb or index finger is like soft, warm cables. Insistent, too: Weaving through the giant grown-up furniture, still learning about his own anatomy, he knows or seems to care little if Dad's fingers were not meant to be twisted this far around. If I stop walking, the cables tighten gently but leave no doubt: *No no, Dad. This way.*

The little hand often comes up as soon as I step through the door. I like that moment before the first tug, when I have no idea if the destination's going to be the kitchen, the TV, or the wooden puzzle on the coffee table.

Ah ha, kitchen. Sink? Water ("a-va-va?")? No, pantry.
"Oh-pa?"

"You want a Goldfish, Alex? What do you want?"

"Oh-pa?" He lets go. He knows I need my hand to ohpa
the pantry door. Isn't he smart? He then leads me to the TV for
more *Mother Goose* videos, and places my hand gently to the
screen. Today, for the first time, he added the command,
"Come." Isn't that adorable?

We take Alex to a "developmental pediatrician," a loud but
kind (to Alex) woman who is a necessary specialist if we're to
learn exactly how ready Alex is for school. New York—the City
or the State, I'm not sure which—wants to know before shell-
ing out for special education for him.

New York will do an evaluation for free, but we got half-way
through that process and decided the government might be more
interested in filling vacancies at specific schools than in filling
any of Alex's special needs. For example, one test on the evaluation involved drawing with a crayon. Jill, who took Alex to this
evaluation, said the supervisor watched Alex try to eat the crayon,
then watched him accidentally make dots on the paper. "Good
enough for me!" the evaluator cried, according to Jill.

We pay $2,000 for a private evaluation. Though it'd be
cheaper to get Alex evaluated by Tony Bennett, I feel this evaluator, Dr. S., will do a thorough job. Alex loves her. He spends
the first part of the ninety-minute session scampering around
her office and yelping with delight. "Oh yes! You're just so excited, aren't you!?" Dr. S. says. She speaks to him in the playful,
high-pitched voice that charms kids.

This evaluation calls for Alex to stack two blocks, drop
puzzle pieces in the right slots, sit in a chair, find a doll, drop a
block in a box and then in a cup, and draw on a piece of paper
with a crayon. If he can do all these things then maybe he won't
even need special education. If he can't do these things, he's a
wreck and this doctor will argue for the most comprehensive

program New York's money can buy. Hard to know what to hope for.

"Alex! Can you come here and sit with me, sweetie? Can you come here and sit with me? Oh, you want to be over there! Oh you *are* orally centered, aren't you?"

Alex puts the blocks in his mouth and wanders over to bang them on the folded metal chair, then wanders around more until I have to scoop him away from Dr. S.'s surge suppressor and Palm Pilot. When he drops a block, which is a lot, he bends to pick it up, every time. Dr. S. tries to get him to drop a block in her plastic cup, but instead he picks up the cup to drink—expecting, queerly, that there will be water in it—and he can't seem to put the blocks on top of one another no matter how the doctor prompts him with playful, high-pitched cries of "One, two!"

"He said, 'me,'" Dr. S. announces. "Did you hear him?" I didn't. He's never said "me" before. He yelps some more and flies around the room. Then he comes and takes my hand and herds me toward the door.

"Oh, he thinks it's time to go. Not yet, Alex," Dr. S. says, then directs him to point to a picture of a dog. The picture of the dog is in a book, next to a picture of a baby. Alex puts his finger on the baby. "Oh no, that's the baby," Dr. S. tells him.

"Bebe," says Alex.

She hands him a baby doll. He chews the toes of the little left foot, then puts the doll down and returns to me for a drink of water. Meanwhile, Dr. S. has slipped the doll behind her back to see if Alex can find it. He does, in about one second. "Oh, can he see its head back there?" she says. Alex starts banging the doll on the folded metal chair, and I tell Dr. S. that Alex is very good with his little brother at home. She makes a mark in her notebook.

"Okay, this one is tough," Dr. S. says, producing still another book and setting it on the table open to a page of black shapes on a white background. "Maybe he'll want to sit on your lap for this one, Daddy. He has to concentrate." She hands

Alex a little piece of white paper with a black triangle on it. Alex studies the paper, studies the book, studies the paper, then puts the triangles together. He does the same thing with the square, the rectangle, and the stop sign. "Good!" Dr. S. cries. She hands him a little wooden puzzle, just a base with an indentation for the red wooden circle and the red wooden triangle. Alex drops the shapes into place without hesitation. Dr. S. spins the base of the puzzle around, but Alex drops the shapes into place no matter how she positions it. She makes another note, checking off what Alex can do. She lets me peek in the book and I see that the tasks are arranged by age: up to twelve months, twelve to eighteen months, eighteen to twenty-three months. Most of the marks are under "twelve to eighteen months." I ask the doctor how she'd assess him based on what she's seen so far. "Oh, there's no doubt he needs a program," she says. Good, I guess. Hard to know what to hope for.

But we keep alive our fantasies of school: helping Alex shop for clothes; holding his hand while helping him onto the bus; watching him and his knapsack disappear up past the driver. Seeing him run toward friends as we mingle at the brownies table during the rummage sale.

A third school has turned him down. The woman who issued today's dump devoted half an hour to her explanation. "Alex certainly has a spark for developing," she began, as I realized that the eventual answer would be "no."

"He has a desire to learn," she said. "He falls down and he gets right back up!"

He sure does!

But they feel he can't interact well with other children, or even with adults. They feel that Alex has trouble concentrating, that he doesn't make eye-contact and that he could become bewildered among eight or nine other children. "Even a teacher/student ratio of one to three wouldn't be enough for Alex," the school official says. He needs closer supervision, "support of all kinds," to nurture that spark that makes him get up when he falls down, and to achieve "what the world will expect of him."

Then she suggests a part-time school program, and perhaps a more "aggressive" schedule of play dates. "He has had no group experiences," she says. Then she gives me phone numbers, making sure I know she knows that it would be wrong to just tell me no and good-bye.

Ending a conversation abruptly can sometimes catch the person you're talking to off guard, and elicit a more candid good-bye. I sign off fast. "Good-bye," she says, cheerful as a game show host.

Jill sways between tears and rage at the news, scouring the kitchen counters and chopping a mound of garlic—imagining, I think, that the fine white cloves are parts of school officials' bodies. My first reaction is to observe that Alex is two years old. I haven't seen many two-year-olds who pump the flesh like a front porch congressman. And I'm thirty-nine and I don't interact much—just ask anybody who rides with me on the 2 train. I thought we were trying to send Alex to school so he could learn to interact. We're not touring these joints because we love construction paper.

"Maybe he was feeling shy that day," Jill adds. "And whoever heard of a two-year-old feeling shy? I never imagined this would become such a depressing, nightmarish thing."

All three schools who've turned him down have stated that they'd be happy to see Alex's application again next year, "when he's a little more up to speed," I think one school said. Well, but school is where he's supposed to get up to speed, or so I thought. I do wish school officials would lay off the tired tactics I've been hearing since those days when doctors pinballed us from office to office with assurances that the next stop would cure all. Then as now, people put us off with a tone I'm sure they think is original and impenetrable: the good news first; the hard "no" and the soft explanation; the phone numbers; the next-contestant-please signoff.

One afternoon, near the bottom of our list and hopes, we cart Alex to the local United Cerebral Palsy offices for an evaluation. Alex doesn't seem to have CP, but apparently they have a special-needs preschool. They take him right off the street. A bunch of evaluators quickly gathers. They watch him play with balls and blocks, walk, reach, jump a little.

Then they're done, and one of them comes to us. "There's good news and bad news," he says. He is a young man with glasses and dark curly hair. He has a kind face; I imagine he'd be great with Alex day after day.

"The good news is, he's too advanced for us to take. The bad news is, he's too advanced for us to take."

Bud-da-boom.

"You know," he adds, "why don't you take him around the corner to the preschool on Nineteenth Street? They might have an opening."

We head to 19th. The sun is warm. Soon it will be the fall of what should be Alex's first school year. Soon. I drop Jill at the door on 19th Street, because I have to get back to work. Work is where you go after you finish school. I go back to my office and shove aside the folder containing all the photocopies of e-mails, all the sheets, all the notes on all the places that have proclaimed there is no place for Alex.

Jill calls that afternoon. "They have an opening," she says. Bud-da-bing.

# JUNE TO SEPTEMBER, 2001

JILL CALLS ME FROM a payphone at work a few days later, after Alex's appointment with another doctor, a neurologist. "He was a good doctor," she says. "He was a nice doctor. I liked him." And?

"He thinks," she said, "that Alex may be mildly retarded."

Just a dream, I say to myself. Jill and I were talking this morning about how all dreams are about anxiety, when really you need relaxation dreams. In a dream, you haven't heard what you think you just heard.

Jill tells me we screwed up, that we should have had Alex in a center-based program and not just getting services at home all this time. What does the doctor mean by "mildly," I ask, feeling that this word could be crucial. Two points below the norm, Jill replies. Then she says, "I'm feeling kind of sad," and her change runs out.

I leave a message for the doctor. He's with patients all day today, his receptionist reports, and he won't get the message until tomorrow. I tell her to try to get him the message today, that he saw my son earlier and gave a disturbing diagnosis. What was the diagnosis? she wants to know. I say the words again. There's a moment of silence that I will not break—let the words linger over someone else's head on this sunny, early-summer afternoon—and she says she'll try to get word to the doctor. I thank her. One part of me is afraid he'll never call back. Another is afraid that he will. All right, let's look at this:

—What's the norm? What does "two points below the norm" mean? What is "mildly"?

—Alex's delays are more like fifteen months, not just a year, Jill reports. But he says little and his language skills are basic. It's hard to fathom what's going on in his head. How can anyone tell where, or how, he is?

—Jill says the doctor agrees with that, and that we won't know for sure for several more months, if not years.

—If this doctor's so good, how come he can't get messages delivered in the same day?

I can't say the news surprises me. Alex still doesn't hug or kiss. He rarely comes when called, or meets your eyes. He falls down. I was just saying to myself the other night that the R word wouldn't surprise me at all. And it doesn't. It does, I'm afraid, open another corridor of care for a troubled child, and maybe later a troubled adult. Walk down the corridor and open the doors to find other corridors. Just as Jill always said that she only wanted Alex not to have to ride the short school bus, now she says she'd be happy to see him on any school bus. Now she says all she wants is for him to be able to support himself. What's behind the doors in this new corridor?

"He has a small head and a small brain. You hear the words 'mildly retarded' and you're not in a good mood," Jill says on the phone when she gets home. "And don't call it the 'R word.' It gives a word a lot more power than it maybe should have."

So now I sit here in my office, and if not for the calendar on the wall and the bags under my eyes, it might be 1998 again. I can't feel my toes or my teeth. The chatter of co-workers seems pointless, the words of people who have not heard what I have heard. Breath is short. My cheeks tingle the way they do when I'm sure I must have dreamed hearing something that was said to me clear as a bell.

Our vacation begins with sucking our household out the front door of our apartment, onto our building's one working elevator, then out the front of the building and into our rented Maxima; then driving, driving, driving, until Jill turns into an vociferous fan of seaside vacationing in spots closer to New York City and ones that promise more beach than the boulder shores of remote Maine. "It's red granite *rocks*," I keep warning her, jamming my sunglasses up my nose and thinking how I have to drive this damned rental Maxima without engaging the COLLISION COVERAGE while overseeing Alex and two babies (Ned and Jill).

Actually, Jill becomes a model vacationer once we get there, but the boys must be changed, watched, fed, changed, bedded down, kept clear of rocks and bad footing in the woods, changed, and slathered with equal parts love, attention, insect repellent and sunscreen. One doesn't "vacation" while caring for the equivalent of little invalids. One of the major tasks of this "vacation" was arranging with a coastal Maine medical-equipment supplier to have oxygen and tubing at the house waiting for us. Alex still uses it when he sleeps.

"I want Alex to see the ocean," Jill says.

He hasn't even seen it by Friday, our last day. Our house is on a scenic inlet of tidal, salty water that seemed sheltered from the wind and so reminded me of a lake. Alex and I do venture down to the rocks of the shore at one point, and he seems to find the seaweed and wet mud a hell of a lot less familiar than the swings in Central Park. After that, it seems we spend every day driving; even a splendid lunch in Acadia National Park was a late affair that limited involvement with the ocean to slowing down to thirty and gawking out our Maxima's windows.

I wake up on Friday to find housemate and fellow vacationer Jon planning a trip to the beach. All week, we hadn't done that much with Jon and his wife Cindy and their two kids beyond a lobster-and-Jon's-relatives cookout. This morning Jon says, "And, well, we want you to come." As that's pretty much a demand from Jon, we plan to be back from the book barns in time to head to the beach.

We follow Jon's car to a parking lot in the woods. We wrangle our stroller (an umbrella job the durability of which pretty much peaks at the potholes on Lexington Avenue) down a rocky dirt path. Alex squeals. "People don't like to walk when they go to the beach," a friend who's with us comments, being sarcastic. Well no, I think, my toe catching on a stone, and here's why.

Gradually the trees thin, the air grows cleaner, and I hear hissing. Alex squeals again as Jill steers the stroller until the sand swallows the wheels. I grab the stroller with Alex in it, she carries Ned and all our other junk, and we haul ourselves around the rim of a tranquil tidal pool until we top a dune, and there it is. White sand, waves as tall as Alex, whispering breakers, hard blue water worthy of some of the smaller spots on Long Island or the Carolinas.

We park Ned with the friend—both of them seem content with that, and our attention is all on getting Alex to the water. We pry off his sneakers and socks and place him on the sand. He curls up the arches of his feet when they hit the wet and the cold, but he takes our hands and begins to move toward the surf.

The cold sea stings at first impact: I figure Alex will retreat, and fast. Instead he splashes forward until one big wave douses the cuff of his shorts. Then he wades deeper, me in tow, until the water soaks my shorts, too, and only a moment later do I realize that my wallet's getting drenched.

I swing him up into the clean, clear air. He looks back down at the foam swirling around Daddy's white legs. "A-wa-wa!" he says.

I set him down, still expecting him to retreat. Not long ago this city kid didn't even trust grass. Yet Alex keeps charging into the a-wa-wa, squealing when the foam crashes into his shorts, his shirt, his face. The sea around him is all motion and noise and wet fun on a warm day. I whirl him up again. "A-wa-wa!" he cries.

After what I think was an intelligent and reasonable amount of time, Alex heads back up the beach. Both Ned and my friend are where we left them. "You certainly had a hard time pulling Alex away," the friend comments, this time with no sarcasm at all. Jill shows Alex how to mold wet sand in a cup. I lose my sunglasses in the surf. We shake the sand from our socks and Alex's little shoes, wondering why we forgot to bring a towel.

One of my biggest memories of that vacation is visiting my parents' grave, I was weeping hard. I held Alex as Jill put her arms around both of us and told him that I was sad because I missed my mother. I was shaking a little too—there were a lot of signs for Alex to see. He kept squirming and looking away and wanting to get down to the grass. Daddy's sadness was nowhere in his world on that sunny day. Jill's first clue came way back in the NICU. "Jeff," she said then, "he doesn't look at me." So we took Alex to be evaluated. No doctor ever mentioned autism, though they mentioned a lot of other bad words. Jill worried and read the Internet. I went on figuring that standard charts don't mean much when applied to Alex, because standard kids don't spend their first thirteen months in the hospital.

My search through Google for "autism" turned up 214,000 entries, or about 80,000 more than a search for "heartbreak." Reads one entry, "Most children with autism are not able to benefit from their environment in the same way as children without the disorder. They tend to be socially unresponsive and to have problems understanding social cues expressed in body or spoken language." Examples of autistic behavior in children include: guiding others to what they want, rather than using gestures to communicate; merely parroting what others say; and insisting on talking about topics of conversation that are of little interest. Pronouns are a minefield.

We have to prepare. For what, we aren't sure. We are sure, however, that it would be good if I learned a little bit about autism, too, beyond *Rain Man*. So I borrowed a title from the library of a local special needs group, an "essential handbook" that promises "answers to the most common questions." The first point is how doctors will do almost anything to avoid calling a kid "autistic." "Like throwing them on the trash heap," says one doctor. "People will never give them a chance." So they make up other words, like "PDD." "Spectrum" is another term.

"Common problems in autism include poor eye contact," the book says, "unusual reactions to sound, and the avoidance of people." Yes, Alex's eye contact is infrequent; he doesn't point or often look to see what your response is; he has little imaginative play; his vocabulary is still quite sparse, and he communicates only to get things he wants or needs; he doesn't kiss or hug us. Yet.

But there are flashes. Once when he seemed to be stoned on antibiotics, Alex did kiss me, right on the cheek in the middle of the night. Now getting him to kiss is a matter of nightly drill after the bath, like teaching him to brush his teeth. He laughs when I touch my cheek to his lips. I think he thinks it has more to do with him than with anyone else.

"A child who can't talk is a popular symbol for autism," the book says.

"He doesn't talk," Jill says. "But make sure you mention how fun-loving Alex is." In her words: Alex has times when he's affectionate, and when he's not well, he always comes and sits on our laps, especially Jill's. He sits to read a story or sometimes to watch TV.

Okay. If my son is on any "spectrum," let's say he's on the mild side for now.

But there's no doubt he's still small. Small head, thin arms and legs. His torso still shows the twin bumps of what an overweight therapist termed "the pigeon chest" common to preemies. His hips are as slender as our hopes whenever we think about Alex and eating.

At school he'll have to hold his own with all the gargantuans Jill and I have seen on the playgrounds, the buses, and the sidewalks. Kids with tree-trunk arms, man-sized hands, heads like birthday balloons.

We ask Alex's pediatrician for advice. "He knows to take in enough to keep him at these proportions," the doctor replies. True, no part of Alex looks small when compared with another part of Alex. And Alex's judgment is what we've always depended on. Which makes our current trials at the table tougher.

Admittedly, Alex's been feverish and irritable over the past week, but in the best of times he's selective at the table. He favors crunchy junk food. At home—he eats better in restaurants—he frets at pizza, chicken nuggets, fish sticks, even fries (all foods he's eaten and enjoyed) if he's in an intractable Goldfish or Bugles mood. "Boo-gulls?" he says softly. A glimpse of anything but water in the drinking cup makes him shake his head and growl like a hinge. (I guess we got him started on this crunchy path, when that same long-gone feeding therapist suggested starting him with Cheetos because they dissolve fast, taste good, and come in a flourescent orange that's easy to spot in the mouth if you suspect your kid is having trouble swallowing.)

Jill says the time has come for us to make Alex's eating decisions. "We can't let him decide, any more than we could let him go outside in January without a coat," she says. Still, I can't imagine broccoli landing anywhere but on the floor.

"Have you tried broccoli in soy sauce?" asks our new feeding therapist. She asks if we all eat together, and how many times we offer him food before we give up. I'm unaware that I've ever "given up," though I have been known to clutch my head and swill a bottle of water while Alex chomps a "dinner" of Goldfish and Milanos.

The therapist recommends feeding Alex things in a plate. "And if he won't eat it, that's it," she maintains. "Don't give him anything else. Should take no more than two meals." Two meals? For breakfast Alex gobbles two bowls of Cheerios by hand (no milk, which I guess is good considering it's by hand) and four strips of bacon. Before we head to the zoo for the afternoon, I fix Alex fries and fish sticks for lunch, and arrange them in two of the compartments of the toddler plate—a kind of round, cartoon-decorated cafeteria tray—and place the tray in front of Alex.

He slowly picks up one fish stick and bites off the end. Then he starts rearranging the food in the compartments. Fries over here one at a time, fish sticks over there one at a time. Jill and I eat most of the fries while Alex stares and stares, then he reaches across the table for *The New Yorker* and, I swear to God, starts flipping through it.

One meal down. "What do we do now?" I ask Jill.

"We go to the zoo," she replies.

Next morning for breakfast, Alex eats two bites of a granola bar and asks for "boo-gulls?" I go to work. Later, Jill calls to say that he's downed about three falafel balls and a few swallows of orange juice—after dumping a full bowl of Cheerios on the floor. In the background I hear Alex's hinge-growl, as well as requests for "boo-gulls?"

"But he's drinking *orange juice*!" Jill whispers into the phone. Good. I hope it goes straight to his proportions.

Alex is curled asleep in a corner of his crib, with a blanket, cannula tubing, Elmo, and one of my T-shirts. He's on his right side. His hair is screwy. His legs are crossed. *Sleep well, Alex. It's a school night.* He's going into the world. What began in an isolette will end, in many ways, in a classroom.

My family's first school night begins at about 10:30 that morning, in the men's room of my office. There I run into Howard. I tell him I'll be a little late the next morning. "First day of school? Oh, wonderful!" he says. "Don't cry too much, Jeff."

I come close to crying at the thought of how close all this came to never happening. I hold out until I read the 2001–2002 school calendar. "Sept. 5: First Day of School for Children." Have you ever read anything sadder in your *life*?! Not sad, exactly. More like a sobering relief after the NICU, the PICU, the surgeries and meds, the bells and the machines, the therapy. The hauling of the oxygen tanks to Thanksgivings and Passovers, the wrenching terms thrown around at the evaluations, the watching of his first stumbles on the playground.

They've given us forms. One for the bus company. One that says, "Daycare Cumulative Health Record." Another is The Board of Education of the City of New York National School Food Program. (My salary overshoots eligibility for the five-cent lunch by $45 a week.) I make up Alex's First Day of School list: diapers, lunch, a change of clothes, a copy of his formal education plan (IEP), and prescriptions for oxygen tanks and perhaps a "para" to shadow him during raucous school activities.

"All clothes must be *labelled* with iron-on or sew-on tapes," the parents' handbook reads. It recommends a blanket and a backpack. "Please send in a notebook for daily home/school communication."

How big a notebook? We don't have labels. Instead, Jill finds a black magic marker. "Do the clothes stay there, or what?" she wants to know. "Do they mean a blanket to sleep on, or under?" Tomorrow looms like my first day of college: a void, details of which are best dreaded.

Some things remain constant tonight. For dinner he has three fish sticks and two chicken nuggets. In the bath, he wants me to turn the faucet on. "What do we say, Alex?" I ask. "Pleeze!" he says. "Pleeze" should impress them tomorrow.

Jill finishes his packing: another of my T-shirts, the forms, his extra clothes, his yellow plastic Bob the Builder lunchbox with granola bars and Goldfish crackers. The lunchbox was a goodbye gift from a home therapist. He's never going to carry a lunchbox all the way to school, I think. We're also sure he won't eat the lunch. But lunchboxes—mine were metal: G.I. Joe or Snoopy; I remember them and want to cry again—have set the tone of this time of year forever, as much as catching the school bus on mornings that are cool with promise.

"I put the diapers in his lunchbox, but hey," Jill says to me. "Don't cry."

Bob the Builder tugs at me. The yellow plastic looks fragile. I frown. "And don't be mad at me," Jill adds. "'Don't cry' is just something married people say to each other."

Next morning, Alex and I crawl out of the municipal bus, which we had to take because we never received the complete paperwork for the school bus until the day before the first day of school. I wheel him four blocks south in his stroller, then make him get out at the school's front door. "You can walk into here," I tell him. He doesn't cry.

We make our way up to the classroom. While I'm busy filling out the forms, he finds a couple of toy buses in his classroom. He runs them across the top of a table and watches the wheels. As his classmates filter in, he doesn't join them. As I talk to the teachers, he keeps bringing me the toy buses. One is a Fisher-Price model, with the little people missing. The other is an electronic music toy. I push the buttons. Nothing happens. "Yeah, we've got to get batteries," one of the teaching assistants says.

Alex will be one of eight kids in this class, with four adults. That's a high ratio of grown-ups, but these kids need it. One keeps lolling his head back and smiling. Another wears a padded helmet. Another, a big boy with blond hair, crawls a lot. He's fast, though, especially when he wants to get out the door.

After a time of accepting the toy buses from Alex, I ask the teacher why she thinks he's not on the carpeted play area with the other kids. "Maybe it's too loud for him over there," she says.

I stay from nine to ten a.m., then I must go to work. I wait until he's not looking to sneak out. Jill comes in at eleven for lunch and to take him home. I wait for her call until noon.

Turns out he did cry. "There will be a period of adjustment," Jill says in the phone message about 12:30. "He wasn't too happy when I got here, but after I was here he perked up."

Oh, dear. Later I find out lunch was a wreck: He ate little, and anyway the school-supplied meal never arrived. "I guess

I'm sad because most of the kids in his class are seriously retarded," Jill says. I ask how Alex is. "Well, relieved that at least
that's over," Jill says. A complete disaster? I ask. Oh, no, she
replies quickly. From her description I decide that, all in all,
probably about a seven or eight. "I'd say a three," Jill says.

The period of adjustment enters its second day with Alex
and me boarding two city buses and going in the wrong direction. It doesn't seem to faze him, as again he's the first in the
classroom. He plays with a bus and a puzzle on this second
morning—again he brings them to me—until he becomes absorbed, apparently, in a wooden stacking toy. So absorbed that
I try to sneak out.

To be certain, however, I return in a couple of minutes. He's
bawling. He holds up his arms to me, and I think how becoming
a parent was a stupid, stupid idea. He stays by himself. The other
kids don't particularly notice one another, either, until they bump
into each other. One boy bumps into Alex. Alex falls and cries.
"He has to get used to things like that," the teacher says, reaching out for him. He cries harder and reaches for me.

Later, while I'm at work, Jill goes by the school. Then she
calls me. "When I arrived, he was sitting and staring into space
over a lunch that he wouldn't eat," she reports. Yet, he had fun
in gym, and one of his new therapists says he gets "high marks"
for feeling abandoned when we leave the classroom. He had
fun in gym, then cried again, I tell Howard. "Well, at least he's
selective," he replies.

We gear up for the third day. Jill won't be in until it's time to
pick him up—after she brought him lunch the second day, he
spent the afternoon watching the door for her to come back. I
will drop him in the morning and sneak right out. He has to
learn how to get along there, Jill and I tell each other. We bring
a bottle of water and a cup from home.

He's cheerful on the bus ride down, and he walks with dignity all the way into the classroom, where he starts to cry. "Alex,"
the teacher says, "Alex, would you like a puzzle?" I tell the

teacher that a wooden puzzle and a drink of water from the cup from home will solve many problems. He gets absorbed in the puzzle. I sneak out.

On the way to work, and through most of the day, it weighs heavy on my heart that when Alex turned around again, he didn't see me there. There's no other way to describe it, either: sneak. Sneak, sneak, sneak.

# SEPTEMBER, 2001

On September 11th, I surface outside the 14th Street subway station and look down 7th Avenue. I have a kamakazi's-eye view of the huge black patch on the silver side of one of the twin towers. It looks like a mattress burning. Orange licks the edges of the patch. I ask someone what happened. Plane, he says, off-course. Pilot error. Standing there, looking south as history rose in thick black ribbons of smoke, I think at least it wasn't terrorists, who would have packed a plane with explosives and aimed for the towers' bases.

I head for work, passing knots of people at all the intersections. I work about a mile north of the Trade Center, and have a clear view all the way. I get to my office at about 9:20. Co-workers say it's like watching a movie. "You can't believe what you're seeing out the window," I hear a colleague tell his wife on the phone. Jill calls twice, saying she'd tuned in to see "Martha Stewart" and just couldn't believe what was on television.

I tell Howard my base-and-explosives theory. "Yes," he says, "but this way the firefighters have a harder time getting at the fire, and it's more spectacular." Howard is a good guy to have around when things get wonky.

At one end of my office is a conference room, with a big, big window that faces south. By the time I get into the conference room one of the towers is gone, and lower Manhattan is dust and smoke at the base of the one tower that still stands. Co-workers who are making any noise at all are crying. "Wow,"

I think, "imagine a world with just one World Trade Center tower."

I tell Howard I'm heading immediately to scoop Alex up from school. I say I'll walk him home if necessary, but I'm sure I'll catch a bus. All the way to the school, I turn often to glance south. The tower is still there, still smoking. I stop into a grocer's and buy a bottle of water. The counterwoman brushes away tears as she takes my $1.25.

At 17th Street and 5th Avenue, I turn around again, and as I watch the smoke and dust billow hard and dark, and from the edges of the cloud rains silver confetti. The smoke and dust balloon in a mass at the base of the tower. Then, above the smoke, against the sky, there is no more tower.

The street moans. "It's gone, it's gone, too," someone says. Most people cry.

At the school, as I ring for the elevator, a sobbing woman tries to touch my arm. She gets in the elevator with me and is still crying as the doors close, but by the second floor she's collected herself enough to say to me, "Your wife called. She said you'd be coming."

I find Alex in his classroom, silent over his mid-morning granola bar. He reaches up his arms to me. He's crying, too, but I suspect it doesn't have much to do with the World Trade Center. He just hates school. I turn to his teachers. Are there any subways, have they heard? Buses, maybe? They start to give me directions to the nearest subway stop, then realize that they've heard no trains are running. I ask if the school will be open tomorrow. "Call us," they say.

"Up for a hike, Alex?" I ask.

We start east, toward Madison Avenue. Jill and Ned are waiting at home, eighty-nine blocks and eight miles north. It takes about a minute to walk a Manhattan block, a little longer if you have to carry a three-year-old boy, his bat backpack, and one of Daddy's T-shirts that he keeps at school to feel secure during naptime.

To pass the time this clear fall day of infamy, I tell Alex how they got the Trade Center, how he and Ned won't remember the Twin Towers, how somebody is going to get the shit bombed out of them for this. People move in a human river north—cars and buses are sparse, but just numerous enough to keep the pedestrians on the sidewalk—and every few blocks a knot is gathered around an open, parked car with a stereo blaring one of New York's all-news stations.

Alex and I have gone about nine blocks, and I'm prattling to him how his grandma wouldn't have thought twice about an eighty-nine-block stroll, when I crash into a knee-high standpipe. The sidewalk gets big as I shoot the heel of my right hand to the pavement and try to keep Alex's head clear. I make it by about two inches. This could be a bad morning to have an injured child on your hands in Manhattan. People offer to help us up.

This is a good day to be a New Yorker and an American, even if you've just lost your biggest building. One church on our way has set up a table on the sidewalk, and offers paper cups of water. "This is nice," says one woman who stops for a drink. "This is New York!" the church water guy answers, then he turns to bellow inside the church, "I need trashbags!"

Every ten blocks, I step into the doorway of an office building, into the cigarette smoke of suddenly discharged office workers, and set Alex down and give us both a swig from the bottle of water. I then step back into the human river flowing north on Madison—flowing smoothly at times, slow at others as mobs of optimists wait for a city bus or cluster around a storefront TV. Many hug cell phones. "You know the World Trade Center towers? They ain't there no more. That's what I'm tellin' you! The World Trade Center is gone!"

I hold onto Alex and keep walking, walking, walking. We stop at Grandma's on 86th Street because I'm worried about her getting to dialysis. At Grandma's, Aunt Julie tickles Alex on the bedroom floor while I instant-message Jill that we are fine and on our way home. (All payphones on the walk up Manhattan were busy, and the regular phone lines were out between Grandma's and home.) Aunt Julie feeds me melon on a fork while I hold Alex; then we start out again.

Soon, my feet burn and my shirt is wet with sweat when, on 100th Street, a messenger asks me, "Is it true about the World Trade Center?"

I say it is, and that I'd seen the second one go.

"I just made a delivery there yesterday," he marvels. Small world.

Eight more blocks, and Alex and I are home. The walk has taken two and a half hours. (Later, I'll find five blisters on my toes.) The TV is on in our living room, broadcasting CBS, the one network that's still reaching non-cable viewers in New York. All other networks and stations had their transmitters atop the first tower. "Can you believe this?" Jill asks, referring, I think, to more than the TV situation.

That afternoon, we take Alex and Ned to two playgrounds. The weather is splendid: cool, leaves sparkling in a light and dry northern breeze, the skies split now and then only by the scream of F-14s low over the city, flying what I think carrier pilots still call Combat Air Patrol. Alex does the ladders and all the slides—he's getting very stable on both—and Ned and Alex ride the swings until my legs begin to cramp from standing up and pushing. We stay late on the playgrounds. "What do you want to do?" I ask Jill. "Go home and watch the CBS tape of planes hitting the World Trade Center over and over?"

"U.S. Attacked" reads the two-inch-high headline in Wednesday's *Times*. Alex's school and my office are closed. Post-impact, two more buildings near the WTC site fall down (later, I learn that one of them housed my bank's main computer). The weather reports begin featuring a gray oval—the smoke cloud—pointing out from lower Manhattan. We pack the double stroller and head across Central Park for more playgrounds. All the way across the park, and often in the days since, I glance down the avenues. Nope, still gone, just like dead people.

"Everything does look different, doesn't it?" Jill says. Sirens make pedestrians turn their head, as do the bangs of heavy boxes dropped accidentally on the floors of delivery vans. As do people just running for a bus, mistaken over and over for the first signs of fresh attacks and a spark of panic. Out with my boys, I look at various buildings and wonder how much rubble each would make. Alex crawls up more ladders, slides down more slides, gets a runny nose, munches corn Bugles. We run him and Ned ragged on playgrounds during afternoons. Alex seems to love the afternoons that I almost think of as idyllic until late Thursday, when the breeze shifts to the south and the playgrounds begin to smell of smoke.

One night, our water turns brown. We call the super and the city, and they both tell us the same thing: that the city, working on "the pipes" to switch over a reservoir, had opened the sluice too fast and raised sediment from the pipes' bottoms. It was reasonably safe to bathe in, I'm told, but, if consumed, could cause a "tummy ache." Jill takes the collapsible tote wagon around the corner and buys three gallons of water. "I don't drink anything that's brown," one city water phone-answering guy offers, "not even soda." So we have that. We boil water, cool it with ice cubes, and, for the first time, bathe both boys together.

In the days that follow, our water turns just a hint of green, and comes to smell faintly like a swimming pool. "Maybe someday we'll have our sweet New York City water back," Jill says.

We're also worrying. I worry about my kids having no future. At work, I click through the news sites, trying to snag that one fact that will let me breathe easier. All that appears on my screen, however, is more and more gruesome and frightening stuff until I realize that, in a war where your worst enemy is still imagination, it's better to just be vigilant and ready. And play computer Hearts. And drink wine each night.

Jill's worry focuses on Alex having a future with special needs. Night after night she cruises the Internet looking for kids like Alex, and finds none. This makes her feel better and worse at the same time. If we could put our two sets of worries in a pot and stir them up in the brown and green water, maybe we could boil them down until they meant nothing.

On his days off from school, Alex is trying to return to his everyday life, which was destroyed not on September 11 by terrorists, but on September 5, by preschool. He tackles every ladder on the playground and insists on a first-hand look at the restrooms. Ned learns to eat new and different things, but since he doesn't walk yet, I guess we can leave his "sturdy shoes" out of the Family Emergency Kit that the *Daily News* suggested we put together. In that kit, we will need batteries; water; baby formula; something for the batteries to power, such as a radio or Alex's fat plastic cassette player; more baby formula; spare clothes; and "high-energy" food. I'm betting Alex would suggest Bugles.

## SEPTEMBER, 2001, TO JUNE, 2002

BY MID-FALL, sending Alex to school has become routine. The bat backpack also carries his little notebook, in which we exchange frequent messages with the school staff.

"9/20: Alex had a terrific day today!" writes one of his teachers. "He fully participated in gym and circle, allowing hand over hand for hand movements in songs. Alex also enjoyed gluing red paper to an apple. After one demonstration, he knew exactly what to do. Alex is adjusting to class routine nicely. He was laughing and smiling most of the day."

"9/21: Hi! Alex is certainly feeling more happy in the classroom. He sits happily during circle time. He is busy exploring the classroom and choosing his own toys. We have begun to hear words from Alex. He actually enjoyed art class. He hesitated for a few minutes, then became busy in the activity of decorating a frame. Alex ate Cheerios & crackers for breakfast and ate Goldfish & the granola bar for lunch. He kept pushing the applesauce away. We've continued to try the school food, but no luck yet."

"We're certainly looking forward to seeing some of Alex's artwork," we write back. "He still cries when he gets on the bus, but we hope he comes to like it soon."

*Best of luck with that,* I think. For the first few weeks, he starts crying in our foyer even as we wiggle the little bat onto him. By the time I hand him through the opened bus door down front, he turns it up to a wail. I scurry off for the subway, unable to look back to see his hands on the glass, his open mouth, his silent scream.

"9/24: Hi! Alex has been coming off the bus smiling in the morning! Please remember to send back Alex's extra set of clothes."

"9/26: Hi! For the last two days, Alex has been eating Crispix cereal. He really seems to enjoy it! I also put a little bit of apple juice in his cup of water. He finished the whole thing! Small steps . . . Can you please send in some hot food to try for Alex?"

Us: "Here are two chicken nuggets. They take about one to one-and-a-half minutes in the microwave. How is Alex getting along with the other children?"

Alex has never had much to do with other kids; he ignores Ned most of the time. But school is a whole new corner in his life. Clues may crop up there that we've never seen before. All we can tell the school, I guess, is what Alex does at home, that suddenly smaller sliver of his life that takes place in the hurried moments of the morning and after he emerges from the bus in mid-afternoon.

"9/28: Hi! Alex ate all the chicken nuggets, crackers & Gold-fish. He really enjoyed it. Alex is getting very comfortable in the classroom. Right now he plays alongside the other children."

They also send home what Jill terms "a boilerplate" news-letter on what September was like for the kids. "Look what we've learned!" the newsletter proclaims, mentioning apples and shaving cream and getting to know one another. "A great big hand goes to (every kid's name in the class) for adjusting to school so well! And thanks to all the parents for entrusting your children to our care." On the bottom I spot the website it was downloaded from.

"10/1: Alex ate all three chicken nuggets. He has quite the appetite when it's food he likes. He loved the parachute today."

That's the first word of Alex's schooling that leaves us com-pletely blank. "We enjoyed the newsletter on what Alex did in September," we reply. "What is 'the parachute?' We are sending a chicken patty cut into three strips for Alex's lunch. Make sure, if you can, to watch him while he eats it. It's a bit dry, and he tends to stuff it in and then choke."

"10/2: Hi! Alex did not eat the chicken patty you sent. He ate a granola bar & Goldfish. A parachute is multicolor fabric circle that we shake, sing and practice our balance on. Can you please send diapers? Alex used the last one."

He's no longer crying when the bus swallows him in the morning. (I almost dare to look back.) I see a swagger in his walk. It comes from somewhere. Two days after the "send diapers" note, we drop by Alex's school for a parents' meeting, and peek through the window. He's sitting quietly during circle time. He allows hand-over-hand when asked to applaud, and he often smiles. His teachers aren't cradling him in their laps, so he's completely free to run around. He sits. He's being herded out to gym when we leave. We don't let him see us.

Jill and I go into a little room with Alex's teacher. Notes aside, I'm eager to hear what she has to say. "He's doing great!" teacher says. "He *loves* circle time!"

I've just read two books on autism; I have come to this conference with questions. How is Alex different from the other kids? How does he get along with other kids? He's tactile at home: could this be a shortcut to teaching him?

And oh yes, does he definitely have autism?

"He comes in smiling every day," says teacher. "He comes down the hall with those little wings flapping . . . He asks for water. He says, 'Want water.' And he's *eating*! And sometimes I sneeeek—" teacher pinches forefinger and thumb together "—a little bit of juice in his water . . ." I know the bat comes home almost empty every night, with all the chicken nuggets and half the granola bar gone, and one or sometimes all three of the plastic snack containers empty. I've never been certain they haven't just thrown out the chicken nuggets.

Does he eat applesauce at home? We reply that he does. "I tried to give him some here at lunch," teacher says, "but he just tosses his head back and it's like, no way. But he takes care of his own tray after lunch! Well, we help him. But he helps carry it right to the wastebasket and throws it away!"

Busses his own plates? I never thought of asking him to do that at home. Jill asks if he eats the school lunch. Teacher shakes her head no. "None of the kids eat it," she says, with a twist of the lips that makes it clear she wouldn't eat it, either. Teacher goes on to say that Alex loves gym, that he's spending more of the day on the carpet when all the kids play (not that these kids actually play with each other at this age, teacher adds), and that he "has his own agenda." Once when the bus got Alex to school too late for the free-play period that opens each day, he insisted on free play right into circle time. Teacher also had to hide all the school bus toys because Alex wouldn't stay away from them.

"If I have a concern," teacher says, "it's about his vision." He looks out the side of his eyes a lot, uses a lot of peripheral vision. "Sometimes he just walks over other kids to get some- where!" A concern of ours, too.

Then teacher says she's made him a class leader: "We kind of put the kids in a higher-functioning group and a lower-func- tioning group, and use the higher functioning group to help show the other kids what to do."

And Alex is in the higher-functioning group? Oh, yes. This good news is hammered home when Jill tells her we've been fearing Alex might be autistic.

Teacher's lips make the school-lunch twist again. "No," she says. "No, I don't see that." Alex is not only some kind of class- room NCO, but according to teacher he's even hung around the door with unusual frequency on days when Jill and I had talked at home about dropping by the school. As if he knows, we marvel.

Then I remember that we've often mentioned autism in front of Alex. We should stop doing that. If we're going to talk about him, let's do it in little rooms with the door closed, and with somebody who seems to like him as much as his teacher.

Jill finds tons of school bus websites on the Net. She has ravaged eBay and the Net for a school bus pillow (I think Grandpa got him one today; Grandma got him a school bus board book). Jill is cutting, pasting, and laminating little counting books using pictures of school buses. Some Elmo, some Ned, but mostly school buses.

"A-buzz," Alex says, "a-buzz, pleeze!"

He has four buses, not counting the real one he rides to school. The first is a seven-inch, die-cast metal model of a full-size school bus. It's realistic: The emergency door has never even shut all the way. Alex has also chewed off the front tires, torn off the stop sign, dinged the paint, and subjected it to what I expect has happened to a New York school bus by this time in the school year. Second is a metal bus, shorter than the first, blue and white, some fruity European tour thing, but he abandoned it after prying off the front grill. Aunt Judie found his yard-long soft plastic bus in her laundry room; Alex lugs it all over the house, even to the dinner table. We allow the bus at the table because convincing Alex that he has to ingest chicken nuggets to board the school bus gets him to eat. And he has a small metal model bus, a model of the twenty-seater he rides to school.

"A-buzz, a-buzz," Alex says.

What is the key to Alex's fascination with school buses? Grandpa wants to know. The color? The shape? The movement? Could be the color: It's the same as NYC taxis, which Alex has loved since he was wheeled around town on oxygen.

It's none of those, Jill responds. "It's where the bus takes him."

Time has come to get Alex to sleep in a bed. Reasons include our unforgiving wooden floor, the height of the crib, and Alex being an excellent climber but a poor flyer.

Crib to bed is a leap, one of the broadest. It suddenly seems to me that parents talk about it only sentimentally. They say it seems like yesterday that they rocked their newborn to sleep in his cradle by their bedside at home. We didn't have that with Alex; I can still see the box and the vent. When did that thin infant crawl from there and suddenly need a bed? This transition is as big as learning to walk, Jill thinks, and just as complicated as we try to iron out the best way to keep a bouncy Alex on his mattress.

We work every angle. I put the city-country-scene sheet on Alex's bed (this sheet fascinates him). Also, only Ned rides a stroller on our weekend outings; we walk Alex everywhere. He needs the practice, he needs the exercise, and we need him exhausted by seven p.m. We set up the boys' bedroom with dimmed lights and a tape of guitar lullabies purring in the air.

I tell Alex "Go to bed," and he heads right for the bed, climbs right up on it—good boy—for five seconds, before he bounces down again and scoots for the living room. I take his hand and guide him back. He crawls up onto the mattress and burrows his face into the blankets. But he's like a new computer owner with the Internet; temptation is too strong. Off the mattress come the legs. I take his hand and guide him back, over and over, to the dimness and the guitar kisses. "Let him just run around until he gets sick of it," says Aunt Julie.

I fortify the edge of the bed with blankets and pillows. Jill spreads blankets across the floor about where Alex might tumble out. If he keeps hopping out, we're going to have to put him in the portable playpen: an incalculable step backward. I tuck him in. Maybe being tucked in is another key factor, I tell Jill. Maybe, she admits. We make the bed to resemble his crib (now owned by Ned, who somewhere during this has dropped off): same blankets, Elmo to hug, one of our T-shirts to snuggle, just as we used to make up the pet carrier to take the cat to the vet. "Alex, you want to help me with this?" I ask, as always, slipping the cannula of his overnight oxygen over his head.

When I spy Alex a moment later, as I'm returning from the kitchen and he's mid-way in his flight to the living room, I see him pause and carefully work the cannula off over his head. Then he's gone like a deer. "Alex, back to bed!"

"I think he just wants us in there while he makes this transition," Jill says. Alex takes my hand as if to say, "Oh yeah, bed. Good idea." He squirms up and buries his face in the sheet. *I knew that sheet would work,* I say to myself as I head to the kitchen. Soon after, though, Alex is still up and hopping. I try one more trip to the bed before resorting to the portable crib. He settles down on the bed without hesitation, and goes to sleep as if this is where he's wanted to be all evening long. Soon he's sprawled and limp as a noodle.

"You were worried he wouldn't fall asleep in the bed?" Jill says. "Maybe that's what we need: One of us has to be convinced it will never happen."

She has several observations about this bed fracas: he may not sleep in the bed tomorrow night, or the next night. But in six months, Jill thinks he will be sleeping there. He's also not "lying in there in wild, crazy baby positions," Jill notes, "with his feet up here and his head down there. He *knows* he's not in the crib." I reply that 7:30 is one thing, but we must be prepared for the middle of the night, when Alex wakes up and finds nothing between him and an Elmo video but a scamper to the TV.

An exhausted boy gets on the school bus the next day. I call to check on him, and ask his teacher for advice on the bed front. "With my two kids, I put up the railing and they stayed right there," she recalls. "They weren't climbers." I reply that Alex is definitely a climber. "Yes," she says, "and he's a *good* climber. I'd be worried about that crib."

On an evening in early January, Jill studies the calendar for the rest of the school year. Each of Alex's future days off is marked with an X. There are many, many X's. "Look at this!" Jill cries. "A week in February and *then* a week in April!"

We're still panting from Christmas vacation: scrambling around the house after our two little animals, caged by the cold outside, surrendering Forbidden Zones of our home to kids' toys and videos and completely undomesticated messes of crap just so we could keep a sliver of sanity. "There's a week in June, too," I say, "unless he gets a lot of days off for snow this winter." We've had no snow. Nor is any expected.

"And *three weeks* in August!" Jill exclaims, studying the calendar with the same expression she'd wear when examining a bad x ray.

Doctor, I'm recovered. There's got to be a mistake!

*I'm afraid x rays don't lie, Ms. Cornfield. My best advice to you is to enjoy the time you have left . . .*

Live, damn it, I tell Jill. Live every day that Alex is in school as if it were your last. Jill laughs. She laughs hard. Perhaps harder than the joke warrants.

We love having him home. We've been at the bottom of a dark winter, and this is better. No oxygen during the day, the only syringe in sight filled with Ned's decongestant, which we were squirting into his mouth. To watch our three-year-old and one-year-old grow, play, and pitch stuff on the floor with abandon and without doctors in our lives. Ned's starting to get bigger, too, learning to do cute kid things like pick another Elmo video and stretch up to try to shove it into the VCR. Alex has also learned how to turn on the CD player.

When I was home over the holidays, I'd try to keep the boys away from our fragile plastic home electronic equipment by taking them down with me when I did the laundry. Alex would run around in the basement, and Ned would sit in his stroller and watch the spin cycles through the portholes of the machines. And by the time the laundry was done it would be almost quarter to five, which meant that we could wiggle them into their dinner-time seats. To Ned we'd present fruit or soup or some such normal thing he could smear on himself. To Alex we'd present a plate of chicken nuggets he could hand back to us until we gave in and opened the Pringles. Nutrition wasn't the point. The point was that the whole affair simply brought our family closer to bath time, bedtime, and a bottle of wine for Mom and Dad.

We love having them home. It soothes the nerves to hear Ned screech out of context, and to be serenaded by Alex's different renditions of "ABCD" or "Twinkle, Twinkle, Little Star" (". . . twin-gle twin-gle LIDDLE stah . . ."; ". . . twinKLE twinkle li-TUL STAR! . . ."; ". . . twinkletwinklelittlestar . . ."). But no unsedated parent is going to sit there and hear a crash from the boys' room and then see Alex rip around the corner into the living room, strewing passengers from the Fisher-Price school bus, and not wish that evening bottle of wine was just a few minutes closer. "Alex, pick something *up*!" I pack Alex's back-to-school bag on Christmas Eve.

The singing tells us that Alex is the one truly suffering from no school, that he's pining to get back to circle time and free play. "The songs are his way of keeping school alive while he isn't there," Jill notes. Hard to believe that this kid wailed at the sight of the school bus in mid-September. Hard to believe three and a half months have evaporated.

Kids do like school at this early age, probably more than they like the holidays. Maybe some schools should hold classes right through the holidays. "Jeff, they can't do that," Jill said. Who's she to be reasonable ("—*and three weeks in August!*—")? I'm not picky about using the same teachers; that's what substitutes are for. Point is, he'd like to go to school seven days, and we'd like to send him.

I tried to explain this to my sister-in-law when I called her on Christmas. "We're even looking for a school that will take Ned this spring," I told her.

"You are *not*!" she replied, thinking I was kidding. She doesn't have kids.

"Oh yes we ARE."

The only drawback to finding such a school, of course, is that soon some sicko would just send us another calendar filled with Xs.

I just bought Alex his first coloring book: "Playtime in Teletubbies Land." I was looking for an Elmo book but couldn't find one, and I figure that when you're trying to guide your Crayolas inside the lines for the first time, better former friends than none at all. The book has the structure and smell I remember: broad black lines, thick paper that I've learned to recognize as newsprint.

I hope Po, Laa-Laa, and the other two What's-Their-Names aren't set on retaining their original colors under Alex's hand. He's more of a color-'em as he sees-'em kind of guy. I hope they aren't fussy about having all their color inside their lines, either. "Alex has a definite vision," Jill says.

We've given Alex ample opportunity to draw. Two blackboards are mounted on the wall between the dining and living rooms. He once had an Etch-a-Sketch, and still has a magnetic board he draws on with a plastic stylus that can be wiped clean with a little toggle. Alex also has had a tin of Crayolas parked on the toy shelf for a long time. It's a commemorative tin from 1993; each side tells a chapter of the century of Crayola, including 1958's now-famous sixty-four-pack with the sharpener in the back. Sometimes Alex reads the sides of the tin while he's eating. When the tin is open, Ned also likes to horn in, grab the lid, and bang it on the coffee table. I have no idea how many crayons the tin originally contained. These days it's got that junkyard look that toy containers get after a few months on the front lines: more colors than a summer dusk, broken crayons, crayons of different widths, scraps of crayon wrapper, chips of colored wax in the bottom.

"Cray-a? Cull-a?" Alex says. He must have learned to color at school, that place from which he keeps emerging with more lyrics from "ABCD" or "The Wheels on the Bus." All I know is, I come home from work one evening and Jill presents me with a piece of typing paper covered with color.

"Who did this?" I ask.

"Well it wasn't me," Jill replies. Soon there are three or four such pieces of typing paper taped to the wall of our kitchen. All are authentic, signed and dated by the artist's mother.

Alex prefers to work on typing paper ("pay-pa?"), probably for the same reason the medium inspires terror in writers: it's a white prairie waiting to be filled. Alex likes to fill it. He often even manages to stay on the paper, except for when he must sharpen his Crayolas on the yellow wood of our entertainment unit. "Get him a *coloring book!*" Aunt Julie commands. "Get him an Elmo coloring book, and teach him that that color is red!"

The first toy store has no Elmo coloring books—in fact no coloring books at all that aren't dog-eared and pawed to softness around the edges. Next I visit a drug store, and after realizing that they have no toy department, I head to the magazines. Makeup, makeup, makeup, celebrities, world news, makeup, makeup, sports. Then my eye hits the lowest shelf. Tucked in the back is "Playtime in Teletubbies Land," 89 cents.

I bring it home. Alex wants to read the book, however, and turn the pages. Even when I put a Crayola in his hand, he hesitates.

Then it strikes me that he hasn't been taught to color in books. "Alex, color, look!"

I haven't colored in a long time. The black lines of the drawings still look huge until I put crayon to paper. I fill in a leg of Po, and our babysitter sets to work on the chest with a nearly new, sharp Violet. Alex pays attention for a few seconds, then grabs Sunflower Yellow and heads for the entertainment unit, which Jill thinks would look cooler if we just let him color the whole thing.

Alex's teachers sent a note home the other day instructing me to send to school a child's Crest Spin toothbrush. "A tube of child's toothpaste would also be appreciated," the note said, adding that students from a local dental school were coming in soon to check the kids' teeth.

If the teachers look to start Alex on the road to tooth brushing, they're in for a shock, sort of. Alex brushes his teeth every night. Sort of. He's taken to having a snack after dinner—we're usually so battered trying to get Ned unconscious that we simply strap Alex into his booster seat with a bowl of Pringles and wish him well. By the time he's done, Ned is often in Dreamland and it's time for Alex to pretend to get into bed. "Alex, time to brush your teeth!"

Tooth brushing is what I think special education calls a life skill. Like most life skills, it is an anti-decay skill, same as washing your own face or hair, or peeling off your own sweaty socks. Alex also does those. Sort of. He takes my hand and we walk to the bathroom. He pushes the stool over to the sink, climbs up and reaches up to take his brush from the holder. The brush has only about half an inch of bristles. Then he reaches over—he gets a little fumbly here—and turns on the water. He holds the brush under the water and then brings it up to his mouth.

Alex's pediatrician brought up tooth brushing about a year ago. "Do you brush his teeth?" the pediatrician asked. I replied that Alex was learning, but that he usually just held the brush in his mouth and sucked the water from the bristles. "That's not good enough!" the pediatrician replied. "You have to brush his teeth for him!" The pediatrician was having a pissy day.

"Does he drink a lot of juice?" my dentist asked. I said that Alex just drinks water. "Oh, don't worry about it so much, then," the dentist said.

It's a notch in Alex's life that he's learning these life skills (it's a notch in my life that I can secretly get one doctor to shoot down the advice of another). Nonetheless, I promptly bought a five-pack of baby/toddler toothbrushes in a dollar store—Spin brushes are $5.99 apiece—and I embark on brushing Alex's teeth during his bath. First, I pass him the brush so he can wave it around. Then gently I take it from him and brush his lips. Some-where in there Alex learns that even baby/toddler toothbrushes from the dollar store soak up a lot of delicious bath water. Get-ting it to his mouth seems half the challenge, and a way paved months before by his home feeding therapist, who used to fiddle with a little brush around his cheeks. From here, I let him watch me while I make an action epic out of pretending to brush my own teeth.

"Alex, watch—" *Chikka chikka chikka*, and I bare my front teeth and pretend to brush. I say "pretend" because who in God's name wants to taste somebody else's bath water?

Alex's brushing is still more a partnership than a solitary end of day in front of the bathroom sink and mirror. I sit on the john next to him, help him take the brush down and turn on the faucet, and help him hold it under the water. When he just puts it between his lips and starts to suck the water, I say, "Alex, open." He usually does, and I work the brush in there and scrub. One side lower, one side upper, then the other. Then I get him a little cup and drink of water. We're not really up to toothpaste yet: he tried one drop in his mouth, and his lips turned into a drooling rectangle and he almost fell off the stool. I feel he'll get to it, though, especially if the tube has a picture of Elmo on it.

I put the brush back in the holder. "All done, Alex." Yes and no. He tries to take the brush back down, turns on the faucet after I've turned it off and leans way over to try to drink from the stream. The fineries of tooth brushing—a.k.a., rinse and spit—remain beyond Alex. Before I put his brush back, I peer at it for tiny specks of food. I see none. "C'mon, Alex, time to dry your hands." I help him down from the stool and hold the towel and rub it over his hands. We're sort of pretending here, too. Then Alex reaches up and turns out the bathroom light like a normal person.

A few days after the Spin brush note, the teachers send home a sticker on Alex's backpack. The sticker reads, "No Cavity

Club!" Sort of, because the report on his check-up lets me in for a shock. Alex may have a cavity.

In the corner of the boys' room sits Alex's oxygen tank. The tubing and cannula are coiled around the stainless steel gauge that crowns the tank. The cannula is dry and dusty; the tubing is turning yellow, and contains little beads of old water. Occasionally, I twist open the gauge and watch the needle jump to "1/2." The tank was also half full when we stopped using it, weeks ago.

One evening back before Christmas I uncoiled the tubing, fished up the cannula, and brought it over to Alex down there in the set-up porta-crib, in the center of the room. I was feeling beaten, I remember, from losing the stay-in-bed fight for another night. "Alex?" I said, holding up the cannula, "you want this?" At that point, I'd long been letting him make the call on whether he needed oxygen overnight. Alex shook his head.

Oxygen has been with us forever. I remember lugging the B tanks in a big canvas bag. Shredding the light-mesh basket under our first stroller with the weight of oxygen tanks. Fearing that the tubing would freeze and crack on cold days. Being woken on his first night home and finding his E tanks nearly empty, and flinching from the *hissss* as I, then still a novice parent, screwed the flow gauge on wrong. I remember the plastic that has always been on his face, and I remember him shaking his head "no" down in the porta-crib.

Alex hasn't needed a whiff off the torpedo in weeks. We keep the tank in case he catches a cold and needs help. Since we decided on that, Alex has had two, maybe three colds. He hasn't needed the oxygen. "We've ignored this huge accomplishment," I tell Jill one night. "We should ring every bell in the village."

We've rung no bells. I don't know why. Perhaps we've been distracted by meetings like the one we had this afternoon with Alex's teacher, the meeting I open by asking, "How is he progressing in school?" and the teacher answering, "Not as well as we had hoped."

Alex has an attention problem. I've seen him stargaze while walking down stairs. The teacher reports that in class he plows right over other kids. He continues to sing one song long after it's over, even after other children have picked other songs. Why he has this problem, and how we remedy it, are pressing questions. Without improved attention, a doctor told us last month at still another meeting, Alex will always have a tough time learning. Still, the teacher's comment is a shock. What happened to "star of the class"?

Teacher wants to promote Alex after this year to a class of similar kids where teachers practice methods of education Jill and I don't currently favor, such as ABA. That's a teaching method that relies on rewards, like candy. "He's not going to consider an M&M a reward," Jill points out. "He doesn't eat them."

How *does* he eat at home? teacher wants to know, her face crinkling as she recounts her own tries to get him to eat banana yogurt. First we've ever heard of Alex trying banana yogurt, but teacher reports that she left some on Alex's lips after lunch so he could lick it. "You should always leave a little of a new food on their lips," teacher says. We didn't know that, either.

How is eating going at home? Jill reports that we've given up, at least for now. "It's been years for us," Jill says, "a long struggle." I know it sounds flimsy, but it's true. We've nonetheless managed to move him off chicken nuggets and back onto fish sticks, but we often neglect to put the green vegetable on his plate—which, theoretically, Alex may at first discard, but eventually will tuck into. It could happen. I saw him eat broccoli once. Two weeks ago he ate pizza. We've tried pizza again just once; he turned it down. He picks pizza rolls apart, but doesn't eat any part. We are trying. "We're doing Alex a disservice if we do one thing at school and another at home," teacher continues. "We're sending a negative message."

I think how Alex has never needed oxygen at school, despite gym class, field trips, and the unceasing play inspired by a crummy attention span. "It's been years for us," Jill says again.

Besides, there are developments elsewhere. Within the past few weeks Alex has, for the first time, used finger-paint, and ped-aled and steered a tricycle. Within the past few weeks, Alex's father has, for the first time, admitted that his son probably has some kind of brain damage.

Probably. Some kind. Who knows? All parents live, in one way or another, with the limitations of their kids. My mother did. "Get good rank in school and become an *engineer*!" she used to say, so I actually began playing Engineer in the back-yard. I imagined I was building a bridge in the Brazilian jungle. I wore a toy pistol. Used it, too.

Alex doesn't play such games, "imaginative play" being one of the categories where evaluators claimed he tanked. While giving a mother's full credit to Alex for the fight he fought, Jill was the first to believe he might have serious problems. In the years since, she's clicked across the Net to verify the dangers of the steroids the NICU pumped into Alex, traded e-mails with parents whose preemies gradually leapfrogged Alex's develop-ment, and traded e-mails with parents whose preemies became hothouses of "issues" with brains, nerves, eyes. Life.

To me, there have always been two sides to Alex: his prob-lems and his future. On one side, my belief that Alex has mere delays, that his hardware is sound and his software rewriting like crazy to catch up from that year in the hospital. On the other side is my fear that he is permanently disabled. In between there has always been a wall, an important wall that gave me hope. In his pictures, I used to see only a smiling boy. In a few recent shots, Alex remains the smiling ham. But in others, suddenly, he looks lost, staring at nothing. In my most haunting picture of Alex, he's sitting in his stroller wearing a somber look, a slightly raised eye-brow, head tilted a little to the left. It is the face of an older boy, perhaps the teenager he'll be. Next time he looks like that, we might be calculating the odds on his living independently.

Maybe I've started admitting what I see in front of me. When he runs he must hold up his arms for balance ("Could cause him great pain in later life," said a physical therapist). He gazes at everything but the steps when walking downstairs ("It's a safety issue," said his teacher). He'll eat nothing strange, like hot dogs or cheese—even pizza took forever, and then we had to starve him on a chilly playground. He doesn't respond to his name. Often, he doesn't meet my eyes. I still do hope that someday Alex will read this, taking time out of his bridge project in the jungle, and wonder what I was worried about with that mystified indifference that adults who were sick babies reserve for their parents.

Nothing changes my mind when we celebrate Alex's fourth birthday. He seemed to be facing his fortieth: sad and frightened, his mouth a big, red rhombus, and he waved and wailed, "Byebye, dungee, byebye, dungee" in shriller and shriller tones. I have no idea who "dungee" is. Sometimes Alex says "bye" when he means hello, but this time I knew he meant "bye." He wailed all though the song both at school and at home, with schoolmates and relatives alike. The relatives I could see, but the schoolmates? These are people who've seen him at his best. Not even the presents could cheer Alex up, not even Uncle Rob trying to rescue the party by murmuring Elmo's theme into his ear. He grabbed his binkie and one of my T-shirts and ran to his bed, where I rubbed his tummy as I'd seen the teacher's aide do at school. "Just very, very upset," Jill said.

Signs pointed to this birthday being Alex's topper. On his third birthday, Alex was a stoic guest of honor, digging into wrapping paper and then studying the Play-Doh mold with Aunt Julie. His second birthday was home with just us; we dimmed the room and the cake mesmerized him, as if he knew the little twin flames had something to do with why his cannula had just been removed. His first birthday was in the hospital; he smeared the chocolate cake and wore a little American flag cap. "Maybe he'll eat cake next year," Jill said then.

There were clues that this year Alex would not build on the mounting happiness of previous birthdays. Last August, Alex fell into tears against Jill's chest when all the kids started singing "Happy Birthday" at another kid's party. Ditto a few weeks ago at the first birthday of another boy.

I write Alex (and Ned as well) a letter every year on his birthday. "In a few minutes, I have to leave my office and head to your school, where we will celebrate your fourth birthday," I wrote to Alex. "Your mom made cupcakes with little flags, and I have to bring the flag-decorated paper plates, cups, and napkins. It should be fun, except sometimes you cry when a lot of people sing 'Happy Birthday' at once. There's not much reason to cry today, Alex."

I guess Alex didn't read the letter. We had no idea when we brought the flags and the cups to his classroom that he'd stiff-arm the cupcakes and spend the party flopped in a beanbag in the corner. We had no idea that, for yet another year, he wouldn't blow out his candles. I had hopes; we'd sort of been practicing by blowing into a whistle in the bath. We'd also practiced him saying "Happy Birthday" and "four." Yet when I looked down during the party at home, I saw that again someone else was needed to blow them out. I took him to his room. Ned entertained the relatives, maybe hoping to stall the twelve months until Alex turns five.

Not long ago, Alex loved being the center of attention. He would cock his head, grin, and stretch for the camera. He would clap in polite incomprehension when groups of grown-ups sang to him. Just last December, he'd rip into a wrapped present whether it belonged to him to not. I don't expect a four-year-old who spent a year in the hospital to sit through a soup-to-nuts tribute dinner in a fine restaurant, but I don't know what this birthday meant at all.

In a few days, Alex's school will hold its graduation. It will be the first graduation of any kind I've attended as a parent. "Won't be a dry eye in the place," one teacher promises. I bet not.

Alex is staying at this school for another year, but he is "graduating" to a different classroom this fall. Still amazes me:

He went to a place in the world last fall, and now he's going to start going to a different place in the world, with different people. "People have taken pictures of him we've never seen," Jill says.

There are photos of a lot of Alex's schooldays that I missed. Jill got to volunteer for the trip to the Central Park Zoo, for instance. She got to see Alex's teacher, a city girl, throw the feed pellets right at the goats. There was the trip to the nearby farmer's market. There were all those gym classes. They taught him to eat pudding in this school, and yogurt. They taught him how to use a spoon, and how to sing songs. There was this whole world here, and in a few days the first part of that world will end. We'll take pictures. Won't be a dry eye in the place.

The chapel-like room is full, and warm. I haven't heard "Pomp and Circumstance" played for real in twenty-two years, yet again I realize that it's an awful sad song to usher in summer. This time, it plays for those graduating from Alex's school.

Banners of paper and bright paint wish success to the grads as they move into the big world of kindergarten. The banners have been made by the other classes of the school; Jill and I can't tell on which banner Alex and his classmates have smeared their own paint.

I look out over the crepe paper streamers, the kids in walkers, the kids on the laps. I scan to see who among the kids pays attention, who looks around, who claps at the Spanish translation of the ceremony, who's ready to move on to the apple juice and cake waiting in the courtyard. I see one of Alex's teachers point to where he sits with his class in the front row, but I can't spot him.

The morning's entertainment opens with the head of the school promising, "We're going to show off a little bit!" One graduating class then belts out, with the help of a recorded song on the sound system, "The Fire Truck Song." I get misty.

Alex comes into plain sight when his class and teachers assemble in a big semi-circle facing the audience. He looks small, sitting on a teacher's lap as she presses a red cushiony tambourine into his hand. He shakes it and waves his hands in enough of the right places to appear to be following along, and, except for occasional staring spells at the ceiling, holds his composure until the applause ends. Then he begins to cry.

The next song, "Move On Back," is a long take, and I admire the fortitude of this class—older? fewer "issues"?—as they plow through it. "Some of these kids have been here for two or three years," Alex's school speech therapist whispers to me. She's worked at the school for sixteen years, and has seen a lot of graduations. "It never loses its emotional component," she says.

A honcho of the corporation that runs Alex's school then takes the mike, and he gets as far as how the school year opened with a tragedy and is ending with a triumph when Jill comes up to me and says Alex is having a fit.

I find him in the courtyard, being walked around by one of his teachers and crying. I carry him back inside—he keeps darting for the ladies' room—and sit beside Jill. "Mommy?" he asks. I hand him to her, and he stiff-arms her and starts to wiggle under the pew in front of us. All the while the room is rocking with cheers and clapping, flashes erupting, a celebration I'm trying to tap Alex into. I whisper the lyrics to "If You're Happy and You Know It" in his ear. That seems to make something click, and he starts clapping and laughing. I hoist him to my shoulders. Between claps, he yanks my hair.

"Doing a good job on Daddy's hair," the speech therapist notes.

"How's he doing?" I ask Jill.

"He's doing great!" she says.

Alex begins to clap with the audience, and laugh. A little manic and he keeps grabbing my hair, but he levels off while the honchos hand out the diplomas. Each kid picks up his or hers to cheering and clapping and a barrage of flashbulbs on a warm June day that most of these parents probably thought they'd never see. One kid covers his eyes when they press the document into his hand. Most kids stride up and take theirs, just like the high school grads for whom they usually play that dismal song. The last of the diplomas goes to the last of the kids, and we have exactly one year to get in shape for when we hear that song again.

# JULY, 2002, TO JULY, 2003

ALEX IS TAKING swimming lessons. Alex's classes are in a three-pool, indoor center about a three-block walk from the bus stop, and all the way he rode on my shoulders as I warned him he was going swimming in a big bathtub. "Alex, you're going swimming," I kept repeating well into the locker room. He must have wondered why T-shirt, denim shorts, diaper, and sandals were swept away right here in the middle of the day, and replaced with a pool diaper and flowered shorts with a string in front.

If Alex was puzzled, he got over it in time to scoot off to the toilets. He loves toilets, though he's only just started to notice a full diaper. He does love to flush. I heard the rush of water, over and over, while I squirmed into my trunks. This class, for special needs kids, takes place in a 200-square-foot pool, the depth of which is adjustable from about one to three feet. I was to be in the water with Alex. We thought he would take to swimming, because he likes to splash and kick in the tub. Also, his therapists have told us that swimming would slow him down and increase his attention span.

The first lesson starts at four o'clock. He wails until 4:30. "Alex, it's just water," I keep telling him. "You know water."

"Noo! Noo!" he replies, his mouth a rectangle of misery and his cries ricocheting off the tile walls. His tears could fill their own pool. The instructors include a patient, cheerful, burly, young man with Crazy Horse's face tattooed on his arm. "Give me five, Alex," he says, and Alex does, limply, while I sneak his feet into the water.

"Stop it," Alex says to me. "Stop it." I want to drown.

"Alex, c'mon." But I have no clue how something as alien as a gigantic swimming pool center—the echoing tiles, the lapping water, the splashes and screeching—settle in Alex's brain. Maybe he just doesn't understand.

I swish Alex from side to side; show him how to blow bubbles; hold him while he floats on his back; have him hug me as I reach under him and make his legs kick; catch him when he jumps from the side of the pool; hold him high and then bring him down with a splash; and show him how to kick off. First, however, I must get his feet wet, then his legs, then carry him to the center of the pool. He refuses to blow bubbles, but he does giggle when I bring him down for a splash. Then he seizes the side of the pool, no doubt thinking he can finally get the hell out of the water and back to the locker room toilets where he belongs.

"Attention's his big thing, isn't it?" the instructor says. "But he's got a bicycle kind of kick, and he's moving all the time. That's good."

When it comes time to practice arm motions, the instructor makes a fine tactical move by breaking into "The Wheels on the Bus." Alex laughs. "He's got an infectious laugh!" the instructor says. He does, and by the end of the first lesson that sound too ricochets off the tiles. A little. "Alex, you're *swimming*!" He looks tired, as if he'll faint in my arms the moment class is over.

"Stop it," he says. "Bye! Byebye!"

I maneuver Alex to the side of the pool. "Everybody, Alex is leaving!" the instructor says. "Bye, Alex!" they call. "Bye BYE!" he calls back, then bolts for the locker room. There, as soon as I have him in yet another diaper and my own hands are occupied prying off my trunks, he heads for the toilets. Across the tiles, over and over, I hear the rush of the kind of water I guess he still prefers.

Down our bedroom hall, out of the darkness, looms his white T-shirt. From the dining room comes a pad-pad-pad where there should be only silence. "And here he comes," says Jill. Alex appears in the night, clears the foot of our bed, brushes the laundry hamper, and bounds onto my abdomen at 1:04 a.m.

"Mommy. Daddy. Go sleep," says Alex, squirming between us and elbowing me in the stomach.

Ever since Ned recently evicted him from his crib, Alex has been sleeping in a fold-out porta-crib. We know this isn't normal for a four-year-old. We tried to get him to sleep in a bed last winter. On school nights, I sat with him on the mattress for hours, rubbing his back and telling him to sleep on his bed, while he sucked his binkie and wormed his way over the railing to scoot for the toy shelf. On weekend nights, after we'd spent the day running him on playgrounds, Alex would actually fall asleep on his bed. Once, I think, he stayed there through the night. Most bed nights, however, we heard the pad-pad-pad and saw the gleam of the T-shirt in the small hours. Jill and I tried returning him to his bed a few times.

Then we hatched the idea of setting up the porta-crib before bed to have it ready in the middle of the night. We'd deposit him in the cage—three-foot-high walls of soft white mesh— give him a sip of water and his binkie, hand him one of my T-shirts and a stuffed Elmo, and watch him burrow into the blankets. We meant to keep trying Alex and the bed. But somewhere in there, doctors and teachers started harping on his terrible attention span, and then we had to get through an endless Christmas vacation. Alex and the bed just fell from being a priority. "I would hate to see your energies go in that direction," said one of his school therapists, who had given us a long list of other things to pay attention to with Alex.

So, night after night I'd pull the porta-crib out from over near the oxygen tank, undo the big rubber bands we used to keep the crib collapsed during the day, and whip the thing together. I hated it for a time: the savage clicks of the locking rails, the way they wouldn't lock unless you had the floor mat positioned perfectly. I hated it and blamed it for Alex, almost four, still not sleeping in a

bed. Then gradually the clicks of the locking rails came to signify
the end of another day. The final moments before a glass of Pinot
Grigio, "Seinfeld," our own dinner, slumber almost never disturbed
by the boys for twelve hours unless one was sick. Night after night,
we'd clear the dessert dishes and step into the boys' room to find
them both out. Alex would be sprawled in the bottom of the porta-
crib; I'd reach down and pull him straight if his head seemed cocked
at an uncomfortable angle. *He's getting tall,* I'd think. *Wonder
when he's going to climb out of there?*

He does climb out of there suddenly one night, and our
energies cascade toward putting him first in the porta-crib, then
in the bed, then back in the porta-crib. Finally, Jill pulls the
door of their bedroom closed. "That sends a message," she says.

I hear the knob rattling, followed soon by the cries of the pris-
oner. I open the door. "Alex," I say, "back to bed!" Back he goes,
bouncing up on the mattress, burying his face in the blanket, clamping his eyes shut in an elaborate pantomime of drifting off that will
evaporate as soon as I close the door again behind me. (Ned, inci-
dentally, can't believe he's scored front-row seats to this. Sensing
something new was unfolding in his household and that soon it
might involve him, he bounces on his rump, rattles the crib springs,
and drinks himself into a stupor on water and Rice Dream.)

Out I go. Rattle rattle rattle. In I go, and place Alex in the
porta-crib. He hoists one leg over the side. "Alex, put your leg
down," I say, careful not to touch him. "I know. You've got this
new freedom and it's exciting. You're growing up, Alex. You're
getting bigger. But it's time for sleep." I set the ottoman beside
the porta-crib, as if I were handing a shovel to a POW. (Jill and
I have both seen him get out, by the way, and he always lands
straight and on both feet.)

Times have changed, I tell Jill. There's another, real bedtime
to consider in this house now, announced by the rattle of the
knob. "He's out of his cage," I say.

"It's not a cage," Jill says.

As part of the ongoing monitoring of Alex's development, I take him to Dr. D., another developmental pediatrician. I steer him into an open room that has carpeted stairs, a gym pad, a two-way mirror, and a door that won't lock from the inside. Dr. D.'s assistant occupies Alex with shopworn toys while she asks how he's doing in school, how he's sleeping, how he's getting along with his little brother?

This is the second time I've watched Alex bounce around this room, flying every two seconds to turn off the light switch or open the door. Now when he opens a door he turns around to machine-gun the room with "Bye! Bye! Bye!"

Dr. D. enters. "Who do you see up on the shelf?" she asks. Alex looks at her. Incredible, but even now there's a germ of impulse in me that wants to please doctors. "Who do you see up on the shelf?" she asks again. "Elmo," I say, looking at Alex.

"Let him answer," she says.

Her forehead creases. "No signs of aggression at all with the baby?" she asks. I tell her no, and in fact Ned is usually the one pushing Alex. I tell her Alex is counting a little, identifying letters in books, saying three-word sentences. Since Dr. D. last saw him, Alex has started eating cheese, ice cream, and some yogurt! To show that as a father I can deliver a balanced report, I tell how he hit the roof during his birthday. I tell her we were told it was performance anxiety. "I wish he was old enough to have performance anxiety," she replies.

Alex ricochets from toys to stairs to door to light switch. "What would he do if you were to leave the room?" Dr. D. asks me. Probably not much, I admit. Play a little, ricochet, probably open the door in a few moments, but more to get out ("Bye! Bye! Bye!") than pursue me.

"What would you do?" she asks Alex in a playful voice. Alex laughs. "Where are your teeth?" Dr. D. asks. Alex busts a gut, and repeats the phrase "Where are teeth?" over and over. Alex actually kisses her.

We go to her office next door for the exam. Alex refuses to acknowledge figurines of Big Bird and Tinky Winky, though he does spy a plastic train on the shelf. "Iwanchocho," he says.

"Did you hear that?" asks Dr. D. "He asked for the train."

Alex laughs. She tries to weigh and measure him. She shines a light in his left eye. "I'm very concerned about what that left eye is seeing," she says. She lassos Alex's skull with a tape measure. He puts up with that better than I've ever seen. He likes her. I do too. Maybe I sense I can talk business to her, as a tired father looking for some doc to finally offer a clue about Alex's life.

"Doctor," I say, as she makes dots on a blue chart, denoting Alex's increasing—or not increasing—skull size, "do you have any kind of a diagnosis?"

And she says, "I do." She spins in her chair to face me. "Alex has, I'm pretty sure, static e-" I confess I didn't keep what she said in my head. It wasn't "encephalitis" or anything easy like that. When I go home tonight, I'll take out the letter she gave us and read the word again. I won't remember it then, either. I'll have years to memorize it. "Basically," Dr. D. says, "it means that at some point, during either the prenatal or perinatal stage, there was a lack of oxygen to the brain."

"Brain damage?" I ask.

Yes. Okay.

I tell her my plan: Get Alex's new school year started. Get the oxygen tank out of our house. ("Are you still paying for that?" she asks, and I like her more: a doctor who talks about money.) Get Alex to a neurologist. Get Alex back to the eye doctor. I further stipulate that I don't like ADD drugs.

"I think Alex would be one child who would really benefit from them," Dr. D. says. "But that's, that's down the road."

"Well," I say, "now we can concentrate on getting him the best life we can, age five to ten, then the best adolescence, then the best young adulthood while we're still around to help him." That's a solid speech. I even ask what this doctor knows about assisted living homes. But that's, that's down the road.

Then she asks: "If you had it to do over again, what would you have done differently?" I like her most of all for asking that question.

Soon Alex has other appointments with his pulmonologist Dr. K., a neurologist, and the ophthalmologist. Alex aces Dr. K., who lights up when he sees Alex. He glows just as he did that Sunday afternoon almost three years ago, when we showed him a NICU picture of Alex and asked if we could please please transfer Alex to his hospital. Our visit today was to see about finally getting the big tank of oxygen out of our home.

Dr. K. scribbled the order, and added that Alex is "much more focused and together than he used to be." He was also pleased that Alex now eats yogurt and ice cream. "With these kids, you have to look for any sign of progress," he said.

The neurologist is next. "She's a neuro-psychologist," says Jill. "Or maybe just a psychologist. I don't know." I don't know much about her, either, except that she broke our previous appointment on twenty-four hours' notice, and that Jill jotted "ADD" next to her name on our phone-side calendar.

"ADD," or Attention Deficit Disorder, is the biggest bugaboo of Alex's educational life so far, the compulsion deep in his head that sets him ricocheting around the classroom when he's supposed to be studying ABCs. Sometimes I can get Alex to stay with a book. Sometimes not. Often he spends whole music-therapy classes screaming around the room, trying to pry open the door, trying anything other than sitting and listening to the music and paying attention to the world he's in. ADD in big letters.

A bugaboo's a bugaboo, I realize, but still I'm afraid that this appointment with Dr. Whateversheis may be the first in a series that puts us on the path of new drugs. It's hard to forget that some of the old drugs did Alex little good.

The eye doctor we know. She's a kind, accomplished woman. Her waiting room features many quality toys, as well as a copy of her book. I like the fact that when it's at last time for the appointment, she stands in the doorway of her office and calls the child's full name, along with "C'mon in!" What happens once Alex is in there, of course, is less hale-fellow: bright lights, icy drops, miniature sneakers hammering at Dad's thighs. But we need some clue about what Alex's left eye sees. His developmental pediatrician is concerned that this eye sees poorly, and impedes everything from descending staircases to his spooning food to his mouth. Any doctor who'd ever seen Alex work a playground ladder and slide might wonder, as I do, if his vision is anything less than perfect. And we did take Alex to another eye doctor some time ago. That doc gave Alex's eyes a clean bill, physically. My theory is that his eyes are fine, physically. The real problem is where they're sending the messages.

By late fall of 2002, we realize that we really should have found a kindergarten for Alex.

Jill and I have gotten to know his current teachers and therapists, the miniscule chairs in his classroom and the miniscule toilets down the hall. We got to know them, and so did Alex. "He's kind of a star around here," his speech therapist once said. But next September, he moves to kindergarten, and his current teachers tell us that's a whole new animal. Ten months from now, he will rise on an early fall morning, munch his granola in the weakening morning sun, step aboard a bus, and go to a place where he doesn't know anybody and they don't know him. And we don't yet know what place this will be.

We've visited only one school so far. It is clean and neat and looks carefully run. Most promising of all, Jill found it by accident after dropping a comment at a yard sale. "What is your tuition?" Jill asks at this new place, after we'd all planted ourselves on three not-quite-so-miniscule chairs on the morning of our tour.

"Twenty-three," the director replies.

I diligently write "$2,300" on one of their brochures. I like this director. "That's twenty-three thousand?" Jill asks with extra gentleness, because her foot couldn't reach my shins under the table. ("That figure's about right," she assures me later. Of course it is. I have a lot to learn.)

The New York City Board of Education has paid for Alex's preschool, in a deal I still don't understand. They'll probably pay for his kindergarten, too, as long as we fill out enough of the right forms at the right times. There will be other forms, as well, because he must again be evaluated by a battery of specialists—speech, neuro, PT, on and on—similar to the throng that gave him a going over in the spring and summer of '01. Actually, two throngs: one recommended by the Board of Education, and the other employed by me and Jill, to ensure that Alex will wind up in a kindergarten that can really help him, and not one that the Board just wants to fill.

"Make sure you use the words 'classroom appropriate to my child,'" advised the speaker in the first of many transition seminars we have attended. "This means you've read the law."

Alex's preschool is holding a seminar on this extremely interesting topic in early December. Two weeks before that, we'll be heading back to the $23,000 school with Alex in tow. Maybe it'll be a quick match, a seamless end to this school holiday for Jill and me. Hope so. Each day is getting a little shorter. Each morning dawns chillier even as Alex boards the bus and disappears into his stardom. Soon we'll make calls. Soon the phone will ring. Jill's virgin 2003 desk calendar will swell with new times and new places. Hope too that I take phone numbers and doctors' addresses down more accurately than I did tuition figures.

I talk to my friend's wife Cindy, who spent a couple of days around Alex two summers ago. With the breathlessness of someone who may be losing his ability to hold a normal conversation, I tell her that I'm coming around to the opinion of the most recent swarm of doctors, one of whom diagnosed Alex with the letters "PDD/NOS," or pervasive developmental delays not otherwise specified.

"I probably know Alex better than almost anybody," I tell Cindy, "and I can see that something's different with him. He doesn't look at you *at all* when you talk to him. He can't stick at anything. When you talk to Ned, even though he's babbling, he pauses, he moves his head, he moves his eyes as if he's really talking to you. Alex doesn't do that. There's something that should be firing there that isn't. And without it, he's just not going to be able to learn. I mean, I listen to him muttering 'All right, okay, all right, okay . . .', and I can imagine a twenty-five-year-old man doing that on a park bench some day. So now we'll have to determine what kind of assistance he'll need to be able to learn."

And so forth. We all know I mean the drugs.

Alex is very independent, Jill has said. She also thinks he has artistic vision. I like him the way he is, but I've seen teachers try to work with him, too. It is not okay, and it is not all right. Even at home, he drags me by the hand to the TV and pleads for "El-MO." I slip the tape in, and once he sees that Elmo is securely on the screen, he's rounding the coffee table with a toy in his mouth. "Not in the mouth, please, Alex," I say, and he takes the toy out and grabs a crayon and starts trying to scribble on the tabletop. "On paper, Alex, on paper," I say. I get him a piece of paper and slide it under his face as Elmo rattles on. Alex makes a couple of scrawls on the paper, usually in just one color—he used to use more—then flings that sheet aside and scrawls on another, then flings that aside. The sheets twirl under the couch. He puts the crayon in his mouth, and it breaks my heart to hear myself saying that I may not be looking at a future senator here.

I've heard of Ritalin. I don't know anybody who swears by it, anybody who's sworn off it, or anybody who knows anybody who's been on it. I don't want to know, either. I've never wanted to know. I do know that not every concoction they shot into Alex in the hospital did him good. "It's hard to imagine a drug that would affect his attention span, and leave the rest alone," says Jill. I would hate to see Alex lose the ignition of independence, hate to see his half-finished slashes of color on the paper turn to tedious, tame drawings, obediently and silently finished. I'd even hate to stop bending over to reach under the couch for the sheets of paper.

"Jeff, we're going to have to start thinking of taking Alex to see somebody," Jill says on the phone one afternoon. She's taking Alex to his music class. I hear Alex screeching at the traffic. She means drugs, too. Jill says she's read that they do keep some kids focused in school, though some of those kids also suffered night terrors. Oh, good. Maybe TV's to blame. Maybe I'm to blame.

Maybe, if we go to the drugs, he'll keep his art, if he has any. Maybe it'd be better if, by the time he's grown up, Alex could pick the hottest stocks. "Well," offered Cindy, "maybe he can do that, too." Maybe, but if we're not careful, we may never find out.

Last night was the spring parent/teacher night at Alex's preschool. This gathering of everyone who knows Alex best sat in tiny chairs and tried to enter Alex's world by discussing what we all knew about him, and how best to take advantage of what we've seen. This arrangement, besides being tough on the knees, presupposes that the child isn't living a double life. For example: "You don't feed him breakfast before he comes here, *do* you?" the teacher asks us.

"What!?" says Jill. "He eats a bowl of cereal. No milk, but still a bowl of Cheerios, and sometimes a granola bar too during 'Sesame Street!'"

"He's starving when he gets here," the teacher says. "*Starving*." Later in the day, when the teachers get soup for their lunch, while all the other kids nap, Alex bums crackers.

Listen, Your Honor, every day I stuff Alex's backpack with what I think he'll eat. I'd send chicken nuggets and fish sticks, but I did that for months and they always came back untouched.

Now most days I send yogurt. ("He finger-paints with the yo-gurt," one teacher reports.) We also learned that at school he eats Rice Krispies, which he never touches at home.

At one point, I gesture toward a construction-paper birth-day cake on the back wall and, like a shrewd prosecutor, ask, "Does Alex have any particular fascination with that birthday cake?" At home, he loves pictures of birthday cakes.

"No," says the teacher.

Some of Alex's physical stuff we know about, like accepting any and all help he can get to avoid coming down stairs by himself, which he can do, and running into walls, which the teacher thinks he does for stimulation. When the teachers re-port that he names all zoo and farm animals by sight, I have a fleeting thought that we are all on the same page: I read a lot of farm and zoo stories to Alex and Ned before bedtime.

At home he bites. At school he pinches. At home he wigs out at groups of people singing, such as during birthday cel-ebrations. At school, he wigs out at the sight of a plastic toy guitar. Alex has never owned a guitar. Mom played a little uku-lele for him back in the hospital and for a few months at home, but she wasn't that bad. At home, he plays constantly with plastic letters, matching them up in the pages of an ABC book. He never touches letters at school, teacher reports.

"Do you think Alex will soon be ready for an interlocking puzzle?" Jill asks as we head out.

"Oh, he does interlocking puzzles!" the teacher replies. "Whips right through them!"

Alex is learning new words! And not saying them at home! Not long ago, one teacher asked Alex, "When do we eat cake?" and Alex replied, "For birthday." "Everything is 'hard,'" the teacher reports. "We ask him to do something, he says 'It's hard, it's hard!' Also, 'Stop.' If he doesn't want to do something, he keeps saying, 'Stop.'" Befuddled parents' response: "I've been telling him to 'stop' at intersections, and wait for traffic." As for "hard": "He must have heard me talking about my new job," Jill says.

Alex's short-circuited attention span soon comes up. Next year, Alex enters kindergarten. "Next year, school is going to be a *lot* more focused and structured than it is here," the teacher says.

We don't doubt it. A few years back, a developmental pediatrician predicted that Alex's attention span would be the number-one obstacle to his education. Nobody needs a long attention span to follow this discussion to the subject of drugs.

"We'd rather begin it while he's here," the teacher points out, "with people who know him and who know what he's like normally." I know that normally Alex pinballs, his powers of concentration limited to occasional fixation on toys of the moment. "Once, to focus his attention, I had to hide the plastic farm," one teacher reports. "That worked for a few minutes. There are herbal treatments they can give him, too, you know. And I have a friend who's a sophomore in college, and she still needs her Ritalin to study."

Parent-teacher night ends for us as I always thought one such night might some day, with words like "neurologist" and "prescription."

The prescription is for tiny tablets of Ritalin, or its knockoff.

The doctor says we give Alex one tablet in the morning and another at noon, if needed. "Keep increasing the dose until you hit the desired effect or a side effect," the doctor says. "How's he sleep?"

"Great!" I say. "Eleven hours a night. I don't want to mess with that. Alex!" Alex is trying to put in his mouth a plastic cap that goes over the thing the doctor uses to look in ears.

This doctor doesn't look in Alex's ears. He doesn't examine Alex at all, and to my relief doesn't even ask his weight. He asks about Alex's medical history and lengthening history of diagnoses. He listens to me, and watches Alex empty a bag of toy solders, plastic policemen, toy cars, and a little green palm tree. I like this doctor. He tells me this drug is a stimulant, which I didn't realize—I'd think you'd pump the opposite into your little boy if you wanted him to stop ricocheting around the room and spilling the doctor's army men behind the examination table.

"Has anyone given you any behavior-modification hand-outs?" the doctor asks. I say no. "I'll see if I can find you some," the doctor says. He watches Alex run behind the table and lean over the thick black electrical cords, stretching for the fallen palm tree. "Flower," Alex says. "Flower . . ."

"Alex, don't go back there!"

"The thing with kids like this," the doctor continues, "is that there has to be a split second between command and con-sequence. With other children, you give them a command and wait a few seconds. With Alex and the attention span he might have, a few seconds can seem like last year."

It would be a lot easier, of course, if Alex could converse. Then, in the weeks to come, he might be able to tell us if he had APPETITE SUPPRESSION, STOMACH ACHE, or some of the other symptoms my new list spells out in caps. Skin rashes and tic syndrome we'd see for ourselves. Ditto, with a bullet, SLEEP DISTURBANCE. How come ALEX DISAPPEARING isn't listed? Many times in adulthood I've thought about taking pills to attack my depression, and I've always wondered if they don't take away as much as they give, if maybe a level temperament makes a classroom run smoother but removes a kid who was there. Some-thing in me is charmed by Alex dropping a toy palm tree behind an examination table.

The doctor concludes that there's no doubt about the PDD-NOS, no doubt that Alex is hyperactive and will get harder to handle as he gets bigger. Others' opinions include:

—Ron, one of Alex's old and dearest teachers, gives a mo-ment of silence when told the plan, followed by "Hmmmm . . . Well, you know, it might help him settle down and bring out his abilities. I think Alex has real abilities." On his own mildly hy-peractive daughter, Ron has tried natural ADD treatments, such as fish oil. Ron spelled the name of the fish oil for me. The last four letters of the name spell A-L-E-X.

—Bernice, a babysitter, doesn't think Alex is right for Ritalin. She says he's very smart, and that she saw this thing on TV where a mother with a kid like Alex developed a new teaching method. Today the kid is fine. There may have been an operation involved.

—Thelma, another babysitter, forms her mouth into an "O" of concern. "But they can get hooked on that stuff," she says. "Oh, I think you'd better think carefully about that."

("Is it addictive?" I ask the doctor. "No," he replies. "If you go out on the street corner, you can't buy Ritalin precisely because it *isn't* addictive. You can also stop if you don't like what it does.")

I leave the exam room with a few soldiers still under the table, and feeling like I have the power to unlock Alex, or submerge his personality. Which will happen? I don't have an answer. I have a prescription.

The pills are bright blue, and bitter. We start with a light dose: half a pill at breakfast, and half a pill at school at midday. I give Alex half a pill one morning before school, and he swallows it while watching "Elmo." Later, the school nurse tells me he takes half a pill at noon with no problem. Next morning, I give him half a pill during "Elmo." He spits it out. I tuck it back in. He spits it out on the end of his tongue. I tuck it back in, the bright blue coming off on my fingertips. The next morning, he twists his head away. I try to force it, but give up when I start having visions of pilling our old cat Mimi years ago. The next morning, he again turns away, and I literally throw up my hands.

"Is he getting the pills?" the nurse wants to know. "He doesn't act like he is. Maybe we should increase the dose?" I never try the pills again. I never mention the pills anymore, and pretty soon neither does the nurse.

## JULY TO SEPTEMBER, 2003

AN ENGLISH TEACHER first handed me *Of Mice and Men* in ninth grade. First thing I noticed was the cover: a watercolor of two men's faces, one sharp and sad; the other, happier, under a broad-brimmed hat. I also noticed the book was thin, which is the handiest kind of classic to a ninth grader. There was also a lot of dialog, and the book ended with a gunshot. We all loved it. We mimicked Lennie whenever circumstances called for us to act stupid, which is also appealing to a ninth grader.

When I grew up and went into tenth grade, my high school drama club put on the play *Of Mice and Men*. I wasn't in the drama club because I hated memorizing. I was nonetheless called to fill in for a missing player for one rehearsal. I had to read for Curley, the troublemaking young semi-boxer who gets his hand crushed by Lennie in a fight. I kept messing up my line, which was "You ever buck barley?" I kept saying, "You ever buckle barley?" Isn't that stupid? Yet it set the tone for my stupendous comic moment: when the kid playing Lennie grabbed my hand, I let out a long, falsetto scream and fell writhing elaborately on the stage. Everybody laughed. I like to think they were laughing with me.

Next to *Elements of Style*, *Of Mice and Men* is probably the best slim jewel in English. If I ever write anything half as good in twice as many pages, I'll be happy. Professionally, anyway. Lennie gets the kindest, most dignified treatment possible in Steinbeck's tragedy. He's a hard worker, gentle, and misunderstood, loyal as the dog who gets shot. He knows what he likes—beans, soft fur, pretty cloth—and when he kills, it's with some comprehension of what the deed will cost him.

I keep noticing five-year-olds who pay attention better than Alex, move smoother, and who look in my face when they speak to me or I speak to them. They don't put toys in their mouths. They talk. Even Ned already picks up on our feelings. Alex fingers a soft, pretty T-shirt when he falls asleep. I know Alex is no Lennie, of course, though he is gentle. I think he's also going to be a hard worker, and loyal. And contemporary New York is a whole lot more understanding toward a person like Alex than hardscrabble California was to a pair of misfit migrant workers. I guess.

My attitude has changed toward most every story involving people who are a little slow. I can no longer watch that "Seinfeld" where Kramer is mistaken for "the mentally challenged" and nabs a ticket to sit at Mel Torme's table at a benefit. It's been a while since I've seen that "All in the Family" where a mentally retarded young man helps Gloria home with her groceries, but I bet I wouldn't watch it the same way I did in 1973. About the only thing I've been able to watch that features the mentally retarded was *Something About Mary*, and everybody said that was a mean-spirited movie. I didn't think so. I think it portrayed the challenged brother with dignity. I don't know why I think that.

I pester Jill into turning off "Friends," and she switches to an old cat documentary on PBS. We'd both seen the documentary years ago, long before we'd even met, and as the mice died and the story unrolled past the farmyards and the vet cages, I remember the documentary, and I see what's coming. The final two segments are about how cats cheer up nursing home residents and autistic children. I remember our own cats and my mom, all lost in 1998, and think of Alex. We cry something awful.

"You know a bad book to read right now?" I ask Jill. "*Of Mice and Men*."

"So what are you reading it for?" Jill asks.

A few nights later we scoop Ned's toys up and guide Alex down from the red chair where he sat staring. We get them to their bedroom, we fetch Alex his blanket and binkie and Ned his bottle, and get them to sleep early. Then we settle down over chili to kill the forty-five minutes before "Scrubs" with a rented Chinese movie entitled *The Shower*. This beautiful movie is about a young professional, Da Ming, who returns home because he believes his father is dying. His younger brother, Er Ming, has sent him a drawing depicting their father lying down. The father is healthy, though elderly, and runs a bathhouse. Er Ming is also an adult, big, and mentally retarded. He carries himself with helpful, gentle good nature, and cocks his head to one side as he stares at a nature program on TV.

Da seems itchy to get back to his life, and he is slow to take to the bathhouse community, including two old men who conduct cricket fights, and a patron who dreams of singing in public but can only belt out "O Sole Mio" in the shower. Interwoven themes touch on death, competition, and the rejuvenating quality of a good soak. The reunited family starts getting along when word comes that their neighborhood, including the bathhouse, is slated to be razed.

Then the dad dies in a bath. Da discovers this, while Er, in his own world, plays in the water nearby. Next, we see Er mopping the bathhouse furiously and shrugging off his brother, once with violence. Finally Da grabs him, stares him in the face, and gets it through Er's big, crew-cut head that their father is dead. Er wails like an animal, and I think of a special needs parent I once heard admit that she hoped her son didn't outlive her.

The scene I have a hard time with, however, comes when Da drops Er off at an institution. Er keeps running his hand around and around and around a tree, and again shrugs off his brother, who gets in a cab and starts to drive away. Next scene, we see him back on the institution grounds, looking for Er, whom he finds writhing from attendants and wailing for his father: "Dad!" the big man cries, "Dad, help me!"

Hard to finish chili after that. "I *cannot* watch this!" I tell Jill.

"Well don't blame me," she says. "Oh Jeff, don't shut the TV off. What about 'Scrubs'?"

Hard to see that and move on to situation comedy. Hard to see that and not hope that I outlive Alex. Jill convinces me, as only she has a right to do as Alex's other parent , to at least turn the movie back on for a minute to see that, yes, indeed, the brothers leave the institution together. "There," says Jill, "I'm sure it's going to have a happy ending. Now let's watch 'Scrubs' and then we'll come back to this . . ."

We do. The brothers stay together. But at the end, the wrecking ball near, Da can't find his brother. He looks everywhere until he finds Er on the rim of the bath where their father died, singing "O Sole Mio" to the tile walls.

To prepare for sleep, I tried to remember two things: the tearing-down of the bathhouse neighborhood was a contrivance, and large parts of "O Sole Mio" sound just like "It's Now Or Never." I never realized that. I don't have much else to fortify myself for bed, beyond slipping into the boys' room. There is Alex, still five, still asleep. *Help me, Dad!* "We're going to have to accept that you and I view things differently than most people," Jill says.

Over the past few years, drain bamage cracks have evaporated between me and Jill, who tells those who ask about Alex that she just hopes he can work in a Burger King someday. I used to think that years from now he would read such remarks from his parents and laugh all the way to the judge's bench. These days, I admit that that's probably not going to happen. Alex can climb a playground ladder without help; school has worked wonders with him: he can sit at "structured play" and use a spoon to eat yogurt; he can almost hold a one- or two-sentence conversation. I'd be surprised to see him drooling. But no, that judge thing is probably not going to happen.

At the same time, Jill and I have found strength in networking. We attend events about special needs, hoping to meet parents and future colleagues, and hear how others survive this knifing experience. Maybe we're also trying to peek into Alex's future. At a conference last spring, an autistic man in his fifties told us that when he was in assisted living, he hated, well, shambling around the sidewalks while a nervous social worker with a clipboard herded him and his friends. He said eye contact was physically painful for him, which he didn't even realize until he was in his twenties. He said he didn't like the way passersby looked at him.

The other day, Jill and I were interviewed by a graduate student in a special-ed program, opening up our lives to the student's questions in exchange for ten hours' free babysitting. One question was, "What's your biggest fear about Alex's future?"

"I guess," I replied, "how people will treat him."

Next morning, we were all headed to the elevator when Ned, who was in the stroller, dropped his bottle. Unasked, Alex bent down, picked up the bottle, and handed it back to Ned. Another time, Alex almost knocked over a lamp, but grabbed it himself just in time. Those are bits of good news. I look for others when I watch Alex play.

"Alex? Want to play with the farm?" We're in the boys' bedroom, after their baths. Ned is on the bed, tossing the little foam-rubber baseball for me to toss back. Alex wanders near the toy shelves, softly chewing the foot of a plastic rabbit. "Alex, you want a puzzle?" We read him books and show him toys—the other night he took a Slinky to bed; last night an old phone—but no toy seems real to him until he puts it in his mouth. Hand him a ball and he presses it between his forehead and the floor even after I show him, again and again, how to throw.

He can learn. We've taught him to take his tray to the kitchen after dinner. Give him paper and crayons and he scribbles with industry. Give him a toy truck and he'll immediately stick his face about two inches from it and study the wheels. How he learns to learn is the key, according to his old speech therapist at school. She would always start by saying that he was doing well with food. She'd say we should continue to wear down his sensory/food problems by moving on to little squares of lasagna, introducing new stuff on the pizza in miniscule doses, and remembering that the longer it takes to get Alex to eat new stuff, the harder it will be.

Then the talk would often move from sensory to behavioral, and there the picture was darker. "He has the potential to do a number of outstanding things," the therapist would say. "But the key is his *availability* for learning." This means his ability to sit still. She recommends giving Alex a lot more practice at sitting still for activities that have a beginning, middle, and an end. She asks, do we have a table and chairs for a structured activity? Yes? Good. We should start with a few minutes of structured activity, which can include coloring, putting little people on a toy bus, fiddling with Play-Doh, or identifying objects on picture cards. It has to be predictable and structured, and something he knows he has to do before he can move on to other fun stuff, like singing a song.

"You could use crayons to make a 'Playtime!' poster that we could put on the table during these sessions," I tell Jill. "Use crayon rather than the computer printer, for the colors." Jill nods. I like that idea, a project that has little tasks to accomplish and gives me the illusion I'm moving forward. That's what I hated about being in the hospital: no details I could knock down, no projects (except finding other doctors and another hospital), and endless generalities that in the end gave us a kid like Alex. I like having something to do. I like having something to fix. And I hope a kid who stoops, unasked, to pick up his little brother's bottle may not be too broken.

It is the first day of kindergarten. Jill wants to get a picture of Alex boarding the school bus, wearing his new Winnie the Pooh backpack. We plan to send the photo to the teachers at his old school, who gave him the backpack. Jill drops the digital camera, however, spattering the batteries across the sidewalk. I could turn this into a continuation of the fight we had last night after Alex had dumped a can of Pringles on the kitchen floor. But instead I collect the batteries and make a mental note to look for a wrist strap.

The bus—short, and identical to the one that took Alex to summer preschool just a few weeks ago—pulls up, and Jill takes him over. She chats with the driver and matron while I make sure Ned doesn't run into traffic. She comes back. "Did he seem okay?" I ask.

"He wasn't thrilled," she replies. "And boy, did they give me a hard time about our babysitter picking him up off the bus this afternoon!"

The plan now calls for me to take a city bus the eighty or so blocks north to his new school. My trip should take about an hour, and I'm interested to see if he'll be there when I arrive.

He is. "They're in the cafeteria," someone tells me in this place, which gleams with first-day shine, and is a bigger version of his old school. Last Thursday, when we visited here to fill out last-minute paperwork, Alex quickly found the gym. So did Ned, and they held the school year's first wrestling match. When we brought Alex back home that day, he cried and cried.

In the cafeteria, I see Alex by the wall, in the big arms of a lady who seems to be trying to get him to concentrate on his first lesson delivered by the New York City Public School System: Eat your Cheerios. I duck behind a big pillar, but the lady aide signals me forward. "Alex!"

"Hi, Poppy!" she says. He's alternating between squirming in her arms and attacking his little carton of cereal with a plastic spork. He scoops, eats, squirms, scoops, feeds me, and squirms. I'm not sure what he thinks he's squirming toward. "Mine's starting today, too," the aide says. "He's in first grade."

Alex will be one of eight kids. One of them, farther down the table, is wailing. (Now a veteran School Dad of three years, I bet he won't wail like that again until June, when he has to leave for the summer.) The teacher, a thoughtful-looking woman with glasses and dark hair, introduces me to Alex's classmate Robert across the table. "Hi, Robert!"

"Hi," he says, and buries his eyes in his hands.

Hard to believe that Alex is entering public school. I always thought that would mean pencil boxes, pens, rulers, and lots of crap you finally get around to throwing away in April. All I stuffed into the Pooh pack last night was granola, pretzels, and a couple diapers. "He's not toilet-trained, right?" the teacher asks.

Teacher agrees with me that the racket of the cafeteria overwhelms special-ed kids—I tell her about Alex's swimming lessons—and she comes around to where Alex is still squirming in the arms of the aide. "Mr. Wiggles," she says.

To the school nurse I try to recall five years of complicated medical history into a minute of talk in a cafeteria that's alive with noise, and then we head to Alex's classroom. He takes a sharp detour toward the gym, but teacher keeps a Jill-like grip and guides him through the corridors, where bright eyes and quiet faces and the bustle resemble a ship of strangers getting ready for sea.

Alex's new classroom has neat stacks of games and puzzles; name tags and posters of colored paper hang straight and somehow inviting on the walls. He heads to the Circle Time area and wiggles into the teacher's plush chair. *This is a happy moment,* I think. *It can't be this easy.*

Alex darts to the big box of balls. "Want to play in the balls, Alex?" teacher asks.

"Wanna go in."

"You want to go in?"

"Don't wanna go in!" and off Mr. Wiggles goes to a stack of puzzles. He pulls down a bendy platter of numerals. "Number three!" he says. "Number three!" His head dives to his work, teacher looks up at me and down to him, and I leave.

# EPILOGUE: MAY, 2004

THE OTHER NIGHT I brought two beach balls home for the boys. The balls were eighteen inches in diameter, and by the time I'd blown one up just halfway, I was winded. I found Jill, who doesn't blow up beach balls, in the kitchen. "You know," I said, "I should blow the other one up using one of Alex's old oxygen tanks."

"You should," she replied.

We still have a tank in the back of the front closet, under the case of wine and the car seat, deep in the shadows. I barely remembered how to screw on the gauge, which tells the airflow and how much oxygen is left in the tank, and I couldn't remember if I had to open the tank by twisting the toggle on top to the right or to the left. I felt as if I was trying to do a puzzle I had once mastered but hadn't seen in years.

Eventually I got the tank hooked up, twisted it open, and watched the needle on the gauge spring to "Full." I attached the ball and was soon listening to the hiss that assured me this tired dad wouldn't have to blow himself into a faint over an eighteen-inch beach ball. I remember when that hiss of oxygen assured me of other things. That my son would be able to breathe, for starters.

Alex is about to finish kindergarten. It's a special-education class, small, three adults to six kids, and Alex is often pulled out for speech or other therapies. The class takes a lot of field trips to places like the New York Aquarium and the Bronx Zoo.

Jill and I have been with Alex on a couple of trips. He lets his hand be held tightly by whatever adult he's in the charge of for the morning. He often looks at the flowers or the animals, though he says nothing. We all met Alex's class at a carnival for special-needs kids the other day, and the only time I saw him smile was when he spotted Ned.

Alex doesn't say much at home, either. He's still not toilet-trained. He still sucks a binkie when going to sleep, and fondles a soft piece of cloth. Chicken nuggets constitute most of his diet. But not all. In the past year he's more often eaten ice cream, yogurt, chocolate, beef from beef and broccoli, chicken picked out from the lo mein from the place around the corner, and the cheese off a pizza. Once he ate baked ravioli. Once he ate shrimp. In the race to gain weight and become a normal eater, Alex is still picky—he'll mutter "banana, banana" over and over while carrying one around the apartment, and he'll even touch the unpeeled banana to his lips, but he won't bite. Nonetheless, suddenly, I feel I can work with Alex on food. Yogurt's a meal in itself if he'll finish a cup, after all. Chocolate opens the door for those protein bars people eat in health clubs. I should also add that we took Alex and Ned to Burger King a few weeks ago, and Alex sat nicely waiting for Jill to come to our table with the food (chicken nuggets), and Ned did not. Alex has learned you wait in restaurants. At least some restaurants.

Alex's pediatrician checks his weight and height, and pens little dots on a growth chart. I used to hate those charts. "Look," Dr. S. says, "he'll still below the norm, but he is consistently following his own curve!" I look at the dots. So he is. This should be no surprise: Alex has lived by his own curve for six years. When he's sick, he knows it. When something is beyond him, he knows it. When he's mad or happy or wants something, he knows it. He sort of shows it, but as his language remains sparse, it's difficult to know when there's a problem. Just last night, after being put to bed, he woke up and coughed and coughed, his face damp and sweaty. We had no idea what was wrong. We never found out, since Alex has only a few words and has uttered, in his whole life, only a handful of what could be called sentences. (I think what went on in Alex's brain that afternoon of his first October was his language center.) He went to sleep, had a quiet night, and after a few quietly concerned moments for his parents this morning, went off to school.

Things work out with Alex, day to day. Yes, he's still obsessed with Elmo, but he's learning to live with it when we all watch "The Simpsons." Yes, his diet is mostly chicken nuggets, but look at Dr. S.'s chart. Yes, he bit Ned for a while, but usually after Ned pestered the crap out of him, and then not hard, and anyway it's kind of stopping. Yes, he screeches, but he also stops, particularly when we let him smell a scented candle. There's the ravioli and the shrimp.

I feel he's getting truly ready for first grade, even if it is special education. On the street, he's bolting less, and taking my hand at intersections. He can do three forty-eight-piece jigsaw puzzles simultaneously. I can't do that. Between Alex and Ned, the toys are gone from our living room floor in about ten minutes (the trick here is to keep looking around, while they're putting things away, for the next thing for them to do). He's needed no oxygen, even during the worst colds, unless you count the arrival of the beach balls. Jill and I are seeing a behavior-management specialist, who thinks up ways to help an autistic kid grow, like charting when he needs the bathroom during the day, and helping him see that the bathroom is where we go to the toilet. We expect he'll be toilet-trained someday. Ned will probably get there first. But we're realizing, month by month, that the only one Alex is racing against is himself.

# RECOMMENDED RESOURCES

## ORGANIZATIONS

This is intended as only a partial list of the resources available to help families with special needs. These organizations, some local, some national and international, have also allowed me to speak and otherwise tell about Alex and what happened to our family.

Association for the Help of Retarded Children, New York City: www.ahrcnyc.org, 212-780-2500, 200 Park Ave South, New York, NY 10003

Canadian Abilities Foundation: www.abilities.ca, 416-923-1885, 340 College St., Ste. 650, Toronto, ON M5T 3A9

Exceptional Family Resources: www.contactefr.org, 315-478-1462, 1065 James St., Ste. 220, Syracuse, NY 13203

The March of Dimes: www.modimes.org, 1275 Mamaroneck Ave., White Plains, NY 10605

National Perinatal Association: www.nationalperinatal.org, 888-971-3295, 2090 Linglestown Rd., Ste. 107, Harrisburg, PA 17110

Parents of Premature Babies, Inc.: www.preemie-L.org

Premature Baby Premature Child: www.prematurity.org

YAI—National Institute for People With Disabilities: www.yai.org, 212-273-6100, YAI/NIPD Network, 460 West 34th St., New York, NY 10001-2382

## WEBSITES

These sites offer excellent discussion boards and memberships to provide support for preemie, special-needs, and other families. (For more URLs, consult the websites section of the credits page.) For many months, they also welcomed announcements about entries in Alex's story. I thank them.

About.com:  www.specialchildren.about.com

BabiesOnline: www.babiesonline.com

The Baby Corner: www.thebabycorner.com

BabyWorld: www.babyworld.co.uk

Fatherville: www.fatherville.com

Fertilethoughts Forums: www.fertilethoughts.net

The Labor of Love: www.thelaboroflove.com

Little One Productions: www.littleoneprods.com

Parenting Your Premature Baby and Child:
www.parentingyourprematurebaby.com

Parents Helping Parents: www.php.com

A Place to Remember: www.aplacetoremember.com

PreemieChat: www.preemies.org

The Preemie Website: http://preemie.info

Resources for Parents of Preemies:
http://members.aol.com/MarAim/preemie.htm

Special Child: http://specialchild.com

Storknet: www.storknet.com

Today's Parent: www.todaysparent.com

Tommy's Cybernursery: www.kingproductions.com